Frank L. Dana

The Great West

A Vast Empire. Comprehensive history of the trans-Mississippi states and territories.

Frank L. Dana

The Great West
A Vast Empire. Comprehensive history of the trans-Mississippi states and territories.

ISBN/EAN: 9783337244842

Printed in Europe, USA, Canada, Australia, Japan

Cover: Foto ©ninafisch / pixelio.de

More available books at **www.hansebooks.com**

THE GREAT WEST

A VAST EMPIRE.

COMPREHENSIVE HISTORY OF THE TRANS-MISSISSIPPI STATES AND TERRITORIES.

CONTAINING DETAILED STATISTICS AND OTHER INFORMATION IN SUPPORT OF THE MOVEMENT FOR DEEP HARBORS ON THE TEXAS-GULF COAST.

BY—
F. L. DANA,
SECRETARY OF THE INTER-STATE DEEP HARBOR COMMITTEE AND EDITOR OF THE COLORADO EXCHANGE JOURNAL.

DEDICATION.

This work is respectfully dedicated to the Inter-State Deep Harbor movement; to the Prairie Schooner Pilots and Pioneers, who discovered a new America; to the Promoters of this Vast Western Empire; and to the "Star of Empire" which has "westward had its way," until it has paused, never to renew its journey, (there is no other West). It stands fixed, perched upon the crown of the Mighty Monarch of the Rockies—Pike's Peak—the geographical center of the Great West. The Star shines with added lustre, as if happy to find its perpetual resting spot; its brilliancy encouraging the toiling millions of the West to persevere in the work of "building an Empire," (Gov. Gilpin's familiar expression early in the '60's), and here will it shine until the Great West shall become the center of the world's supply of breadstuffs, meats, cotton and woolen fibre, gold, silver, copper, zinc, tin, lead, iron, coal, oil and building material.

"THE GREAT WEST,"

PUBLISHED MONTHLY BY THE

GREAT WEST PUBLISHING COMPANY,

F. L. DANA, Editor.

Price Fifty Cents Per Number; Six Dollars Per Annum—Cash in Advance.

Advertising Rates Furnished on Application to the Publishers.

J. W. Nevatt, Manager Publishing Department.

August, 1889.   Denver, Colorado.   Part Third.

IN presenting this the third edition of The Great West to our readers, we do so with a marked degree of pride. We are proud of our success with the first two numbers; we are proud of the multitudinous press opinions that our first effort brought forth; we are proud of this issue, which contains a graphic description of Pueblo, Colo., the "Pittsburg of the West," a city in which every citizen of Colorado takes pride. Likewise do we devote considerable space to Canon City and Monte Vista, Colo., two enterprising, progressive cities, that are destined to be a power in this our magnificent commonwealth. In connection with Monte Vista, we publish an original poem by Mrs. Clara Troth, to whom we acknowledge our indebtedness, etc.; it is a brilliant production, and worthy a place in the annals of that charming valley of which Monte Vista is the capital.

OUR NEXT NUMBER.

The fourth edition of this work will contain a complete history of Kansas and descriptions of several of her wonderful cities, and will be dedicated to the Deep Harbor Convention, which assembles in Topeka October 1st next.

DEEP HARBOR ENGINEERS.

The Inter-State Deep Harbor Committee has succeeeed in getting a board of United States engineers appointed to survey the Texas-Gulf coast, with a view of reporting to the next session of Congress the most feasible point on that coast to construct a deep harbor. The engineers are now on the coast, and have visited nearly all of the prospective harbor sites, and will be able to report to Congress, even if called in extra session in October next. Their report will form a basis upon which the Inter-State Deep Harbor Committee will work during the coming winter, to have Congress appropriate sufficient money to accomplish the work in the shortest possible time, let the report favor whichsoever part it may. Since our last number an Inter-State Convention has been arranged for, to assemble at Topeka, Kansas, at 4 o'clock p. m., of the 1st day of October next. The basis of representation is such as to ensure an extraordinary convention, composed of the most representative politicians and business men west of the Mississippi River, and is as follows:

APPORTIONMENT.

The following are hereby designated as delegates to the Inter-State Deep Harbor Convention, to be held at Topeka, Kansas, October 1, 1889, and are all earnestly requested to attend:

The Governor of each State and Territory west of the Mississippi River, who shall be authorized to make all appointments from his State or Territory hereby designated not otherwise selected.

Four delegates at large from each State, two of whom shall be its United States Senators.

Four delegates from each Congressional district, one of whom shall be the member of Congress or Territorial Delegate-elect.

The Republic of Mexico shall be entitled to five delegates, to be appointed by the President thereof, who is also earnestly invited to head the delegation.

The president of each Chamber of Commerce or Board of Trade west of the Mississippi River, who is authorized to appoint an alternate if he is unable to attend.

It is earnestly requested that all members of the Permanent Inter-State Deep Harbor Committee, and including the secretary, will attend the convention and participate in its deliberations.

All correspondence in relation to the convention should be addressed to F. L. Dana, secretary, Topeka, Kansas.

In behalf of the Permanent Inter-State Deep Harbor Committee.

F. L. DANA, Secretary.   JOHN EVANS, President.

The Governor of Kansas, Lyman M. Humphrey, issued his proclamation, upon the invitation of the Permanent Inter-State Deep Harbor Convention, calling the convention together, and has written each of the several governors west of the Mississippi to be present at the convention. Topeka is making elaborate preparations to entertain the delegates, and will not leave one stone unturned to make of this the second Inter-State Deep Harbor Convention one of the greatest that ever assembled in the West. The Kansas corn and wheat crop this year is "simply immense." Of corn, 250,000,000 bushels; of wheat, 32,000,000 bushels; surplus corn, 150,000,000 bushels; surplus wheat, 25,000,000 bushels; surplus cattle, 300,000 head, or 1,500,000 tons; surplus pork, 1,000,000 head, or 100,000 tons; surplus of corn, wheat, cattle and pork, 5,200,000 tons. With a Gulf port as is proposed, Kansas would save $4.88 per ton of surplus, which amounts to $25,376,000 per annum. That accounts for the extraordinary interest displayed in that state toward the movement.

INDEX.

	Page
CHAPTER I. The Great West	9
CHAPTER II. Lousiana	13
CHAPTER III. Missouri	15
CHAPTER IV. Arkansas	17
CHAPTER V. Iowa	19
CHAPTER VI. Texas	26
CHAPTER VII. California	34
CHAPTER VIII. Minnesota	39
CHAPTER IX. Oregon	42
CHAPTER X. Kansas	45
CHAPTER XI. Nevada	49
CHAPTER XII. Nebraska	51
CAAPTER XIII. Colorado	54
CHAPTER XIV. Pueblo	83
Arkansas Valley	88
Climate	89
Health Attractions	91
Coal and Oil	92
Railroad Advantages	94
Pueblo Buildings	97
Pueblo Banks and Banking	98
The First National Bank	98
Stockgrowers' National Bank	99
Western National Bank	99
Manufactures	100
Colorado Coal and Iron Company	100
Smelters	101
Pueblo Street Railway	103
Business Conveniences	103
Schools	104
Loretto Academy	106
Social Life in Pueblo	107
Pueblo City Government	108
Andrew A. Grome	110
T. S. Smythe	111
W. P. Gartley	111
A. T. Stewart	111
George F. West	111
J. H. Elspass	112
Charles H. Lamkin	112
Thomas P. Lloyd	112
Hotels	113
Pueblo Journals	113
The Chieftain	115
The Daily Pueblo Press	115
Manufactories and Business Firms	117
Monte Vista	121
Poem by Clara Troth	124
Canon City	126
CHAPTER XV. Utah	129
Delegate Cain, on Irrigation	131

		Page.
Chapter XVI.	New Mexico	135
Chapter XVII.	Washington	141
Chapter XVIII.	Dakota	145
Chapter XIX.	Idaho	147
" XX.	Arizona	150
" XXI.	Montana	152
" XXII.	Wyoming	154
" XXIII.	Alaska	157
" XXIV.	Oklahoma	160

INDEX TO ILLUSTRATIONS.

Wharf Scene, Galveston	31
Fishing on the Rio Grande	73
Long's Peak	76
Entering Boulder Canon	81
Central Block, Pueblo	84
Fremont Pass	93
Colorado Smelting Company, Pueblo	102
Central High School, Pueblo	104
Hinsdale High School, "	105
Loretto Academy, "	106
Pueblo City Hall	109
Daily Chieftain Building	114
Residence of J. J. Lambert	116
Wilson & Barnard	119
Bird's Eye View of Salida	120
The Hotel Blanca, Monte Vista	123
Toltec Gorge	125
Mount of the Holy Cross	127
Mother Grundy	128
Round-Up Scene in New Mexico	139

INDEX TO APPENDIX.

A summing up of the Resources and Possibilities of the Great West:

Food Production and Distribution, (table)	IV
Export and Surplus, (table)	V
Distance, (table)	V
Distance, (table)	VI
Inter-State Deep Harbor Convention	IX
Committee of Arrangements	X
Governor Adams' Address	X
Convention Resolutions	XII
Permanent Committees	XIV
Commercial Congress	XIV
Irrigation Reservoirs and Duty of Water, by the State Engineer	XV
Duty of Water	XX
Major Powel's Report	XXI
Measuring Flow of Water, (illustration)	XXIII
Opening the Ditches, (illustrated)	XXV
Burlington & Missouri River Railway	XXVIII
Flume in Main Canal, (illustrated)	XXIX
Mileage and Traffic of the Great West	XXX
St. Louis & San Francisco Railway	XXXI
Northern Pacific Railway	XXXI
Chicago & Northwestern Railway	XXXII

THE GREAT WEST.

CHAPTER I.

WHAT is the "Great West?" It is not "Buffalo Bill's Wild West," as is generally supposed in the East and in England. It is all of that portion of the United States lying west of the Mississippi River, and is usually understood to include Illinois and Wisconsin. Without the last two States, it comprises in area nearly two-thirds of the United States of America, and nearly one-third of the present population of the United States.

In wealth the great West is nearly equal to one-half of the entire United States; in natural resources it is equal to its area—two-thirds of the natural resources of the Union. Contrary to all heretofore published authorities, barring Dr. Strong in his work entitled "Our Country," the Great West is capable of sustaining a population in proportion to its vast area, and will ere many years dominate the Union. Its political, its financial and its social features—the significance of which is growing upon the civilized world, is having the effect that will bring about, within a few years, the greatest political revolution the world ever witnessed.

Ten or twenty years will probably witness the West in control of the government. The West has been accustomed to have its wishes and demands for justice in the apportionment of appropriations disregarded, its financial interests forced into Wall Street, and representation in national affairs denied. That is gradually being changed. The East is slowly relaxing its severe discipline of the West; the citizens of that division begin to feel the public pulse beating time to the onward march of progress, and in truth very soon will we realize that "Westward the Star of Empire hath its sway."

This mighty empire is well defined—the Mississippi river on the east, the Pacific ocean on the west, the Gulf of Mexico and the Mexican Republic on the south, and the British possessions on the north; and if the signs of the times be true, the northern boundary will ere long be the Arctic ocean and the southern line the Panama canal.

Erastus Wiman, of R. G. Dun & Co., has a communication in the January, 1889, number of the *North American Review*, upon the "Greater Half of the Continent." Referring to Canada, he attempts to justify commercial union, and at the same time combat political union between the United States and that British province. We commend the spirit of union, but believe it should be both political and commercial, agreeing with that eminent American statesman, John Sherman. The greater half of the continent lies west of that line of demarcation which is generally applied when speaking of the Eastern or Western States of the Union, viz: the Mississippi River. The line extends south to the Gulf, and, extended north to the Arctic Ocean, would give the greater half of the continent to the West, the East representing less than one-fourth of the North American continent.

Long east and west lines are unnatural boundaries betweeen peoples, and by actual comparison one may see how very remarkably true to this theory have the nations of Europe applied their map making. An east and west boundary line in either American continent is repugnant to nature. The Creator made these continents to lay lengthwise, north and south, connected by a narrow strip of land, which, pestilence ridden, forms a boundary almost impassible between the two continents.

Hon. T. F. Sorrells, of Arkansas, in a recent speech referred to the interchange of commodities as naturally belonging between zones, north and south; that the natural channels of trade were from north to south, and *vice versa*. This is quite easy of comprehension. The same zones have similar products, and consequently have no legitimate interchange. Unnaturally, however, the great east and west trunk lines have diverted traffic through a combination of capital and circumstances to the positive detriment of the Western people. Nature is gradually gaining the ascendancy in the matter of traffic, and these monster monopolies see the hand writing upon the wall; the centre of population and wealth is gradually creeping westward; the time approaches when the West will not pay tribute to New York or the railroad kings. The Santa Fe has a north and south line which connects their immense system with the Gulf; the Denver, Texas & Gulf railway connects Denver with the Gulf, which opens up a vast country north and west to the natural course of trade. Already the good effect of conforming to Nature's law of traffic is felt, though the great east and west trunk lines are dissipating as much as possible the bountiful blessings the Great West is sure to enjoy.

The 49th parallel of north latitude divides a people and outrages nature. It forms a barrier to traffic. As Mr. Wiman states: "The American has limitations on the north by a line drawn at the St. Lawrence and the lakes, and along the 49th parallel, against which his commerce beats as against an impenetrable wall, and like a wave rolls back upon itself. A night's journey from Boston or New York, and the limit of his boasted areas towards the north are reached; two nights and a day, even from Chicago, in the centre of his territory, and the ground to the north covered by the trade of that great city is exhausted."

Therefore, political and commercial union will speedily follow the present agitation; otherwise, annexation will be forced by the commercial demands of the great marts referred to by Mr. Winnan. There is growing a West that can not be trifled with. The North and South has disappeared in smoke and death. The East and West have taken their places. The South, like the East, were for a time masters; their power waning, they resorted to violence to retain their ascendency. Even now the power of our Eastern masters begins to wane, and they, too fond of their money bags to even resort to violence to retain their power, have been practicing extortion upon us, exacting excessive toll for transporting our persons, our products and necessities, demanding exhorbitant interest for the use of their gold, and, Shilock like, exacting the pound of flesh nearest the heart for the least deviation from their own heathenish laws.

A Western Empire is forming; a financial centre (Denver) is established at the base of the Rocky Mountains, where nearly thirty millions of gold and silver annually concentrate, gathered from the everlasting treasure vaults of the Rocky Mountain range; where money goes begging for borrowers at from six to eight per cent. per annum interest ; where palaces are being erected for the homes of the Western millionaires; where massive stone and brick blocks are being constructed to accommodate the present urgent demands of a constantly increasing commerce, made inevitable by the revolution taking place— natural currents of trade dominating the artificial, unhealthy and vicious channels formed by a greedy, grasping East. aided by monopolistic carriers.

Man can conceive of no mightier empire than the "Great West." That empire must have a capital. That capital must be central and accessible. The Star of Empire in its westward march has paused at Denver, and smiles upon that city, which it has christened and designated the empire's capital. Here wealth and learning, social and moral culture, have become firmly planted, and distinguished travelers have dubbed this city the

"QUEEN CITY OF THE PLAINS,"

—founded by tried men and true—men who waded in blood to reach this delightful mecca—travelled across the then great American desert, almost every step being disputed by the savage. Thousands of lives were lost in those trying days, and the prairies were strewn by bleaching human bones. It required a hardy, determined people to reclaim this Great West from the savage. It is accomplished, and many are now living who should receive the hero's badge of honor, having braved the hardships of explorers, that future generations might occupy in peace and plenty this grand empire destined to rule the nation.

The progress of the West stands as one of the marvels of the age. Prior to 1859, except the states bordering on the Mississippi and California, this immense interior was regarded as a great desert, barren of vegetation and abounding in great useless mountain ranges of perpetual snow. Thirty years has witnessed a wonderful transformation, beginning in 1859, by discoveries of gold where Denver now stands. The greed of gold stimulated the hardy pioneer to penetrate this trackless plain, and all at once it dawned upon the world that this plain was not a desert, but fertile and desirable public lands. These began to appreciate in value, until the land between the Mississippi and Missouri Rivers was practically appropriated by the western flow of population. The same irresistible tide of immigration moved westward, and is still moving westward at the rate of 25 to 30 miles per annum. Meanwhile a hardier class has outstripped the slow tide of immigration, and the coast and mountain states have been peopled, though sparsely, with a sturdy, progressive population, whose numbers are daily augmented, and whose wealth (especially Colorado) is greater per capita than any other people on earth. Colorado is the central state of this vast Western Empire, and might be said to concentrate within her borders the essence of wealth, contained west of the Mississippi River, which is equal to saying the entire Union.

Denver is the capital of the state, and admirably situated to become the capital of the Great West; (we accede to Pueblo the manufacturing business of this vast region.)

Fuller descriptions of states and cities will claim our attention later on in this article, which has an ultimate bearing upon the great subject of commerce and transportation, which is soon to occupy the undivided attention of this New West, and compel the National Congress to appropriate our share of the public "pap" to construct deep harbors upon the Gulf coast of our sister state—Texas, and otherwise improve transportation facilities, opening up to the entire west a direct and short line to the sea, and consequently to the markets of the world. Appropriately the first Western Commercial Congress assembled in Denver (the Inter-State Deep Harbor Convention), the latter part of last August. The movement was perpetuated, and by a happy arrangement the managing officers reside in Denver, and consequently the headquarters are firmly established here.

CHAPTER II.

LOUISIANA—1541 TO 1889.

TAKING up the Great West in detail, we naturally turn to Louisiana first.

"Louisiana" was the name given by La Salle in 1682 to all of that portion of the United States west of the Mississippi River (except Texas and New Mexico, then a part of Mexico), that lies between that river and the Rocky Mountains, including Idaho and Washington Territories and the State of Oregon.

This portion of the Great West was first discovered by De Soto in 1541, who, however, did not ascend the Mississippi beyond New Orleans. He died the following year, and was buried in the waters of that mighty stream. His followers were scattered, and no permanent settlement was effected until 1682, when La Salle descended the river from the Canadian settlements and took possession of this vast region in the name of Louis XIV, in whose honor he named the country Louisiana. It is generally believed, however, that no settlement of importance was effected before 1699, and not until 1706 was New Orleans established. The little colony, headed by Bienville, in that year unfurled the flag of France. The French crown retained possession of this territory until 1762, when it fell into the hands of the Spanish crown, and was severely ruled until 1800, when it again fell into the possession of France, and in 1803 was purchased from the French by the United States for $15,000,000. In 1804 the United States divided this territory and named what is now known as Louisiana, the Territory of Orleans, which was admitted in 1812 as a state, under the name of Louisiana. In the same year war with England was declared, and in 1814 New Orleans became famous because of its noble defense by General Jackson, with 5,000 men, against Sir John Packenham, with 12,000 Britishers. The state grew rapidly thereafter, and to-day ranks very high, New Orleans being second only to New York in amount and value of domestic and foreign exports, amounting to about $100,000,000 per annum. The inward bound coastwise cargoes to New Orleans are valued at about $200,000,000 per annum, imports about $20,000,000. The coastwise and foreign trade together amounts to nearly $500,000,000 per annum.

The Eads jetty system has made it possible for deep-draught ocean-going vessels to enter the port at New Orleans. The only drawback to New Orleans as a port is the necessary towage of ninety-five miles from the jetties. The establishment of deep harbors on the Texas coast will not affect the importance of New Orleans as a port of entry, as many suppose. The traffic that the proposed Texas ports will attract will be of a different class, affecting New York more than any other eastern port.

Louisiana contains 41,346 square miles, or 26,461,440 acres. Much of the State is lower than the high-water level of the rivers, and is protected by dykes or levees from inundation. The land is generally of great richness, produces sugar cane, cotton, rice, corn, tobacco, oranges, figs, bananas, peaches, etc.

Louisiana produces annually about 200,000 hogsheads of sugar, about 10,000,000 gallons of molasses, and about 500,000 bales of cotton, which is most all exported from the State. Other crops are most all consumed at home. The forests are extensive, containing several kinds of oak, hickory, locust, sassafras, mulberry and pine.

Louisiana has 1,256 miles of coast on the Gulf of Mexico; the Mississippi River flows through and along the State border for nearly 800 miles, and floats the commerce tributary for nearly 2,000 miles, and the Red and Washita Rivers are also navigable for quite a distance, bringing wealth to the great city of New Orleans.

The school facilities of Louisiana are second to no other Southern State, and are gaining rapidly upon some of the Northern States.

Rail connection has opened up a traffic between New Orleans and Denver which heretofore came by rail from New York, and has placed tropical fruits and sugar into Denver as cheaply as into Chicago. Denver and New Orleans are closely allied. We take their fruits, sugar and molasses, while they take our gold and silver, and the intervening sections our coal. The opening of the proposed Texas deep harbors will not materially affect the relations of New Orleans to Denver, but will materially affect Denver, as it opens up an European and South American trade to Denver which the disadvantages of New Orleans as a port of entry has heretofore barred us from. Texas deep harbors are a necessity, and we demand the immediate attention of Congress in their institution.

Soon after the completion of the Denver, Texas & Gulf Railroad, the direct rail connection, the New Orleans merchants held an exposition of their resources in Denver Chamber of Commerce. Their favorable reception caused the establishment in Denver of branches or agencies of their large mercantile houses, the result of which has been beneficial to both commercial cities.

CHAPTER III.

MISSOURI—1682 TO 1889.

WE take up Missouri second in our review of States and Territories, in the order of her seniority of State-hood. We will conform to that rule in our treatise of the sister-hood comprising "The Great West."

LaSalle descended the Mississippi River in 1682 and took possession of the country west of the Mississippi River in the name of Louis XIV, naming it Louisiana. Missouri was included in the cessions made by France to Spain in 1762, and by Spain retroceded to France in 1800, and purchased by the United States in 1803.

St. Louis was known as a fur-trading point as early as 1755, and had less than 1,000 inhabitants, and St. Genevive had about 500 inhabitants. St. Louis was the capital of the District of Louisiana of the Territory of Orleans. When the State of Louisiana was admitted into the Union (1812) the Territory of Orleans was obliterated, and the Territory of Missouri was organized with St. Louis as its capital, which in 1817 contained about 5,000 inhabitants, while the Territory contained about 60,000. In that year the Territory knocked at the door of Congress for admission as a State, and precipitated a fierce excitement regarding the extension of slavery into the unorganized territory of the United States, and that came near disrupting the Union. A compromise was, however, effected, and the State admitted in 1820 under conditions set forth in what has ever since been known as "the Missouri compromise." The President's proclamation was not issued completing the admission, however, until August 10, 1821.

The State prospered, and at the breaking out of the rebellion in 1861 contained upwards of one million people, which has been augmented until the State contains nearly or quite 2,500,000 population.

The State contains 69,415 square miles, or 44,425,600 acres, and has 114 counties. Its chief cities are St. Louis, Kansas City. Hannibal, St. Joseph, Springfield and Jefferson City (the capital).

The Mississippi River runs the entire length of the State on its eastern boundary line (470 miles). The Missouri River forms a portion of the west boundary line, and deflects above Kansas City to the east, and flows across the State from west to east near its middle, and empties into the Mississippi River just above St. Louis. Both streams are navigable throughout their entire course through or along the State, the Missouri for 450 miles, and the Mississippi for 470 miles—over

900 miles of navigable waters available to the commerce of this great State. The profitable use to which this great natural commercial facility has been utilized, one need only point to the magnificent commercial centers. St Louis and Kansas City.

Missouri contains immense natural resources in the form of the baser metals and coal, the south half of the State being rich in coal, iron and lead, also timber. Notwithstanding the fact that the great swamp 100 miles wide starts in about Cape Girardeau and extends into Arkansas, Missouri produced more lead than any other State in the Union, until recently. Colorado now takes the lead by many thousand tons. The north half is rich in agriculture and some coal.

In 1880 there were in Missouri 215,575 farms, averaging 129 acres each, a total of 27,879,276 acres. Of these 16,745,020 acres were improved. Estimated value of farms, $375,633,037.

In 1887 Missouri had in corn 6,406,785 acres, producing 140,949,000 bushels, valued at $52,151,135. Wheat, 1,712,603 acres, producing 27,744,000 bushels, valued at $17,201,280. Oats, 1,358,119 acres, producing 39,793,000 bushels, valued at $10,346,185. All other field crops amounting to a value approximating $200,00,000, or in round numbers, Missouri produced in 1887 from field crops a value approximating $100,000,000.

On January 1st, 1888, Missouri had 782,124 head of horses, valued at $45,040,996; 225,563 head of mules, valued at $15,019,534; milch cows, 737,259 head, valued at $14,344,215; oxen and other cattle, 1,429,453 head, valued at $26,077,367; sheep, 1,087,690 head, valued at $1,894,973; hogs, 3,798,799 head, valued at $15,043,246. Total value of live stock, $117,420,331.

The total value of farms, farm animals and farm products of Missouri January 1st, 1888, amounts to $572,752,228.

Such vast resources deserve competitive seaboard markets, and is one good argument for the establishment of a deep harbor on the Texas Gulf Coast, and is there any wonder Missouri joins the progressive movement with Colorado and the Great West in demanding of Congress appropriations for commerce that directly affects two-thirds of the area of this glorious Republic. Colorado has a great many native Missourians within her borders; in fact, Colorado is mainly peopled with immigrants from the older States of the Union, from the progressive, energetic portion of the population of America. While the resources of this great State are similar to the products of Colorado, our interests are common, and together we pull for the main interest—Deep Harbors on the Texas Gulf coast.

Missouri is represented on the Inter-State Deep Harbor Committee by Hon. D. H. Armstrong, vice-president, St. Louis, Mo.; Hon. A. L. Tomblin, Stanberry, Mo.; Col. H. F. Fellows, Springfield Mo.; Hon. J. S. Logan, St. Joseph, Mo., and Hon. W. W. Anderson, Louisiana, Mo.

CHAPTER IV.

ARKANSAS—1680 TO 1889.

ARKANSAS was the third State west of the Mississippi River to to be admitted into the Union. It formed a portion of the original Territory of Louisiana; later Territory of New Orleans; later Territory of Missouri; and after the admission of Missouri into the Union, became a Territory by the name of Arkansas, which then included the State of Arkansas and the present Indian Territory, and was included within the original purchase from France by the United States in 1803. The State is 240 miles in length, by an average breadth of 225 miles, containing an area of 53,850 square miles, being about the size of England proper, or an equivalent of 33,406,720 acres. This portion of the original Louisiana was nominally colonized in 1680 by the French at the junction of the St. Francis River with the Mississippi; but in fact, it was little better than a wilderness at the time of the purchase by the United States in 1803. It became a Territory March 2nd, 1819, named after the principal river, the Arkansas, which is navigable throughout its entire course in the State. It flows from near the northwest to near the southeast corner of the State, where it empties into the Mississippi River, which river flows from the north to the south along the entire eastern border. The other rivers in the State are St. Francis, White, Big Black, Washita and Saline, all more or less navigable. Nearly all of the counties of the State are either bordered or traversed by navigable streams, and probably no other area in the world, not surrounded by an ocean, of equal dimensions with Arkansas, has one-half of the natural commercial ways enjoyed by this State. The state is well watered but has no lakes worthy of name.

The surface is, in the eastern portion along the Mississippi, very low and flat, subject to overflow, and very swampy; while the north and west portions are rolling, often terminating in small mountains reaching an elevation of two thousand to three thousand feet.

The climate is exceptionally salubrious in the western portion and malarial in the eastern counties. Vegetation is prolific. Yellow fever has never been epidemic in Arkansas, which often devastates the states to the east just across the Mississippi River.

The State abounds in valuable timber, there being large forests of cypress, oak, pine, red cedar, black walnut, locust, maple and mulberry trees. Besides these are grown beach, sycamore, ash, elm, hickory, laurel, juniper, ironwood, palmetto, holly, butternut, scrub oak, etc. All fruits common to the latitudes of 33° to 36° grow in abundance.

Game is still very abundant in some portions of the state, such as deer, bear, quail, prairie chicken and wild turkey.

The streams afford an abundance of fish, while alligators are occasionally encountered in the bayous.

Arkansas has fewer miles of railroad than any of her western sisters. That, however, is overbalanced by her excellent natural channels of commerce.

The Territory had in 1820 only 14,273 inhabitants. The number increased gradually, and March 1st, 1836, a State Constitution was formed, and the State admitted into the Union June 15th of the same year. The State is bounded on the west by the Indian Territory and Texas, on the south by Louisiana, on the east by Mississippi and Tennessee, on the north by Missouri.

Arkansas is not known for its precious metals; however, there appears to be some considerable mineral found there carrying 70 per cent. lead, and as high as 50 ounces silver per ton. Experience has not been such as to encourage mining for metals in the State. An inferior quality of coal underlies about 8,000,000 acres. It is mined for domestic use only, as it is regarded unfit for commercial uses.

Arkansas produced in 1886, 42,140,000 bushels corn, valued at $20,648,600, on 2,069,176 acres of land; wheat, 231,357 acres produced 1,815,000 bushels, valued at $1,542,750; oats, 263,848 acres, produced 4,749,000 bushels, valued at $1,994,580; other field crops, exclusive of cotton, 5,875 acres, produced crops valued at $1,091,748; cotton, 1,354,788 acres, produced 660,872 bales, valued at $26,662,228; a total agricultural product, exclusive of farm animals, valued at $51,939,906.

Arkansas had January 1st, 1888, 179,055 head of horses, valued at $10,678,480; 122,457 head of mules, valued at $9,063,660; 304,404 head of milch cows, valued at $4,453,431; 469,057 head of oxen and other cattle, valued at $4,603,415; 220,167 head of sheep, valued at $310,127; 1,588,560 head of swine, valued at $3,938,202; or a total valuation, exclusive of farm lands, approximating $100,000,000 January 1st, 1889.

Arkansas is noted for its world-renowned hot springs at the city of that name. There are fifty to sixty mineral or medicinal springs at Hot Springs, varying in temperature from 93 to 148 degrees, strongly impregnated with carbonates and carbonic acid, and are famous for the benefits afforded to thousands of invalids who annually visit there.

The greater portion of the arable lands of the State are directly tributary to the proposed Texas Deep Harbors, and consequently the State takes a deep interest in the Deep Harbor movement, such distinguished citizens of Arkansas are prominently identified with the movement, viz: Judge T. F. Sorrells, Judge William Fishback, Governor Simon P. Hughes, Hon. J. W. T. Tiller, and Hon. William M. Duffy. They are members of the Inter-State Deep Harbor Committee.

CHAPTER V.

IOWA—1788 TO 1889.

IOWA was included within the original Territory of Louisiana, purchased from the French by the United States in 1803. The first white settlement within the present limits of the State was effected in 1788 by Julian Dubuque, a French Canadian, at a point on the Mississippi River, now occupied by the city of Dubuque, so named in honor of its first founder, who, in about the year 1790, erected a fort to defend his possessions granted him by the Spanish crown in the year 1788. The grant was a large tract of land, and included the city now bearing his name.

Iowa lies midway between the Atlantic and Pacific oceans, and in the latitude of greatest migration it is as near as any State of the Union can be, the geographical centre of the United States. It is drained by two great rivers—the Mississippi on its eastern border, and the Missouri on its western border. It is bounded by the great States of the American Union, Wisconsin and Illinois on the east, Minnesota on the north, Nebraska on the west, and Missouri on the south.

The State is the most purely agricultural of all the United States. Lead was at one time quite extensively mined near Dubuque, and was the direct cause of the settlement there of Julian Dubuque in 1788; he mined the lead and traded with the Indians until his death in 1810.

In 1833 a small settlement was established by Illinoisans near where Burlington now stands, and thereafter the eastern portion of the State was rapidly settled until the war of the rebellion broke out, when immigration was checked for about four years, after which an unprecedented rush for farms in Iowa was made by sturdy eastern farmers. Following close upon the heels of the farmer came the business man and manufacturer, and although almost purely agricultural, Iowa is a State of wonderfully diversified interests, never tending, however, to build large cities. Moderate sized cities are scattered throughout the State, while on the two great rivers forming the eastern and western border are such magnificent commercial centers as Keokuk, Fort Madison, Burlington, Muscatine, Davenport, Clinton, Bellevue, Dubuque, Sioux City, and Council Bluffs.

Notwithstanding Dubuque was the first settler, as early as 1673 whites had explored the country. The aboriginal owners of this lovely region, in their appreciation of its beauty, fertility and location, bestowed upon it the very appropriate name of Iowa, signifying in their language, "The beautiful land." The first Europeans who trod the soil of Iowa were two zealous French Jesuits, of Canada, James Marquette and Louis Joliet, who had heard from the tribes of the northwest, assembled in council, of the noble river, on the banks of which they dwelt. Marquette and Joliet were stationed at the mission of St. Marys, the oldest settlement in the present State of Michigan. Marquette formed the purpose of discovering this great river, and the Indians who had gathered in large numbers to witness his departure, endeavored to dissuade him from his perilous journey, representing to to him that the Indians of the Mississippi Valley were cruel, and would resent the intrusion of strangers into their domain. But he was not to be diverted from his purpose, and on May 13th, 1673, with Joliet and five French Canadian boatmen, he left the mission, and proceeding westward to the Wisconsin, they descended that river to the Mississippi, and on the 25th of June landed a little above the mouth of what is now the Des Moines River, where they remained six days with a part of the Illinois nation, and on their departure Marquette received from them the calumet, the emblem of peace and a safeguard among the nations. The first settlement of the whites in Iowa was made by Julien Dubuque, in 1788, who purchased from the Indians the land where the City of Dubuque now stands, and engaged in mining and trading at that place, where he died in 1810.

Although Marquette and Joliet in their exploration of the Mississippi River looked over the luxuriant border of Iowa as early as in 1673, yet the French and Spaniards left this country to the undisturbed possession of the aborigines. Even the enterprise of Julien Dubuque was not inaugurated until more than a century later.

When the United States came into possession of the Mississippi Valley, by the "Louisiana Purchase," the territory now comprising the State of Iowa was in the possession of the Sacs, Foxes and Iowas, with the savage and warlike Sioux Indians in the northern and western portions of the territory. After a long contest with these tribes under the leadership of the renowned Black Hawk, known in history as the "Black Hawk War," the treaty by which the whites at last obtained possession of Iowa was concluded at Rock Island, September 21st, 1832, and ratified February 13th, 1833, to take effect June 1st, 1833, when the Indians left the ceded territory known as the "Black Hawk Purchase," thus opening the way for its settlement by the white man.

The territory embraced within the limits of the State of Iowa was, as is well known, a part of the immense empire which France sold to the United States in 1803, and which had been previously for a time a part of the possessions of the crown of Spain, to which it was conveyed by France in the year 1763.

On the 31st of October, 1803, an act of Congress was approved, authorising the President to take possession of the newly-acquired territory, and provide for it a temporary government; and another act approved March 26th, 1804, authorized the division of the "Louisiana

Purchase," as it was then called, into two separate territories. All that portion south of the 33rd parrallel of north latitude, was called the "Territory of Orleans," and that north of the said parallel was known as the "District of Louisiana," and was placed under the jurisdiction of what was then known as "Indian Territory."

On the 4th day of July, 1805, another change occurred, the district of Louisiana becoming on that day the "Territory of Louisiana." The legislative power was vested in the governor and three judges, to be appointed by the President and Senate, the former for three years, the latter for four. This government continued until the 7th day of December, 1812, when the Territory of Louisiana became the Territory of Missouri.

In 1819 a portion of this Territory was organized as "Arkansas Territory," and in 1821 the State of Missouri was admitted, being a part of the former Territory of Missouri.

The admission of Missouri carried with it the abolition of the Territory of Missouri. All that part of the latter not included within the limits of the State of Missouri, was therefore left without civil government, and remained in that condition until June 28th, 1834, when the portion east of the Missouri and White Earth Rivers, which limits included all of the present Wisconsin, Iowa and Minnesota, and most of the Territory of Dakota, became a part of the Territory of Michigan.

In July, 1836, the territory embracing the present States of Iowa, Minnesota and Wisconsin was detached from Michigan, and organized with a separate territorial government under the name of "Wisconsin Territory."

By virtue of an act of Congress, approved June 12th, 1838, on the 3rd of July, of the same year, the Territory of Iowa was constituted. It embraced the present State of Iowa, and the greater portion of what is now the State of Minnesota. Robert Lucas, who had been one of the early Governors of Ohio, was appointed the first Territorial Governor, and William B. Conway, secretary. The latter died during his term of office, in November, 1839, and James Clarke was appointed to the vacancy. The first Legislative Assembly convened at Burlington, November 12th, 1838. That place continued as the seat of the Territorial Government until the Fourth Legislative Assembly, which convened at Iowa City, December 6th, 1841. The latter place continued as the capital of the territory and state until the permanent location at Des Moines, in 1857.

On the 17th of January, 1846, the Legislative Assembly passed an act providing directly for an election, in April following, of delegates to a constitutional convention. The convention thus provided for met at Iowa City on the 4th day of May following, and formed a constitution with the present boundaries of the state, which had meantime been proposed in Congress. This constitution was adopted by the people August 3rd, 1846, by 9,492 affirmative votes against 9,036 negative votes. Governor Clarke, by proclamation, called an election of state officers for October 26th, 1846. On that day Ansel Briggs, of the county of Jackson, was elected Governor, Elisha Cutler, jr., Secretary of State, Joseph T. Fales, Auditor of Public Accounts, and Morgan Reno, Treasurer. These officers entered upon their respective duties December following.

On the 28th of December, A. D. 1846, Iowa was admitted into the Union as the twenty-ninth state.

It is a matter of some interest to glance at the various changes of ownership and jurisdiction through which it has passed.

It belonged to France, with other territory now belonging to our national domain.

In 1763, with other territory, it was ceded to Spain.

October 1st, 1800, it was ceded, with other territory, from Spain back to France.

April 30th, 1803, it was ceded, with other territory, by France to the United States.

October 31st, 1803, a temporary government was authorized by Congress for the newly acquired territory.

October 1st, 1804, it was included in the District of Louisiana, and placed under the jurisdiction of the Territorial Government of Indiana.

July 4th, 1805, it was included as a part of the Territory of Louisiana, then organized with a separate Territorial Government.

June 4th, 1812, it was embraced in what was then made the Territory of Missouri.

June 28th, 1834, it became part of the Territory of Michigan.

July 3rd, 1836, it was included as a part of the newly organized Territory of Wisconsin.

June 12th, 1838, it was included in and constituted a part of the newly organized Territory of Iowa.

December 28th, 1846, it was admitted into the Union as a State.

Among the first important matters demanding attention at the first session of the Iowa Territorial Legislature, was the location of the seat of government, and provision for the erection of public buildings, for which Congress had appropriated $20,000. Governor Lucas, in his message, had recommended the appointment of commissioners, with a view to making a central location. The extent of the future State of Iowa was not known or thought of. Only on a strip of land fifty miles wide, bordering on the Mississippi River, was the Indian title extinguished, and a central location meant some central point in the Black Hawk Purchase, and on the 21st day of January, 1839, an act was passed appointing Chauncey Swan, of Dubuque county; John Ronalds, of Louisa county, and Robert Ralston, of Des Moines county, Commissioners, to select a site for a permanent seat of government within the limits of Johnson county.

Johnson county had been created by act of the Territorial Legislature of Wisconsin, approved December 21st, 1837, and organized by act passed at the special session at Burlington in June, 1838, the organization to date from July 4th following, and was, from north to to south, in the geographical center of this purchase, and as near the east and west geographical center of the future State of Iowa as then could be made, as the boundary line between the lands of the United States and the Indians, established by the treaty of October 21st, 1837, was immediately west of the county limits.

The commissioners, after selecting the site were directed to lay out 640 acres into a town, to be called Iowa City, and to proceed to sell lots and erect public buildings thereon, Congress having granted a section of land to be selected by the territory for this purpose. The commissioners met at Napoleon, Johnson county, May 1st, 1839, selected a site, section 10, in township 79 north of range 6 west of the Fifth Principal Meridian, and immediately surveyed it and laid off the town. The first sale of lots took place August 16th, 1839. The site selected for the public buildings was a little west of the geographical center of the section, where a square of ten acres on the elevated grounds overlooking the river was reserved for this purpose. The capitol was located in the center of the square.

On Monday, December 6th, 1841, the Fourth Legislative Assembly met at the new capitol, Iowa City, but the capitol building could not be used, and the legislature occupied a temporary frame house that had been erected for that purpose during the session of 1841-2.

By an act of the Territorial Legislature of Iowa, approved February 12th, 1844, the question of the formation of a State Constitution and providing for the election of delegates to a convention to be convened for that purpose, was submitted to the people, to be voted upon at their township elections in April following. The vote was largely in favor of the measure, and the delegates elected assembled in convention at Iowa City on the 7th of October, 1844. On the 1st day of November following, the convention completed its work and adopted the first state constitution.

The constitution adopted by this convention was rejected by the people at an election held in April, 1845, and also at one held on the 4th day of August, 1845, there being at the latter 7,235 votes cast "for the constitution," and 7,656 votes cast "against the constitution."

A second constitutional convention assembled at Iowa City on the 4th day of May, 1846, and on the 18th day of the same month another constitution for the new state with the present boundaries was adopted, and submitted to the people for ratification on the 3rd day of August following, when it was accepted.

The constitution was approved by Congress, and by act of Congress approved December 28th, 1846, Iowa was admitted as a sovereign state in the American Union.

The first General Assembly of the State of Iowa was composed of nineteen senators and forty representatives. It assembled at Iowa City November 30th, 1846, about a month before the state was admitted into the Union.

At the first session also arose the question of the re-location of the capital. The western boundary of the state, as now determined, left Iowa City too far toward the eastern and southern boundary of the state; this was conceded. Congress had appropriated five sections of land for the erection of public buildings, and toward the close of the session a bill was introduced providing for the re-location of the seat of government, involving to some extent the location of the state university, which had already been discussed. It provided for the appointment of three commissioners, who were authorized to make a location as near the geographical center of the state as a healthy and eligible site could be obtained; to select the five sections of land donated by Congress; to survey and plat into town lots not exceeding one section of land so selected; to sell lots at public sale, not to exceed two in each block. Having done this, they were then required to suspend further operations, and make a report of their proceedings to the Governor. The bill passed both houses by decisive votes, received the signature of the Governor, and became a law, and in 1851 bills were introduced for the removal of the capital to Pella and to Fort Des Moines. The latter appeared to have the support of the majority, but was finally lost in the House on the question of ordering it to its third reading.

On the 15th day of January, 1855, a bill re-locating the capital within two miles of the Raccoon Fork of the Des Moines, and for the appointment of commissioners, was approved by Gov. Grimes. The site was selected in 1856, in accordance with the provisions of this act, the land being donated to the state by citizens and property holders of Des Moines.

Gov. B. R. Sherman says of the state: "The Iowa of to-day is a vast empire, the joy of every citizen, and containing within itself all the essential elements of political and personal greatness, which needs only the watchful and liberal care of the state to make it the realization of the hopes of the most sanguine of its people. Our growth in population and development, in resources and possibilities, has been without parallel, and it is not too much to say that our people have been exceptional in prosperity, as unrivalled in business energies. Our prairies, so lately a wilderness, are teeming with a population unusually intelligent and industrious, being constantly added to from the over crowded East; and in the near future the many thousands of untilled acres, fertile beyond description, and only awaiting the touch of the husbandman, shall be made to laugh in abundant harvests, alike the joy and profit of the hardy pioneer. The products of our soil, yielding in such wonderful abundance, are sent to the uttermost parts of the globe to make glad the inhabitants of earth, and our very name has finally become the synonym for superiority and plenteousness, and the enterprise of the people has accomplished results none the less astonishing to ourselves than a marvel to the nation."

Iowa is by actual United States statistics the richest agricultural state in the Union, and has twice the agricultural resources of all the New England States combined, and in surplus products equal to the New England and Middle States combined.

Iowa, in 1886, produced 198,847,000 bushels of corn on 7,927,019 acres, valued at $59,654,100; wheat, 2,657,105 acres producing 32,455,000 bushels, valued at $19,473,000; oats, 2,298,752 acres, producing 78,454,000 bushels, valued at $18,044,420; hay, 3,673,875 acres, producing 4,137,844 tons, valued at $20,689,220; other field crops, 514,125 acres, product valued at $6,690,520; a total of field products amounting to $124,551,260.

January 1st, 1888, Iowa had 1,003,022 head of horses, valued at $74,032,082; mules, 45,649 head, valued at $3,936,540; milch cows, 1,255,432 head, valued at $29,251,566; oxen and other cattle, 2,095,253 head, valued at $42,633,795; sheep, 408,478 head, valued at $985,249; hogs, 4,148,811 head, valued at $27,969,624; a total valuation of live stock amounting to $178,808,856, or twice the value of all the New England States combined, and unsurpassed by any state in the Union. Total farms cultivated in Iowa in 1888 amounted to 185,351; almost as many as all the New England States, where farms are cut up into such small acreage that a western farmer would call a garden patch. The surplus agricultural product of Iowa is simply enormous, and amounts to more than all of that of the New England and Middle States combined. In 1887 the agricultural product of Iowa was increased by about $25,000,000 over that of 1886, while the product of the New England and Middle States was not materially advanced. Iowa's surplus product has been forced east by the force of circumstances which governs this great Western empire, viz: the dominating influence of the monopolistic transportation companies over the American Congress, which withholds a just proportion of public appropriations for the improvement of the water ways contiguous to the "Great West," such as harbor facilities on the Texas Gulf Coast. The day is dawning that will revolutionize the channels of exportation of the surplus grain products of America, and in consequence stimulate the industry and enhance values of farm products and farm properties of this Western empire. Iowa is deeply interested in the movement for Deep Harbors on the Texas Gulf Coast, and consequently has placed on the permanent committee to secure Deep Harbors, such able citizens as Hon. J. M. Pierce, Hon. A. P. Chamberlin, and Hon. D. W. Smith, of Des Moines; Hon. W. O. Kulp, of Davenport; and Hon. B. Zevely, of Council Bluffs.

CHAPTER VI.

TEXAS—1687 TO 1889.

La Salle, the French explorer, first settled Texas in 1687, erected a fort on Matagorda Bay, and spread the French flag to the gentle breezes. Without doubt this vast state was included within the French cessions to the United States in 1803, under the name of Louisiana.

France in 1670 ceded all the Territory of Louisiana, including Texas, to the Spanish Crown. The country was retroceded to France in 1800, and by France sold to the United States in 1803. Spain, however, claimed Texas as Spanish territory not included in the retrocession to France in 1800.

The United States made several unsuccessful attempts to wrest Texas from the Spaniards, between 1806 and 1816; in one battle in 1813 the American and Mexican loss amounted to 2,500 killed, while 700 citizens of San Antonio were massacred. In 1819 the Sabine River was established as the boundary.

In 1820, an American citizen, named Moses Austin, obtained from the Mexican government a grant of a large tract of land, and began a settlement which rapidly increased, but some were of such a lawless character that in 1830 the Mexican government forbade any more Americans coming into Texas.

In 1824, the Mexicans overthrew the tyranical power of the Spaniards, and adopted a constitutional mode of government, recognized by every foreign power except Spain.

In 1833, a convention of settlers, then 2,000 strong, attempted to form an independent Mexican State; the attempt was unsuccessful.

In December 1835, a small gathering of Texans assembled and declared the independence of Mexico, and professed to have established the Republic of Texas. Santa Anna, the President of Mexico, at once prepared to invade Texas with an army of 7,000 men.

February 23rd, 1836, he with 4,000 men invested the Alamo at San Antonio, garrisoned by 140 men, under the command of W. B. Travis; thirty-two other Texans forced their way through the Mexican lines and joined Travis; therefore Travis could muster but 172 men, with which force he defended the Alamo for eleven days, repulsing the Mexicans repeatedly, and killing 1,600 of the attacking force, while his own little band was reduced to a mere handful. On the 6th day of March, 1836, the Alamo fell into the hands of the Mexicans, all of its defenders were slain, only a woman, a child and servant being spared from the wholesale slaughter. They were concealed in a strong inner room, and escaped the tremendous cannonade and musketry fire. Here the brave Davy Crocket fell surrounded by scores of dead Mexicans, slain by his own hand, while defending himself in the final assault.

General Sam Houston soon after succeeded in raising 800 picked men to repel the invaders. April 21st following he gave battle to twice the number of Mexicans headed by Santa Anna; the battle resulted in the total defeat of the Mexicans, who lost 630 in killed, 208 wounded, and 730 prisoners. Santa Anna escaped from the field, but was captured the following day. This decisive battle practically determined the independence of Texas, and a Republican form of government was at once adopted; General Sam Houston was chosen President and inaugurated October 22nd, 1836.

March, 1837, the United States acknowledged the independence of the Texas Republic, followed by the acknowledgment by France in 1839, and England, Holland and Belgium in 1840. Thus was the Republic firmly established.

In 1845, Texas was annexed to the United States by act of Congress in December in that year. Mexico had never acknowledged the independence of Texas, and an invading army started from the City of Mexico to invest the Texas Republic. The United States authorities proposed to hold by force of arms the new territory acquired by annexation, and the result was the Mexican war of 1846; it lasted into 1848, the Mexicans were defeated, and their capital fell into the hands of U. S. General Scott; peace was established, and Texas became one of the states of the American Union. It seceded with the other Southern States in 1861, and joined the war of the rebellion, and not until 1870 was the state re-admitted to the Union.

The physical features of Texas are its Gulf coast line, extending 800 miles from the mouth of the Sabine River, which separates the state from Louisiana, to the mouth of the Rio Grande River, which forms the boundary line between Texas and Mexico. From a low swampy coast on the Gulf, the surface gradually rises to 3,000 and even 5,000 feet above sea level in the northern portions of the Pan Handle, and quite mountainous in the northwestern portion, near the city of El Paso and near San Antonio. The shore is protected by a chain of long narrow and flat islands from the severe Gulf storms. Large lakes or lagoons are formed between the islands and the main land, and form a safe refuge for small crafts, and in some instances they are deep and afford safe anchorage for large ocean-going vessels.

The islands are from 50 to 200 miles long. The channels connecting the lagoons with the Gulf are of variable depths, that at Galveston Island being of the greatest width and depth, the channel is over two miles wide and twelve feet deep at its greatest depth.

This channel has had millions of dollars expended upon it by the National Government in order that the channel may be narrowed and deepened upon the Eads plan of jetty system. The work is now in the hands of a competent U. S. Engineer, Major Earnest, and progressing with as much success as the limited appropriations made by the National Congress will admit of.

The City of Galveston is situated on Galveston island, and is already a magnificent commercial city, deeply interested in the final success of the engineering skill of Major Earnest. Here is a magnificent roadstead capable of accommodating the commerce of the world; much cannot be said of the harbor as a refuge for distressed vessels in severe weather owing to the deep water being in the channel and not landlocked; while commodious, it could not be regarded a perfectly secure harbor. It will be necessary to construct two jetties, known as the North and South jetties, in order to control the channel as proposed, each of these jetties of solid stone work will be extended six miles to the deep water in the Gulf. The south jetty is nearly one-third completed; under most favorable circumstances, with ample appropriations the work could not be completed under three or four years; at the present rate this generation will scarcely enjoy the benefits of the proposed harbor, or for that matter, any of the proposed harbors of the Gulf coast.

At the mouth of the Sabine, similar work is being constructed by the Government, the general features being similar to Galveston; no city is there, however, and the commercial necessities do not compare.

At the mouth of the Brazos River, private capital has taken hold of the matter by permission of the government. The bill giving them permission to construct a harbor, also provides for payment by the National Government a stipulated sum per foot of depth obtained as the work progresses, until 24 feet of water is obtained, when final payment is made by the Government, and the harbor management reassumed by them. A great many persons believe that the friends of Brazos Point have solved the question of economical and speedy construction of harbors upon the Gulf coast. The friends of Aransas Pass also favor development by private capital in a manner similar to Brazos, and Congress will undoubtedly be called upon to pass a bill of similar tenor to enable private capital to improve Aransas Harbor and Pass.

Galveston friends and friends of Sabine professes to be satisfied with the National appropriation idea, but are divided upon the present system of appropriations in homeopathic doses. The true friends of either place are heartily in accord with the Inter-State Deep Harbor movement,* while the enemies to progress and public interest are in favor of continuing the present long-drawn-out system which probably affords them place or profit as individuals. Aransas Pass, while very conspicuous as a prospective deep water port, has received but a few hundred thousand dollars from the National Government, and no continuous work has been performed at that point; unlike Galveston, the

---

*See Appendix for purposes and accomplishments of the Deep Harbor Committee.

harbor is land-locked, but limited in good depth and also limited in anchorage; the friends of this point claim, however, that the harbor is of sufficient capacity to hold safely all of the merchant marine that will ever traverse the Gulf, in addition to *all* of the American navy. (The latter is only a slur at our present navy, they have been so accustomed to speak slightingly of our navy that they cannot read the signs of the times, viz: The future American navy will be larger and more effective than any other single government on earth can produce).

We grant that Aransas Pass has more in her favor, naturally, to make a greater port than any other point on the Gulf coast, but in the same connection we must say that men of energy, enterprise, and strategy move the world and not conditions. Conditions do not make or build cities, it is individual and collective enterprise, and they are which conquer conditions, as evidenced by our great Chicago. Almost anywhere within twenty miles of Chicago's present site could have been builded a city with one half the difficulties to overcome that has marked the era of that magnificent metropolis. Was it conditions then that made Chicago? No, it was the man, and it will be man that makes Aransas, irrespective of conditions, or it will not be made at all. Macauber like, the friends of Aransas appear to be waiting for something to turn up.

Turning from the coast we follow the gradually rising and gently undulating prairie lands, except a few counties in the eastern portion famous for their pine; the state is purely agricultural and stock raising. Texas contains a greater area than any other state or territory of the United States, (except Alaska), 274,356 square miles, divided into 229 counties, some of which are larger than some two or three New England States combined.

The principal rivers of the state are the Red, Sabine, Trinity, Colorado and Grand, collectively supplying some 400 miles of navigable waters, all flowing southeast into the Gulf.

The principal cities are Galveston, San Antonio, Fort Worth, Dallas, Houston, Waco and Austin, the latter, the state capital. Galveston is the principal seaport. Houston is also a seaport city, reached by Galveston Bay and Buffalo Bayou; Houston is also a great railroad center. Dallas is a large wholesale point, only surpassed in the state by Fort Worth, which city claims to be the greatest railroad center in Texas, some thirteen roads centering or diverging from there. San Antonio is a winter resort, a "quaint old town" of great historical renown; here is the famed Alamo, and various other missions of the early days of the Montezumas.

Texas produces every species of grain, vegetable or fruit known to agriculture, except bananas, oranges and pineapples, and they are raised to a very limited extent. Cotton is principally produced, Texas ranking first of all the United States. In wool, Texas is in the lead, in fact in all live stock and live stock products Texas leads the Union.

PUBLIC SCHOOLS.

The public schools of Texas are rapidly approaching a degree of perfection that approaches the boasted New England systems, and as compared with other Southern States are vastly superior. The following facts gathered from reports of Hon. F. B. Chilton, Secretary of the Texas State Bureau of Immigration, and can be relied upon:

The permanent free school fund, invested in state and county bonds, is $5,873,174.02; 40,000,000 acres of land controlled by the state, and four leagues, or 17,712 acres, to each county organized and unorganized, controlled by the counties, making a total of 47,288,676 acres, which at $3 per acre would bring $141,866,028, added to the above makes a grand total of $147,739,202.02. The interest on the bonds and land notes for which school lands have been sold, rentals from the lands leased, one-third of the state tax, and one dollar on each poll, forms the available fund which is used each year for the maintenance of public free schools. The available fund is increasing rapidly each year. In 1881 the amount appropriated for maintenance of public free schools was $103,933.44; in 1885 it was $2,050,000; in 1887 it was $2,255,415; a letter from the treasurer of the state says, the appropriation for 1888 will be about $2,300,000. This fund will soon be sufficient to give free education to ten times as many children and persons as now live in Texas, between the ages of five and twenty years. We have a State University located at Austin, the capital, which is one of the best endowed educational institutions in the United States. It is open to both sexes; tuition free. The Constitution of the state provides for the establishment of a university for the education of colored youths; steps have been taken to put it in operation. The University lands will permanently endow these institutions, making them in time the equal of any in America. The University Permanent Fund is at present $523,411, invested in bonds; this with an available fund of $21,680, and cash on hand of $10,825, makes a total University Fund of $555,916. Besides this, it has 2,221,400 acres of land, most of which was located at an early day, and is very valuable, worth from $3 to $20 per acre. At an average of $6 it would bring $13,328,400, making a grand total of $13,884,316 for university purposes. The State Agricultural and Mechanical College, located near the City of Bryan, Brazo County, is endowed with $209,000, invested in bonds, also a large endowment from the United States Government. Ninety-four students, one-half of whom take a mechanical, and one-half an agricultural course, receive free board and tuition. The cost of board and tuition for other students is $130 for the scholastic year. The Sam Houston Normal School for the education of white teachers, and the Prairie View Normal School for the education of colored teachers, are supported by the state, and 155 white and 45 colored students receive tuition and board free, in proportion to white and colored population.

WHARF SCENE, GALVESTON, TEXAS.

Texas produced, in 1886, 69,213,000 bushels of corn on 4,417,-688 acres, valued at $38,759,280; wheat on 529,104 acres producing 5,353,000 bushels, valued at $4,844,700; oats, on 552,966 acres, producing 11,369,000 bushels, valued at $5,684,500; cotton, on 3,771,-740 acres, 1,499,698 bales, valued at $61,102,188; other field crops, on 125,444 acres, products valued at $1,524,686; or a total value of field products, $111,915,354.

January 1st, 1888, Texas had the following live stock: horses, 1,225,803 head, valued at $38,115,135; mules, 193,488 head, valued at $10,032,254; milch cows, 772,716 head, valued at $10,972,567; other cattle, 6,336,504 head, valued at $63,077,993; sheep, 4,523,789 head, valued at $6,864,744; hogs, 2,279,082 head, valued at $6,436,128; a total live stock value of $135,498,821; grand total of agricultural and live stock products amounting to $247,414,175.

The total of assessed values of all properties in Texas for 1888, $730,225,123.

The total commerce of Texas, imports, exports and coastwise trade, amounts to nearly $200,000,000 per annum, even with the limited harbor facilities now enjoyed. Deep harbors would add from 100 to 200 per cent, and make Texas second to no state in America in commerce, etc.

The following recapitulation of Texas statistics we glean from Hon. F. B. Chilton's reports of January 1st, 1888. They are, somewhat, but not materially at variance with United States statistics, owing probably to the fact that the following is one year later than the government reports:

Area of Texas, square miles	274,356
Area of Texas, in acres	175,587,840
Area of mineral lands, acres	20,000,000
Area of timbered lands, acres	40,000,000
Of which there are pine and cypress, acres	26,000,000
Number of acres of public free school lands, controlled by the State	40,000,000
" " " " " " counties	4,237,596
State University lands	2,221,400
Other school interests	839,680
Asylum lands (Deaf and Dumb, Lunatic, Blind and Orphan), 100,000 acres each	400,000
Number of counties (none less than 30 miles square)	203
And enough territory to organize an additional	60
Number of bales of cotton raised, 1887	1,352,377
" bushels of corn raised, 1887	63,416,300
" " of oats raised, 1887	10,000,000
" " of wheat raised, 1887	4,374,000
Estimated live stock in 1887	12,000,000
Shipped live stock in 1887	1,500,000
Exported pounds of wool	8,000,000
" " of hides, 1887, about	60,000,000
Estimated population of 1887	3,000,000
Number of miles of railway, 1887	9,500
And number of miles to be built in 1888	1,280
Taxable values of 1887	$650,225,123
Rate of taxation	37½cts. on the $100
Value of farm products	$172,000,000

Value of live stock	$150,500,000
" stock shipped	$10,000,000
" hides shipped, 1887	$5,400,000
" wool exported, 1887	$1,000,000
" free school fund, bonds and lands	$147,769,202
Available school fund, 1887	$2,285,451
Probable fund for 1888	$2,300,000
Value of State University fund, lands and bonds	$13,884,316
Available fund for 1887	$32,505
Endowment fund of the State Agricultural and Mechanical College	$500,000
Value of Asylum lands	$12,000,000
Estimated value of railways	$215,000,000

While Mr. Chilton estimates the value of railways in the state at over $200,000,000, it is a remarkable fact that no Texas railways have ever yet paid a dividend, accounted for probably in the marvelous amount of railroad extensions indulged in by the various railroads, and the vast mileage necessary to traverse the state, some of which must unavoidably pass through large stretches of unoccupied territory.

Texas is almost an empire within itself, and forms no small portion of the vast empire that stretches from the "Father of Waters" on the east, to the Pacific Ocean on the west. It is the key to the great treasure vaults of the Great West. The establishment of deep harbors on the Texas coast will open the door which will admit of the West; "the greater half of the continent" interchanging commerce with the world without the intervention and extortion of the east, and build up a Texas such as the early Texas fanatic never dreamed of, or the most sanguine of present sages ever conceived.

In size and resources Texas surpasses almost any European country, and the Great West collectively surpasses all of Europe combined.

CHAPTER VII.

CALIFORNIA—1542 TO 1889.

PRIOR to 1542 California was practically unknown, and the name, probably, originated through a Spanish romance, published in 1510, in which the author speaks of an island which he called California Island, a place where an abundance of gold and precious stones was to be found.

The Spaniards, the great explorers, fitted out a fleet in quest of the island of so much abundance, under the command of one Cabrillo, and in 1542 they coasted along what is known as California, as far north as Cape Mendocino, in 42 degrees north latitude. In 1579 Sir Francis Drake, in command of an English fleet, plundering Spanish commerce, coasted along California as far as 48 degrees north latitude and it is believed sailed into San Francisco bay to overhaul his vessels; he claimed the country in the name of England, and named it New Albion. The country, however, remained unoccupied, except by a few Jesuites, until 1767, when the Franciscan friars entered and occupied California, driving out the Jesuits with the aid of a proclamation of the King of Spain, backed by armed coadjutors. They succeeded in establishing various missions, succeeding in bringing under their submission the mass of the aborigines, and prospered well until Mexico became independent (in 1822); that marked the turning point in the Franciscan rule, and their power gradually waned until 1840, when they were entirely broken up.

The Indians were treated by these missions as little better than slaves; they were, however, taught frugality, and prospered in a worldly way, intellectually they were very little aided by the missions. In all there were twenty-one missions, the first being established in 1769, the last in 1820. They were all well located, the priests having displayed excellent judgment in selecting the best garden spots for their settlements. The Indian population was large, even up as late as the cession of California to the United States by Mexico in 1848. The mission Indians numbering at that time about 30,000. In 1880 there were but 11,630 Indians in the entire state.

Just prior to the United States coming into possession of California, there was great rivalry between England, France and the United States over this Mexican possession, and in 1842, Commodore Jones, of the American navy, captured the fort at Monterey, and raised the stars and stripes; the next morning, however, he hauled down his flag and made satisfactory apology for the mistake. Both European countries were charged with attempting to wrest this country from Mexico; such a thing the United States would not tolerate. The result being that when war was declared with Mexico by the United States, that General Fremont, who had been upon a scientific investigation on the Pacific coast, abandoned his explorations in May, 1846, and made his way to Sonoma, where he organized a battalion of mounted riflemen, and on the 5th day of July recommended a declaration of independence. Commodore Sloat, on a United States frigate, put in at Monterey on July 2nd, and on the morning of the 7th, invested and took possession of the fort, and hoisted the stars and stripes, with no intention of imitating Commodore Jones' example, by hauling them down again. He immediately issued a proclamation declaring California to be a part of the United States. General Fremont in obeying the orders of Commodore Stockton, (who had superceded Sloat), instead of those of General Kearney, who ranked the Commodore, and assumed command, got himself into trouble and was court-marshaled, found guilty of "mutiny and disobedience." The President rejected the finding as to mutiny, and remitted the penalty on the other count, but General Fremont refused the clemency and resigned. He afterwards conducted several successful expeditions overland to California, and served the government most faithfully in his exploratoins in the Rocky Mountains, and he is regarded almost universally as the conqueror of the territory.

At the close of the war with Mexico California was ceded to the United States in the treaty of peace ratified May 19th, 1848, and immediately the question came up whether it should be admitted to the Union as a free or a slave state. Congress adjourned March 4th, 1849, without settling the question, or even forming a territorial government. San Francisco was, however, made a port of entry and the customs laws were extended over the country.

Meanwhile, in 1848, gold had been discovered, and a grand rush had been made to the new Eldorado; the population had increased rapidly, the matchless harbor at San Francisco had attracted the commerce of every nation, presenting a centre of attraction for the restless and energetic of every race and clime.

September, 1849, the people held a convention, which framed a State Constitution, in which slavery was expressly forbidden.

September 7th, 1850, congress passed a bill admitting California as a free state, but as a compromise left New Mexico and Utah, (organized on the same day as territories), open to its introduction. The gold excitement was now at its height, fortunes were made in a day, and a constant stream of gold flowed eastward, intensifying the excitement. Speculation ran rife, and property in San Francisco was held at fabulous prices; lots were worth gold coin enough to carpet them; all forms of gambling were regarded as legitimate business; adventurers and crimimals flocked in, and society was in a chaotic state. Self-preservation being the first law of nature, order became necessary, which could only be enforced by stringent measures, and was the direct cause of the formation of the celebrated vigilance committee, which soon assumed the proportions of a regular government, and successfully resisted the state authorities up to 1856, when they formally resigned, after having hanged several and driven hundreds of the worst characters from the state. The vigilantes held their courts and pronounced judgment which was speedily executed, while their judgment was often severe, it has never been charged that injustice was done, while such methods are to be deplored, the exigencies of the times demanded speedy justice and a general fear of the consequences of sin.

California is one of the largest states of the Union, being 750 miles long by an average of 200 in width, containing 155,980 square miles. The state is blessed with several fine harbors, the best being at San Francisco; the others at San Diego, Humboldt, Santa Barbara, Monterey, Bodega, San Luis, Obispo and Tomales; the first named being the best harbor on the Pacific coast, if not the best in the world. The bay is completely land-locked and of ample room to float the combined navies of the world.

California has but two prominent rivers, the Sacramento and the San Joaquin, both empty into San Francisco Bay, one from the northeast and the other from the southeast, both are navigable for considerable distance. There are two great mountain chains in the state, the Sierra Nevada and coast range. The state is interspersed with mountains and large fertile valleys. The principal mountain peaks are Shastar Tyndall, Brewer and Dana, ranging in height from 13,000 to 14,500 feet. The valleys have the appearance of having been at one time immense lakes that would compare with Lakes Superior and Michigan, having been drained into the ocean, left a rich sediment which accounts probably for the remarkable fertility of these valleys. The state is noted for its wonderful scenery, especially that in the great Yosemite valley, which is world renowned. The valley is about 150 miles southeast of San Francisco, at an elevation of 4,000 feet above sea level, in the center of the Sierra Nevada mountains, hemmed in by almost perpendicular walls or cliffs, from 2,000 to 3,000 feet high. The great falls of Yosemite creek are the most wonderful in the world; the creek falls 2,600 feet in three leaps, the highest being 1,500 feet. Mt. Dana, which towers above and dominates the Yosemite valley, is over 13,000 feet high, and is easily ascended; from its summit a magnificent panorama of the Sierra Nevada range and Yosemite valley is obtainable. "The big trees" also attract much attention: these giants of the forest may be seen in groups, the most important being near Visalia. The common name for these trees is giant red wood; they vary in height from 100 feet to 400 feet, and in circumference at five feet from the ground, varying from 25 to more than 100 feet: one now standing measures 104 feet in circumference, and 376 feet in height, remains of fallen trees indicate that much larger trees have grown there. The other native species of timber are pines in large variety, black oak, ash, hickory, elm, beach, white cedar, spruce, fir, laurel, tamarack, cypress, yew, juniper, chestnut, acacia, poplar, cottonwood, walnut, maple, buckeye, and innumerable varieties of shrubs, the most remarkable being the "chaparral."

The wild animals of California are varied and quite extensive, although they are being gradually exterminated, especially those animals valuable for their fur or flesh.

The largest and fiercest of the animals of this state—the grizzly bear—is now almost extinct; next comes the black, brown and cinnamon bears, followed by the less harmful wolves, badgers, coyotes, foxes, wild cats, otter, beaver, gopher, skunks, martins, weasels, elk, deer, rabbits and other minor animals, probably the most attractive of all California animals is the sea lion, which frequents seal rock at Golden Gate in countless numbers, whose noise and gambols attract thousands of sight seers daily. Birds of every variety, indigenous to the varied climate, are in great abundance, the California quail and sage hen being remarkable for plumage and food qualities, other species being not unlike those found all over the Western States.

Fish in great abundance and variety are found in the rivers, bays and in the ocean, and their catch and preservation form the important industries of the state.

The precious metals are all found in the Sierra Nevada mountains in the northeast portion of the state, gold being the most prominent and found in greater abundance than in any other field in the world, the average annual output for thirty years being upwards of $20,000,000, approximating in the thirty years nearly $1,000,000,000. It is mined principally by placers, although some good quartz lodes have been discovered and worked. Quicksilver is largely used in placer mining, and is found near at hand in great abundance, and one mine has yielded as high as 3,500,000 lbs. quicksilver per annum, and is the largest mine of the kind in the world.

The volcanic character of California is manifest in the formation of the mountains, and there are occasionally earthquakes now of more or less violence, upheaving and cracking the ground. In consequence of this uncertainty, the traveler will see that the great majority of houses in California are of frame, or if of stone, the foundation and upper walls are of unusual width and strength.

The state boasts of a very superior climate, the leading feature being the remarkable uniformity of temperature, the mean summer temperature of San Francisco is 60 degrees, and mean winter temperature 51 degrees; there are but two seasons, the dry and rainy, corresponding with the eastern summer and winter, the dry season being from May to November, and the rainy season from November to April.

Not much more than one-third of the state is adapted to agriculture, and only about one-half of that is being cultivated. In 1886 California had 3,104,640 acres of wheat, producing 36,165,000 bushels, valued at $26,400,450; 722,450 acres of barley, producing 16,038,000 bushels, valued at $10,424,700; hay, 967,479 acres, producing 1,296,284 tons, valued at $10,564,307; other crops, 328,489 acres, producing crops valued at $7,076,300; a total value of crops amounting to $54,465,757.

January 1st, 1888, the state contained 345,828 head of horses and mules, valued at $25,098,644; 250,773 head of milch cows, valued at $8,275,509; oxen and other cattle, 692,267 head, valued at $14,194,447; sheep, 5,462,728 head, valued at $10,291,779; hogs, 1,047,842 head, valued as $4,886,000; or a total of 7,799,488 head of live stock, valued at $62,696,379, or a grand total of farm products amounting to $117,166,136.

California abounds in fruit, and especially excels in oranges, peaches, apricots and grapes, which fruit is shipped in large quantities either green, dried, canned or in juice wine, etc.; the total value of which forms no small proportion of the state's farm product, and would place the entire product well on to $200,000,000.

The principal commercial cities of the state are San Francisco, Sacramento, Los Angeles and San Diego.

While California has not yet entered very actively into the movement for deep harbors on the Texas Gulf coast, yet their interests are identical with all of "The Great West," and in a short time they will add their influence to build up a western commercial Congress that will shake the nation, and insure recognition from the great National Congress at Washington. California has received almost her proportion of national appropriations, owing to the intimate commercial relations San Francisco has ever had to the great City of New York, these relations are being gradually shifted to a nearer and dearer relationship which is springing up in this grand Western Empire, to which San Francisco is destined to be what New York has been heretofore to the entire Union, dividing honors only with the Gulf port.

CHAPTER VIII.

MINNESOTA—1680 TO 1889.

WHILE Minnesota lays on both sides of the Mississippi, which river finds its source in the north central portion of the state, it is usually and in this history rated as Trans-Mississippi, or a portion of "The Great West."

It was first explored as far north as St. Anthony's Falls in 1680, by French fur traders, and the falls received their name by a Franciscan Priest named Louis Hennepin, after whom the county in which Minneapolis is situated was named. The French succeeded in establishing several fur trading stations in Minnesota about that time; the settlement of the state, however, did not commence until 1845. England became possessor of this portion of North America in 1763, the French having in that year ceded it to Great Britain.

The United States came into possession of this territory at the conclusion of the Revolutionary War in 1783, and was included in what was then termed the Northwest Territory, and which included Wisconsin and Illinois. In 1820, Fort Snelling was built, and two years later a mill was erected at St. Anthony Falls, where Minneapolis now stands. In 1823, the first steamboat ascended the river to St. Anthony Falls, and about the year 1830 a small Swiss colony settled near where St. Paul now is. In 1838 the Indian title to the lands east of the Mississippi River were extinguished, and in 1842 a settlement was effected at Stillwater.

The territory of Minnesota was organized by Act of Congress in 1849, the territory then containing 5,000 white population. Soon after the Indian title to the lands between the Mississippi and Red River of the North was extinguished, barring a few small reservations, the settlement of the territory then began in earnest, immigration being so rapid that Congress, in 1857, opened a way for the territory's admission into the Union, which was immediately acted upon by the people, and on May 11th, 1858, the state was admitted, and rapid progress was made in population, wealth and intelligence.

The boundaries of the state as established by the Act of Admission included 83,531 square miles, one-third of which is valuable timber land, including all varieties of deciduous trees found anywhere in the northern states, including valuable pine forests.

The state contains innumerable lakes of more or less importance, in fact about one-thirtieth part of the state's surface is covered with water; the most important lake being Minnetonka lake, near Minneapolis, and White Bear lake, near St. Paul. The state contains several rivers, the most important being the Mississippi, Red river of the North, Minnesota and St. Croix, all of which are more or less navigable, there being within the state 1,350 miles of navigable streams. The waters of the state flow south into the Gulf, east into the great lakes, and north into Hudson Bay, the great divide being in the northwest portion of the state; this divide, the highest portion of which is a table land at an elevation of 1,680 feet, but not more than 100 feet above the surrounding country, nothing resembling mountains in the state. The streams have an unusual fall, and often flow over precipitous places, making waterfalls of such importance as to supply the state with abundant water power, the principal of which is situated at Minneapolis (St. Anthony Falls), where the largest flour mills in the world are situated, the combined output of which aggregate over 8,000 barrels per day.

Minnesota ranks well in the front of agricultural states of the Union. Spring wheat is the principal cereal, and in that commodity the state excels all others, and likewise in oats, excepting Iowa.

In 1886 the state produced 19,905,000 bushels of corn from 668,380 acres, product valued at $6,767,700 from 3,067,851 acres; 42,856,000 bushels of wheat, valued at $26,142,160, from 1,184,032 acres; 40,735,000 bushels of oats, valued at $10,183,750, from 367,601 acres; 8,455,000 bushels of barley, valued at $3,551,100, from 480,000 acres; 600,000 tons of hay, valued at $2,820,000, from 63,161 acres; 5,306,000 bushels of potatoes, valued at $1,963,220; other field crops, 39,374 acres, product valued at $246,480; or a total value of field crops amounting to $51,674,410.

January 1st, 1888, the state contained 390,458 head of horses and and mules, valued at $32,479,714; 433,966 head of milch cows, valued at $10,306,693; 489,886 head of oxen and other cattle, valued at $9,974,076; 283,725 head of sheep, valued at $674,698; 549,793 head of hogs, valued at $3,254,775; a total of 1,947,828 head of live stock, valued at $56,689,956; or a grand total of farm products valued at $107,264,366.

Minnesota is also regarded as a health resort notwithstanding the long cold winters. The atmosphere is dry and bracing and the cold equitable. The summers are delightful, warm days and cool nights, and attract thousands of tourists during that season. Lake Minnetonka has become a very popular summer resort, and there are several very large and comfortable hotels situated about the lake where every creature comfort is supplied. Several excursion steamers ply about the lake for the accommodation of visitors, besides numerous sailing crafts and row boats.

The lake is reached by a motor line from Minneapolis, likewise by the popular St. Paul, Minneapolis & Manitoba Railway which connects St. Paul and Minneapolis with this beautiful lake.

The school facilities of this state are unsurpassed by any. There are public schools and colleges adequate for the rapidly increasing population, where a finished education may be had which vies with the great institutions of learning in the Eastern States. Society is of the very best and highly refined.

The principal cities are St. Paul, (the Capital), Minneapolis, Winona, Red Wing, Duluth and Fergus Falls. The state is well provided with railroad facilities, the principal lines being the St. P. M. & M., C. B. & Q., C. M. & St. P., C. & N. W., N. P. St. P. & D., and the C., St. P., M. & O. railways.

Minnesota is awakening to the importance of the movement for deep harbors on the Gulf coast. Gov. McGill, in his last biennial message to the Legislature of that state, recommended the appropriation of at least $1,000 dollars to aid in the agitation. As yet no representation of that state has been had on the permanent Standing Committee, known as the "Inter-State Deep Harbor Committee;" we are assured, however, that they are with us, and will ere long have their full quota of representation on the committee which is fast assuming the importance of a Western Commercial Congress.

CHAPTER IX.

OREGON—1592 TO 1889.

OREGON at one time embraced all that portion of the United States north of California and west of the main range of the Rocky Mountains, including a portion of Idaho Territory, and all of the present State of Oregon, and the lately admitted State of Washington. The coast of Oregon was first discovered by De Fuca, a Greek navigator, no claim, however, was made to the country until the Spanish Admiral Fonte, in 1640, coasted along the west coast of America in the interests of Spain, which country she pretended to claim as Spanish territory until 1790, when she ceded to England, by treaty, any rights she might have to that portion of America. Notwithstanding several explorers had coasted along the entire west coast of America, the discovery of that noble stream, the Columbia River, was made by an American navigator, from Boston, Captain Robert Gray, who commanded the merchant ship "Columbia." Captain Gray had sailed past the mouth of the Columbia River twice on his trading voyages; the first time in 1789, without discovering the river, and the second time in June, 1791, at which time he marked the location of what he believed to be a large river; he did not sail in, however, owing to the surf which broke with violence across the mouth of the stream. Soon after he encountered Captain George Vancouver, of the English Navy, to whom he related his discovery. Vancouver, however, scouted the idea, as he had searched the whole coast, trying to find such a stream, and believed it was impossible that he could have missed it. Captain Gray soon parted with Vancouver and sailed south, hoping to effect an entrance to the river that he was certain he had discovered; he soon sighted the mouth of the river, (May, 1792), and with all sails set he steered the "Columbia" boldly for it, and safely ran in, between the breakers into a basin where no other sail had ever been; he continued his course up the river some fifteen or twenty miles, followed by a swarm of canoes filled with curious natives.

The anchor being let go, Captain Gray found himself floating on the peaceful bosom of a fresh water river, which he named Columbia, after his noble ship. This river's existence had been surmised for some years previous, and the phantom river was called the Oregon, after the country through which it was supposed to flow.

Captain Gray made a report to the United States Government of the discovery he had made, and it was a basis upon which the Government claimed the valley of the river. France had likewise a shadowy claim to all that portion of North America west of the Mississippi River, and north of the Spanish possessions, under the name of Louisiana, all of which the United States acquired by purchase in 1803.

President Jefferson ordered a survey of the Columbia, and started out a continental exploring party in 1804, in charge of Captains Lewis and Clarke, who ascended the Missouri River to its source, crossed the grand continental divide, and encountered the Columbia River in about 49 degrees north latitude. They surveyed it to its mouth, including its tributaries, and thereby gave the United States a substantial title to the country. It was not, however, until 1846 that all dispute regarding the title was settled; it was then determined by treaty with Great Britain, fixing the 49th parallel north latitude as the boundary line between the United States and British America.

Oregon was sparsely settled with fur traders, principally English, who discouraged immigration and succeeded in keeping the country practically a wilderness up to the year 1833, when a few settlers found their way overland to this delightful and rich state.

In 1834 Dr. Marcus Whitman, a missionary, succeeded in planting a colony near Walla Walla, after which the country began to settle up gradually, but no considerable immigration took place until the excitement caused by the finding of gold in California in 1849, the overflow of disappointed gold seekers then found their way to Oregon.

The few settlers who were in the state succeeded in organizing a Territorial Government by the adoption by their votes of a Territorial Constitution in the year 1845. It was, however, not until August 14th, 1848, that Congress passed the act to organize the territory, the delay being caused by the open question between England and the United States as to the title, which was settled, as before stated, by treaty in 1846.

Joseph Lane, the first Governor of the territory, arrived March 3d, 1849, when the government was inaugurated. The act of Congress creating the territory of Oregon, included within that territory all of the present states of Oregon and Washington; the latter was, however, created a territory in 1853, which left Oregon its present dimensions, which was admitted into the Union as a state February 14th, 1859.

The state contains 96,030 square miles. The principal rivers are the Columbia and branches, Williamette, Fall River, Snake River and the Owyhee.

The Columbia is the only navigable stream in the state, which is only navigable 96 miles, to the Cascade range of mountains, which has several extinct volcanos, ranging in height from 4,000 to 10,000 feet above sea level; here is found some gold, silver and platinum. Coal has also been discovered in limited quantities. The forests abound with game, including the grizzly and black bear, panther, wild cat, elk, deer and antelope. The feathered game is quite plentiful, and vies with California for variety, etc. The rivers swarm with salmon, which has aided the state very materially in a great industry, that of canned salmon.

The chief cities are Salem, (the Capital), Portland and Oregon City. The climate of Oregon resembles California; it is believed, however, to be superior in some respects. The death rate is small, and the state is regarded a sanitarium to some extent, and is certainly beneficial to a large class of diseases.

The immense forests of pine form no inconsiderable portion of the state's resources. Oregon pine being considered superior in many respects to any other found on the American Continent.

The principal agricultural products of the state are wheat, oats, potatoes and fruit.

In 1886 the state produced 11,133,000 bushels of wheat, valued at $7,570,440, from 884,640 acres; 5,102,000 bushels of oats valued at $2,142,840, from 199,199 acres; other crops 431,371 acres, product valued at $5,467,030; total field products, $15,180,310.

January 1st, 1888, the state contained 180,947 head of horses and mules, valued at $9,090,543; milch cows, 78,997 head, valued at $2,338,311; oxen and other cattle, 598,218 head, valued at $12,172,122; sheep, 2,930,123 head, valued at $4,987,069; hogs, 220,723 head, valued at $664,819; total live stock, 4,009,008 head, valued at $29,252,864, which, added to the value of product field crops, 1886 gives a total of farm products amounting to $44,433,174, exclusive of fruits, which would increase the product, if statistics were obtainable, to nearly or quite $50,000,000; then add the fisheries' industries, and the state's annual product would be increased considerably.

As yet the state has not joined the progressive movement for deep harbor facilities on the Texas Gulf coast, owing to the prevailing opinion of its people that the proposed harbors are too far away to benefit Oregon. That, however, is a mistaken idea, as from practical demonstration an interchange of commodities has taken place between Texas Gulf ports and Oregon within the past year.

Oregon will, ere long, awaken to the importance of joining this grand western alliance which is formed to advance the interests of the Great West.

CHAPTER X.

KANSAS—1682 TO 1889.

KANSAS was included within the Louisiana Territory purchased from France by the United States in 1803, discovered by La Salle in 1682. It was successively a part of the District of Louisiana, of the Territory of Orleans, then of Missouri Territory, and after the admission of the State of Missouri, in 1821; it formed a part of the great unorganized portion of the Louisiana purchase until 1854, when a semblance of a Territorial Government was established under the famous Stephen A. Douglas' Kansas-Nebraska Bill. A fierce contest, however, raged between the slavery and anti-slavery inhabitants of the territory until 1859, the anti-slavery element gaining the ascendency, after a bitter strife and much loss of life to both sides. During this turbulent period the famous John Brown, of Osawatomie, figured quite prominently, and waged a relentless war upon the slave trade men. Afterwards he went east, and in 1859 attempted to seize the arsenal at Harper's Ferry, arm the negroes, and incite the slaves to rebel against their masters; he was captured after being wounded, and by the United States authorities executed very promptly. This one incident, probably, more than any other, started the Northern people to thinking seriously of the abolition of slavery.

Kansas Territory at this time comprised the limits of the present state, and a large portion of Colorado, including where Denver now stands, as far west as Leadville, and south to the southern boundary line of the state, and containing 114,793 square miles. In 1859 a constitution was adopted for the proposed state, prohibiting slavery. This settled the question; Congress passed an enabling act, and January 29th, 1861, Kansas was admitted to the Union as a free state. At the same time the seceding states went out. Kansas furnished her quota of men to preserve the Union, and did her part bravely. With the cessation of strife the state enjoyed an era of prosperity scarcely equalled in the history of the nation. Population doubled and quadrupled in an incredibly short space of time, and it soon ranked among the leading states of the Union.

The boundaries of the state defined by the admission act of Congress cut off nearly 40,000 square miles from the west of the territory, the western boundary being the 102nd degree of longitude.

The state is bounded on the east by Missouri, north by Nebraska, west by Colorado, and south by the Indian Territory. Contains 82,080 square miles.

The surface is generally undulating, rising gradually from the valley of the Missouri 700 feet above sea level to 4,000 feet on the western border. Nearly the entire area is a rich prairie covered with grass, and almost devoid of timber, the little timber that is found is along the streams, and is principally cotton wood, a very poor class of timber, having very little if any commercial value. The interior of the state has no navigable streams; there are a large number of small rivers abounding in fish, and affording sufficient water for stock raising, etc.

The Missouri River on the eastern border furnishes navigation for about 50 miles along the state. The early settlement of Kansas was much aided by the possibilities of navigation that this river afforded, several towns being started before the "iron horse" made his appearance in Kansas. Coal of an inferior quality is found throughout the entire eastern portion of the state, comprising an area nearly 17,000 square miles in extent. A fair quantity of building stone is obtainable in almost all portions of the state. None of the precious metals are found, however, some of the baser metals are found in limited quantities. Immense deposits of salt are found in the central portion of the state, notably at Hutchison, Kansas, where at a depth of 300 feet a salt deposit has been discovered which appears unlimited, the vein being more than 300 feet in thickness, and covers quite a large area; quite extensive works have been established here, and salt forms one of the important industries of the state. Negotiations are pending whereby it is believed a strong English company will take hold of this property and develop it upon such a scale as to make Hutchinson the greatest salt producing city in America.

The climate of Kansas is very pleasant, in winter the temperature rarely falls below zero, and in summer ranges from 80 to 100 degrees, even in the warmest weather the nights are unusually cool, which makes the heat of the day tolerable. Occasionally severe wind storms sweep over the prairies, rarely, however, doing serious harm.

Wild game was formerly very plentiful, such as deer, elk and buffalo, all of which are practically extinct, as far as Kansas is concerned. Small game, such as ducks, geese, prairie chicken and quail, may be found in their season, and are quite abundant.

The soil is very rich and yields abundantly of all agricultural products, where drouth does not interfere, that, however, does not occur very frequently, and the state rates one of the best of the Union in agricultural products.

In 1886 the state produced from 5,812,615 acres, 106,129,000 bushels of corn, valued at $34,212,240; 1,272,300 acres, 14,556,000 bushels of wheat, valued at $8,442,480 from 964,930 acres, 25,516,000 bushels of oats, valued at $8,201,030; from 99,031 acres, 5,744,000 bushels of potatoes, valued at $3,733,600; from 1,320,000 acres, 1,-884,000 tons of hay, valued at $8,131,200; other field crops, 221,512 acres, product valued at $1,152,720; a total field product valued at $62,051,240.

January 1st, 1888, Kansas contained 724,997 head of horses and mules, valued at $49,928,929; 640,081 head of milch cows, valued at $14,344,215; 1,583,915 head of oxen and other cattle, valued at $32,271,946; 830,139 head of sheep, valued at $1,457,558; 2,377,561 head of hogs, valued at $13,457,469; a total of 6,156,693 head of live stock, valued at $111,460,117, which added to the field products makes a total valuation of all farm products aggregating $173,511,357.

The principal commercial cities of the state are Leavenworth, Atchison, Lawrence, Topeka and Wichita.

Kansas, as much as any other state west of the Mississippi River, is deeply interested in the deep harbors on the Texas Gulf coast, and in all movements looking to that grand consummation has figured conspicuously, and is ably represented on the permanent Deep Harbor Committee by Hon. Howel Jones, of Topeka; Senator A. Caldwell, of Leavenworth; Judge J. E. Emery, of Lawrence; Hon. W. E. Hutchinson, and Hon. Marsh M. Murdock, of Wichita.

The following statistics are compiled from the official reports of the Secretary of the State Board of Agriculture for the State of Kansas, for ten years, showing the number of bushels of grain grown, and value of the crop:

Year	CORN.		WHEAT.		OATS.	
	Bushels.	Value.	Bushels.	Value.	Bushels.	Value.
1879	108,704,927	$26,562,674	20,550,936	$18,448,711	13,326,637	$3,397,416
1880	101,421,718	24,920,079	25,279,884	20,980,667	11,483,796	2,918,089
1881	80,760,542	44,859,963	20,479,679	21,705,275	9,900,768	3,855,749
1882	137,005,722	51,838,366	35,734,846	24,003,820	21,946,284	5,766,579
1883	182,084,526	47,492,663	30,025,936	22,322,119	30,987,864	6,135,788
1884	190,870,086	39,512,734	48,050,431	20,516,560	20,087,204	5,568,332
1885	177,350,708	40,428,327	10,772,181	6,829,945	31,561,490	6,558,303
1886	130,569,132	37,966,081	14,579,093	8,482,503	35,777,365	8,860,603
1887	75,791,454	26,836,422	9,278,501	5,759,548	46,727,418	12,232,243
1888	108,754,087	....	16,720,719	....	54,665,055	....
Totl	1,382,313,497	$340,423,259	231,472,206	$149,049,147	276,579,591	$55,298,702

I hereby certify that the above is correct as taken from the official reports of this office.

Dated, Topeka, Kansas,   M. MOHLER,
    October 30th, 1888.   Secretary.

The following statistics are compiled from the official reports of the Secretary of the State Board of Agriculture for the state of Kansas, for the year 1888:

Population, 1,518,552.

	LIVE STOCK, 1888.			LIVE STOCK, 1887.		
Horses	700,723	head.	....	648,037	head.	$58,323,330
Mules and Asses	92,435	"	....	89,957	"	8,995,700
Milch Cows	742,639	"	....	692,858	"	13,857,160
Other Cattle	1,619,849	"	....	1,568,628	"	31,372,560
Sheep	402,744	"	....	548,767	"	1,077,534
Swine	1,433,245	"	....	1,817,394	"	12,931,758
Total No. 1888.	4,991,635	"	1887,	5,385,641	Value, 1887,	$126,558,042

I hereby certify that the above is correct as taken from the official reports of this office.

Dated, Topeka, Kansas,   M. MOHLER,
    October 29th, 1888.   Secretary.

CHAPTER XI.
NEVADA—1848 TO 1889.

PRIOR to 1848 Nevada had no white settlements, the only inhabitants being aborigines; not even a mission had been established within the borders of the state.

In 1848 the United States acquired by treaty with Mexico the territory embraced within the limits of the state, together with California, New Mexico and Utah. The Territory of Nevada was not established until 1861, up to that time it was included within the Territory of Utah. At that date Nevada contained 17,000 inhabitants, attracted thither by the discovery of rich silver mines. The Comstock lode, in Storey County, was discovered in 1859, its annual output of silver for several years averaged $15,000,000. It made and lost fortunes within a short space of time by stock jobbing operations, and finally, having practically exhausted the rich ore, the mine was abandoned. At times since, it has been operated on low grade ore, but has yielded only insignificant returns. The other principal mines are the Consolidated Virginia, California and Sierra Nevada, two of which have been worked to a depth of 2,870 feet, men being able to work at that depth not more than an hour or two at a shift.

The State of Nevada was admitted into the Union in October, 1864. It is bounded by California on the west, Oregon and Idaho on the north, east by Utah, and south by Arizona, contained 110,700 square miles. The surface is an elevated valley or basin, which stretches from the Rocky Mountains to the Sierra Nevada range, interspersed with mountains of minor importance, and varies in altitude from 2,000 to 7,000 feet, average being about 4,000 feet above the sea level. Extensive forests are encountered in the mountains, affording an abundance of the best pine lumber; several varieties of pine, spruce and fir are the principal growth. No hard wood timber in the state, none being found on this slope of the Sierra. A few mountains reach the height of 10,000 feet, none above timber line, the very summit being covered with a heavy growth of timber. The lumber interest is destined to become one of the state's principal industries. The precious metal output is still quite large, though insignificant as compared with the palmy days early in the '60s. The decrease in that industry has caused the agricultural and stock raising interests to receive more attention, and while inconsiderable as compared with some of our more advanced states, yet its increase and development is an evidence of progress, and adds hope to the already substantial worth of the state.

In 1886 there were 192,013 acres in crop, value of product amounting to $1,955,280.

January 1st, 1888, the state contained 47,701 head of horses and mules, valued at $2,505,098; 18,037 head of milch cows, valued at $631,295; 323,400 head of oxen and other cattle, valued at $5,819,648; 660,996 head of sheep, valued at $1,259,660; and 21,087 head of hogs, valued at $111,846; a total of 1,071,221 head of live stock, valued at $10,327,547, which, with the field crops, aggregates $12,282,827, the value of farm products January 1st, 1888.

There are no considerable cities in the state, Virginia City and Carson City (the Capital), are the principal ones. The climate is not as severe in winter as would be supposed at such an altitude; the summers are delightful, and on the whole the climate is regarded as very healthy. The educational advantages are very good, comparing with equally populous sections in the East. Society averages well, but can not be said to compare with adjoining states.

Nevada should join in the progressive movement for deep harbors on the Gulf coast, and ultimately the firm establishment of a "Western Commercial Congress." The Great West must have inter-state reciprocity, a partial success at that has just been accomplished by the Grand Inter-state Deep Harbor Convention, which brought together in Denver, in August last, over 700 delegates from thirteen of the twenty-two states and territories west of the Mississippi River.

CHAPTER XII.

NEBRASKA—1682 TO 1889.

NEBRASKA was included within that territory discovered by La Salle in 1682, and by him named Louisiana. This tract was purchased from the French by the United States in 1803, and was successively a portion of the Louisiana and Missouri Territories up to the time that Missouri was admitted as a state, with its present boundaries, in 1821. From 1821 until 1854 it was within the limits of that vast unorganized territory, which has since become rich and populous states; we refer to that portion of the United States which lies between the Missouri River and the Continental Divide.

In 1854 Nebraska Territory was organized under Douglas' Kansas-Nebraska Bill. It extended north to the British line, west to the main range of the Rocky Mountains, east to the Missouri River, and south to the 40th parallel of north latitude, which included all of North and South Dakota, part of Colorado, Wyoming, Montana and its present dimensions. In 1863 it was reduced to its present limits, the Missouri River on the east, Kansas and Colorado on the south, Colorado and Wyoming on the west, and South Dakota on the north. The state is 420 miles long by 138 to 207 miles in width, and contains in area 76,855 square miles.

Exclusive of a few soldiers who were stationed in Nebraska to protect the overland freight teams, this state, in 1854, contained no white settlers, and not until the building of the Pacific railroad was there any settlements formed of any consequence; that stimulated immigration to a large extent, but not until Nebraska had been admitted as a state did she experience any very decided or rapid increase of population. From that time since, the state has progressed with wondrous strides, and to-day not less than 1,000,000 people find homes within her borders.

The surface resembles Kansas' gently rolling prairies, beginning at the Missouri River, at an altitude of about 800 feet, it rises gradually as you proceed westward until, at its western boundary line, it reaches an altitude of upwards of 4,000 feet, the ascent being so gradual as to be unobservable without the use of an instrument. There are no mountains in the state. The Missouri, Platte and Niobrara Rivers are the only considerable rivers in the state, the Missouri being navigable throughout its entire course along the eastern border of the state, about 350 miles. The other two extend through the state from the western border to their confluence with the Missouri; they are not navigable; their special benefit to the state being their supply of water for stock, and in the western section for irrigation. They are sluggish, and in no portion of the state have sufficient fall for any considerable water power. Their valleys are broad and very fertile, producing an abundance of all cereals, and grass for hay grows luxuriantly. The uplands in the eastern portion of the state are almost as productive as the rich bottom lands, while the up-lands in the western section furnish rich grazing for the many thousand herds of cattle that are ranged there.

The state contains no minerals of commercial value. Coal in small quantities and of a very inferior grade has been encountered by boring for water in a few localities.

A fair quality of building material is found; sand-stone and a soft lime-stone, which hardens by exposure.

Nebraska has been noted for its immense live stock interests, grazing and shipping. Ogallala, on the Union Pacific railroad, was for some years the objective railroad point for stock men, and it is estimated that some seasons have witnessed the shipment, east from this point, of upwards of 200,000 head of cattle. The numerous railroads that now extend from the Missouri westward have intercepted the inclination to concentrate the great range interests in any one point, and Ogallala has lost most of her old time prestige. Nebraska also produces many head of hogs per annum, besides vast supplies of grain

Omaha has become a great cattle, hog and grain market, and is fast rivalling her sister city (Kansas City) lower down the Missouri River. Here, too, is centered the manufacturing interests of the state, which is not inconsiderable. The other cities of importance are Lincoln (the Capital), Hastings, Grand Island, Fremont, Beatrice and Nebraska City. The climate is mild and dry, drought, however, rarely affects the crops, owing to the strength of the soil which retains the moisture longer than the soil of eastern states of the same latitude, and in this respect Nebraska is a better state for agricultural pursuits than Kansas directly south. The temperature in summer rarely reaches 100 degrees Far., and in winter it seldom drops below zero.

In 1886 Nebraska had in crops as follows: 3,879,123 acres of corn, producing 106,129,000 bushels, valued at $21,225,800; 1,579,727 acres of wheat, producing 17,449,000 bushels, valued at $8,201,030; 742,051 acres of oats, producing 21,865,000 bushels, valued at $4,154,350; 172,088 acres of barley, producing 3,786,000 bushels, valued at $1,173,660; 54,630 acres of potatoes, producing 3,278,000 bushels, valued at $1,311,200; 960,000 acres of hay, producing 1,392,000 tons, valued at $5,220,000; other field crops, 72,089 acres, valued at $303,480; total value of field crops, 1886, $41,589,520.

The state contained January 1st, 1888, 454,145 head of horses and mules, valued at $34,033,331; 857,202 head of milch cows, valued at $9,108,651; 1,979,646 head of oxen and other cattle, valued at $22,763,600; 422,112 head of sheep, valued at $852,456; 2,334,526 head of hogs, valued at $13,341,813; total, 4,647,630 head live stock, valued at $80,099,851, which added to the field crops, makes a total of farm products January 1st, 1889, aggregating $121,689,317.

The educational and social advantages of the state are exceptionally good, comparing with Illinois or Ohio.

Nebraska produces a very large surplus of farm products that go to foreign markets, exported via New York. Eleven dollars per ton could be saved to the producer if facilities were provided for exporting via the Texas Gulf coast. An interest has been awakened, as was evidenced in the late Inter-state Deep Harbor Convention, wherein Nebraska was represented by a large delegation of distinguished men, and is now represented on the Permanent General Committee by Hon. Champion S. Chase, of Omaha, Chairman of State Committee; Hon. O. E. Goodell, of Lincoln, Secretary; Hon. Herman Kountze, and Hon. W. N. Nason, of Omaha, and the Hon. Joel Hull, of Minden.

CHAPTER XIII.

COLORADO—1682 TO 1889.

WE now come to the Centennial State, so called because it was in the Centennial year (1876) that the state was admitted to the Union. Colorado is the central state of "The Great West," and is appropriately the seat of the grand movement for a Western Commercial Congress, the first session of which was held in Denver, August 28th, 1888, lasting three days, and was designated "The Inter-State Deep Harbor Convention."

The state derived its name from the Colorado River, which river was so named owing to the color of the water; Colorado being the Spanish for red. The territory embraced within the boundary of the state from 102 to 109 degrees west longitude, and from 37 to 41 degrees north latitude. Was originally about equally divided between Spain and France, the United States coming into possession of the eastern half in 1803, through the great Louisiana Purchase, and the western half in 1848, by treaty with Mexico. That portion which was included within the Louisiana Purchase was successively a portion of Louisiana District (1804), Louisiana Territory (1805), Missouri Territory (1812), unorganized until 1854, when it was nearly equally divided between Kansas and Nebraska Territories.

In 1861 the State of Kansas was admitted into the Union, and the Territory of Colorado created, including the present boundaries, taking in a portion of the Territory of Utah, and some of the Texas cession of 1850. The first Governor of the Territory was William Gilpin, a pioneer, and sometimes called the founder of Colorado. When he was asked what he was doing out this far west, his answer was invariably, "Founding an Empire." While but a phrase, and used more than half in jest, the venerable Governor Gilpin is living to-day, and views an empire so vast in extent and resources that it promises to outshine the whole world besides. (The Governor referred to all that territory west of the Mississippi River, there was no Colorado then.)

Governor Gilpin may be seen any day walking the streets of Denver, a hale and hearty old man, esteemed by all. He is sufficiently well off in this world's goods to make him independent. His favorite pastime is to visit old acquaintances, and talk over reminiscences of the early days of "The Great West," or discourse upon his proposed map of the world, in which, as he says, he proposes "to blot out the d—m

Atlantic Ocean from off the face of the earth." The Governor builded better than he knew, and the West has outstripped his prophecy, which, in 1860, or even fifteen years later, was regarded almost universally as the utterances of an enthusiast and incredible. Gradually the day began to dawn, and in 1880, the sun began to shine. The day had arrived when "The Great West" could justly claim to be an Empire; its natural products were then balancing the East, (the Mississippi River the dividing line), while the center of population was scarcely leaving Ohio on its steady march westward.

Hon. John Evans was the War Governor of Colorado, appointed by President Lincoln to succeed Governor Gilpin, and was, therefore, the second Governor of the state. While Gov. Gilpin is generally called the founder of Colorado, it is universally conceded that Gov. John Evans is the father of the state and its greatest benefactor, having inaugurated more and greater enterprises than any other citizen of this great state. Governor Evans still survives, and is in good health, abounding in wealth created by his own energies and successful enterprises. His home is in Denver, where an eight-story stone block, and several lesser ones, stand as monuments of his great worth to Colorado.

"The Star of Empire," attracted by a Colorado sky, and the loadstone of western natural wealth, is gradually creeping westward; in fact, it might be said to have passed even now to the central state of this new empire, and paused to move no more, being unable to pass that massive wall which nature has erected just west of Denver, and which extends north and south through the state, dividing it quite equally into east and west. This unsurmountable wall is variously named, "the Backbone of the Continent," "the Continental Divide," "the Water Shed of America," or more properly, "the Rocky Mountain Range."

The sources of the streams of Colorado are high up in the mountains, varying from 10,000 to 12,000 feet above sea level. The North Platte and South Platte Rivers, have their source in the north central part of the state, only separated by a mountain range; the north fork flows out of the state on the north boundary, in a northeasterly direction; the south fork flows south and east, the two streams being separated where they issue upon the plains by some 300 miles; they approach each other until they are united a few miles east of the northeast corner of Colorado. The Kansas' and Grand Rivers have their sources near the center of the state, and within a few feet of each other; the Arkansas flowing south and east to the Mississippi River, and thence into the Gulf of Mexico, while the Grand flows west and south into the Colorado River, and thence into the Gulf of Lower California. The Rio Grande River has its source in the southern part of the state. flows almost directly south into the Gulf of Mexico, forming the boundary line between Texas and Old Mexico. Thus it will be seen that Colorado might well be termed the central state of "The Great West."

Colorado's chief industry is mining. Gold was first discovered in 1859, near where Denver now stands, and every year since the precious metal output has been on the increase. The record for 1887 surpasses the first ten years of Colorado mining by some thousands. The following is a record by years from the first discovery up to January 1st, 1889:

Year.	Gold.	Silver.	Lead.	Copper.
1859-69	$27,200,000	$ 330,000	....	....
1870	2,000,000	650,000	....	$ 20,000
1871	2,000,000	1,000,000	....	30,000
1872	1,725,000	2,000,000	$ 5,000	45,000
1873	1,750,000	2,190,000	25,000	65,000
1874	2,000,000	3,096,000	75,000	90,000
1875	2,150,000	3,125,000	60,000	190,000
1876	2,725,000	3,323,000	80,000	170,000
1877	3,150,000	3,725,000	250,000	300,000
1878	3,500,000	6,310,000	625,000	275,000
1879	3,200,000	12,375,000	525,000	315,000
1880	3,200,000	18,615,000	1,675,000	480,000
1881	3,300,000	17,100,000	3,250,000	425,000
1882	3,250,000	16,500,000	4,400,000	520,000
1883	4,000,000	17,370,000	4,100,000	490,000
1884	4,300,000	16,000,000	3,750,000	475,000
1885	4,200,000	15,300,000	3,850,000	450,000
1886	4,450,000	18,250,000	4,675,000	510,000
1887	4,500,000	16,292,000	5,000,000	1,000,000
1888	5,700,000	23,500,000	5,000,000	900,000
Total...	$88,300,000	$190,792,000	$37,365,000	$6,745,000

A grand total to January 1st, 1889, of $332,202,000. The first quarter of 1889 shows a decided increase over the same time in 1888, and, if continued, will place Colorado's metal output for the year close on to $50,000,000. Another important and growing industry is the petroleum fields being discovered.

OIL WELLS.

Oil was first discovered in 1862, near Canon City. No practical use was made of it until 1880. When a well was put down 1,225 feet boring for water, at that depth a flow of petroleum was struck, yielding about 40 barrels per day; since then about twenty wells have been bored, and the daily flow has been increased to 1,000 per day. The total output of these wells to date is probably upwards of $2,000,000, which, added to the coal and metal output, makes $359,202,000. Then add the building stone output to date, about $11,000,000, and we have the enormous amount of $370,202,000 wealth extracted from the mountain regions of Colorado through mining alone, nearly the entire amount extracted within the past 20 years. It is almost incredible, but nevertheless indisputable figures show it. The iron industry, although in its infancy, would probably increase the wealth extracted from Colorado mountains by nearly or quite $5,000,000, making a grand total of $375,000,000.

Colorado combines the essence of wealth which requires nearly all of the states east of the Mississippi River united to compare with it. In this connection the following regarding the industries of the Great West, and of Colorado, will prove interesting to the reader, and may induce some idle capital to be invested in the field of industry that this Great West offers to the wealth of the East.

English journals have already conceded that the World's Exchange is destined soon to be drawn on New York, rather than London, and with the single exception of iron products, the United States have far exceeded Great Britain in every staple manufacture; and what is more to the point, has almost illimitable resources, yet undeveloped for future growth. It is this certain prospect of remunerative industries, such as the Standard Oil Co. presents, that is bringing foreign capital here for investment in manufacturing and mining industries. For more than ten years some thirty alien landlords and foreign syndicates have owned over 20,000,000 acres of our arable lands; but now the inquiry is for good stone quarries, iron and coal measures, oil lands, tin, mica, and copper plants, as well as gold and silver properties, all of which are found in abundance in Colorado. Where the great metal deposits are, there must the furnaces come, the foundries be opened, and the product worked to its highest commercial form. The West will excel in the manufacture of woolen goods, as the South must in the merchandise of cotton fibre. And the sugar and rice of Southern commerce will be met by such vast Western values in lumber and metal products as the world's market never saw before, from Puget Sound to the Gulf; such a highway of riches will yet annually pour, as will heavily tax our freight ships' bottoms to carry. Men and money are all the elements required to effect more than any mercantile prophet can now foresee.

Already in the markets of the world American calicoes and cutlery successfully compete in price with the British; while our wheat, cotton, meat and lumber make the price for all other countries in similar staples. But the day of bulky export of raw products must soon merge into a brighter one, when the American artisan and mill shall convert the bulk of our crude material and crops into the highest commercial form for inter-state and inter-national export, and multiply our sixty billion dollars worth of United States exchange in 1888, into one hundred billion dollars, and more by 1892, with such overwhelming advantage to American production, that the French, Belgian and English chemist, mechanic and manufacturer will be forced, from self-interest, to emigrate hither, and combine his skilled labor with our material resources. American industries are not exactly in their infancy, needing an exhorbitant tariff to protect them; but a better economy is requisite in their manipulations. Raw products must be taken, as near as possible, to their original site, and manufacturing facilities applied. The eastern states now having a monopoly of home manufactures, so called, may object to this, but the Middle and Western states, especially the latter, are sure to win in this controversy, even as Southern cotton mills have proposed paying 20 to 30 per cent. dividend annually, where New England factories could scarcely net 5 per cent; so the Great West, with her boundless cheap food supplies and unlimited deposits, will bring the wool, stone, lumber and metal workers of the world eventually to develop her quarries, forests and mines. Other things being equal, the land that has the largest landcrops and smallest population is ahead in the race for independence. Our population is from sixty-three to sixty-four millions, and our agricultural, forest and live stock products of all kinds amount annually to about nine billion dollars worth; this is about $140 to every man woman and child. No other country is so well fed and has so much food products for export. Nowhere is the class of high livers so large. No other nation eats seven hundred millions in animal food alone annually. Our average citizen buys daily in meat 22 cents' worth, of bread 5 cents' worth, and in coffee, tea, sugar, fruit and vegetables, 9 cents' worth.

The population of the globe is carefully estimated at very nearly fifteen hundred millions, no hundred millions of that number are living upon such a wonderful area for productive resources as are the citizens of the United States. According to the brilliant and eccentric Ex-Gov. Gilpin, of Colorado, "we straddle the axis of the temperate zone;" and we certainly have developed during the past one hundred years as no country within the zone has. Asia has yet four-sevenths of the earth's population, about 52 to the square mile, and many millions periodically starving.

Europe has one-fifth of the earth's population, and most of them poorly nourished, and thousands half starved. She is crowded with a population of nearly 90 to the square mile, and represents the extremes of poverty and wealth, as no other country does.

Africa has one-seventh of the earth's population, or about 17 to the square mile. Two hundred and fifteen cities of the world number over 100,000 population each; thirty number over 500,000; the most populous in the order named, being London, Paris, New York, Vienna, Berlin and Canton; each a million and upwards; the great British metropolis swarming with four and a half millions, all but half a million of them pauperized to a greater or less degree.

What wonder then that the tides of emigration to our country are so large, or that the proper advertising of the Great West and her advantages should be regarded as philanthropy upon the broadest scale.

Every state and territory west of the Mississippi River, except eight, being watered by streams which have their source within this state. The fall is very rapid in these streams; waterfalls and rapids are common, and the water in its mad course has, in past ages, worn deep channels in and through the mountains, which cuts or canons often measure from 1,000 to 2,000 feet in perpendicular depth. The most notable probably of all being the Grand Canon of the Arkansas, which canon has been compelled to yield to the almost superhuman skill of the civil engineer, and the whistle of the locomotive of that great pioneer railroad, the Denver & Rio Grande, is heard in shrill discord with the music that has been made for thousands of years by the laughing, sparkling waters of the noted Arkansas. The wonderful engineering feats performed in this grand canon are only equalled by the same enterprising railroad in building their line over Marshall Pass, Veta Pass and the line through the Black Canon of the Gunnison River. Much praise is due the Denver & Rio Grande management for the rapid development of Colorado and her mineral resources. It is the greatest narrow gauge system in the world. The third rail is being put down, and standard gauge cars can be run over much of the system.

The extensive irrigation system of Colorado is due entirely to the rapid fall of streams, and their everlasting supply of water taken from the perpetual snow banks high up in the mountains above timber line. The Platte and Arkansas Rivers fall several thousand feet from their source before emerging upon the plains, and through considerable of their course they flow through large parks, or valleys, several miles in extent, which have only a slight fall, consequently the average fall for 40 to 50 miles would be 200 feet per mile. The power capable of being developed by water wheels in these two streams alone would suffice to turn the wheels of every factory in New England. The day is approaching when electric wires will be utilized to distribute this power equitably throughout the state, to drive the loom and spindle of the cloth manufacturers which are sure to be established sooner or later, where raw material is cheap and native to the soil; where power can be supplied at a minimum of cost, and where consumption is greater per capita (owing to the nature of employment, mining) than any other people on earth. All of these are concentrated in Colorado. The state produces annually over 10,000,000 pounds of wool, every pound of which, if manufactured here, would go rapidly into home consumption. The greatest cotton state in the Union joins us on the south, viz., Texas, which for lack of cheap power must export her entire crop. Add to the above the boot and shoe industry, the same conditions govern cheap leather, tanned with a native weed, said to be superior to any other tanning material in America. Here, too, are hides almost without number, taken from the hundreds of thousands of cattle marketed per annum. Cheap water power obtainable, and cheap fuel if preferred, coal as low as 80c. to $1 per ton, owing to proximity of mines. Cheap fuel has stimulated the iron and smelting industries of state to a wonderful degree. Side by side with the best grades of heating and cooking coal in this state lies immense iron deposits, sufficient in amount to supply the world for a century, and coal to manufacture the same, beside furnishing the world with coal for heating and manufacturing purposes for a thousand years to come. Hayden's survey for the United States Government developed the fact several years ago, that Colorado contained 80,000 square miles of coal area, veins varying in thickness from 3 or 4 feet to 14 feet in thickness, often ten or fifteen veins lying one above the other, with only a thin shale between, and varying in quality from common lignite to the best bituminous and cooking coals, and in quite a large area anthracite coal, unsurpassed by the famous Pennsylvania hard coal. Hayden's survey defined the coal limits then known; subsequent developments and discoveries have proven that Hayden overlooked the small amount of 10,000 additional square miles of coal area in the state, of equally as good if not better quality of product than was included within the 80,000 square miles established by his survey.

We quote from the March number of the Commonwealth extracts from an article by Alfred Dexter, which will prove of considerable interest in connection with Colorado's coal interests:

OUR COAL MEASURES.

"No more conspicuous example than the State of Pennsylvania can be found showing the wealth in coal mining. Next to food and raiment, shelter and fuel are necessaries of daily life, and the state that has coal products in all-sufficient abundance, both for home consumption and export, is sure of a royal revenue therefrom. Pennsylvania has long been on record as producing half the coal mined in the United States; but it is now officially announced that the area of the coal beds of Colorado is nearly equal to the entire territory of the Keystone State, or fully 40,000 square miles. Meager as are our appliances for getting the product out and to market, yet the output for 1888 was between 2,000,000 and 3,000,000 tons; and it is rationally asserted that this state has deposits sufficient to supply the increasing population of the entire Union for centuries to come.

"One hundred years ago, and Pennsylvania stood only third in point of population; but 50 years past she has ranked easily as second —New York, of course being first. Pennsylvania ranks first in coal and petroleum, iron and steel; second in rye, buckwheat and potatoes, also in printing and publishing values; third in milch-kine, hay, and also in soap manufacture and in railroad-lines mileage; fourth in tobacco and oats; fifth in malt and distilled liquors, and in the manufacture of silk goods; sixth in the production of salt and copper, and the same in agricultural implements; and eighth in the breeding horses and sheep.

She produces about 5,000,000 tons of pig iron annually, and fully 50,000,000 of tons of coal, which certainly must mean as many millions of dollars yearly revenue. In these immense resources of diversified and staple values, Pennsylvania, more than any other state, is the prototype of the Centennial State; and in no feature so particularly like this as in her great coal fields.

Great Britain still yields double the quantity of coal produced in the United States, and over one-half the product of the world, and holds very nearly the same superiority in its annual output of pig-iron. Without her coal resources England could never have so excelled in iron and steel values produced, and the logic of like conditions there must bring the same results finally to Colorado. For, in addition to coal, iron and tin, this state will find her home market largely in the endless and constantly increasing local industries involved in the reduction of metal and coin of our precious ores. And to secure this end most successfully we import nothing, but find all the necessary elements within the state.

With the past fifteen years Colorado has made an output of 13,-000,000 of tons of coal, at the very minimum estimate; and this has figured immensely in the economy of her aggregate production of gold, silver and base bullion products during that time, which products very considerably exceed $330,000,000 in value.

As illustrated by the cases cited of iron and steel production in England and Pennsylvania, so, through the fuel possibilities of this modern Aladdin, coal, we have transformed seemingly barren and worthless mountain rock into the shining and perpetual tokens of commerce, by which the barter of the world's merchandise is effected.

It is undeniable that in estimating the great natural resources of Colorado, her coal fields, which range throughout an area of about 100,000 square miles, and comprise coal-bearing strata of 40,000, must ever stand among the first and most important certainly known; and these figures are likely to be exceeded, rather than cut down, by developments constantly being made.

The working veins run on an average six feet in thickness, at the cost of mining at present is from $1 to $2 per ton, according to locality and conditions.

According to the following statement Colorado coal, at the mines, is worth $2.29 per ton, a very handsome figure when compared with Ohio coal, but still admitting of a favorable comparison with Pacific Coast coal. The figures doubtless may be accepted when apportioned among the mines, but would scarcely hold good if tonnage was taken as a basis. In nearly all the leading producing districts, good coal at the mines can be secured at from 75 cents to $1.25 per ton, the price at Trinidad varying from 50 cents to $1.00 per ton.

PRODUCTION OF COAL IN THE UNITED STATES IN 1888.

States and Territories.	Quantity Short Tons.	Value at Mines.	Per Ton.
Pennsylvania,			
Anthracite	43,578,000	$84,977,100	81 95
Bituminous	32,500,000	30,875,000	0 95
Ohio	11,950,000	11,114,000	0 93
Illinois	11,855,188	11,300,030	1 12
West Virginia	5,498,800	6,048,680	1 10
Iowa	4,842,220	6,304,110	1 30
Maryland	3,479,470	3,293,070	0 95
Indiana	3,140,979	4,397,370	1 40
Missouri	3,909,967	8,650,000	2 21
Kentucky	2,570,000	3,084,000	1 20
Alabama	2,900,000	3,335,000	1 15
Tennessee	1,907,297	2,164,026	1 10
Colorado	2,185,477	4,808,049	2 29
Kansas	1,850,000	2,775,000	1 50
Wyoming	1,480,487	4,811,583	3 25
Virginia	1,073,000	1,073,000	1 00
Washington	1,215,750	3,647,250	3 00
Indian Territory	891,000	1,737,450	1 95
New Mexico	635,042	2,003,887	3 25
Georgia	230,000	345,000	1 50
Utah	205,000	430,500	2 10
Arkansas	193,000	289,500	1 50
Texas	90,000	184,500	2 05
Michigan	65,000	104,000	1 60
California	85,000	340,000	4 00
Oregon	50,000	150,000	3 00
Dakota	25,000	43,750	1 75
Montana	41,467	155,501	3 75
Rhode Island	7,500	17,875	2 75
Nebraska	1,500	3,375	2 25
Idaho	600	2,700	4 50

COLORADO INDUSTRIES.

The story of the cranky old Bay State farmer, who had a son graduate from Harvard College, at an expense of thousands of dollars, and on the return home of the expensive hopeful, bluntly asked him at the dinner table: Wall, John, what's the good of all your larnin'?" "What kin ye make?" is a good story for Colorado; till lately the youngest of states, and richest naturally in variety and value of crude products; but what can she make out of them? Our worthy Labor Commissioner, and the Secretary of the Chamber of Commerce, have displayed a good deal of well-directed activity in collecting much accurate information from year to year, concerning our already established manufacturing institutions; also, the occupations followed by our working classes, male and female; number of hours employed; wages by day and piece work; expense of board or housekeeping; sanitary condition of their dwellings, etc., etc.; but still the cry comes up from the ranks of the unemployed: "Who will give us work? What can we earn? and at what?" and while this mountain air sharpens the appetite, promotes digestion, and runs the nervous system at a higher rate of speed, food is its nutritious fuel, and labor must be in harness to obtain it. Eastern workmen and their families are coming by the thousands from their over-crowded conditions there to this land so highly reputed for health, and with so many industries to institute and develop. Fortunate will it be for us as a state if sufficient capital shall come with the skilled labor, and which will turn aside and occupy the favorable sites for manufacturing, to be found here on the right hand and the left, and so materially add to our practical and revenue-bearing productions. Arizona copper waits to be compounded with Colorado aluminum for bell metal. Steel cutlery and tools, axles and springs should be made to supply carriage works with material for further manufacture, and the public generally with home products. Window glass and household wares of that crystal material have been made here to a small extent, but have not been encouraged as they should have been in a country that has the superabundant and superior character of sillica deposits that Colorado has. All our own consumption of clay, iron, lead, water and gas, and oil piping, should be supplied from and through our own manufacture, with tens of thousands of car loads for export throughout the adjacent states and territories. Bronze and spelter founders and moulders should find welcome conditions here for the prosecution of their specialties. The City of Newark, N. J., has a surplus of those who are perfectly familiar with all the diversified industries that may be based upon these metals.

We have for years been advocating the establishment of oil, paint and glass works here, which should employ the native mineral paint rock which lies in immense deposits throughout the state. One local manufacturer is worth to a city a dozen mere merchants in foreign productions. A better field for a large leather tanning manufactory than this is was never known in this or any other country; for tanning, for tawing, for coloring and setting the dyes with mordants in the shortest possible time, and in the most effective way.

The reports made from time to time on the kaolin and kindred deposits about Canon City, and other points in Colorado, have had the result of interesting eastern pottery manufacturers to investigate, and having done so to their satisfaction, we may expect from correspondence had, that branch manufactories will be eventually established here, and certain it is that with practical management they can sustain themselves with very handsome profits. A company should be able to put up a series of two and three story buildings in which to do all the fine finish and decorative work in the best modern style of the art, with a proportion of four decorating kilns, to eight burning kilns, and take the highest standard of porcelain and semi-porcelain for the products.

There is also large profits in manufacturing sanitary earthenware, and which consists of all the goods entering into the plumber's trade. Ordinary brick can also be faced with one porcelain side, so that when laid in a wall with porcelain face exposed, like it should be in hotel courts, or naturally dark passage ways, the light reflected from the porcelain surface would illumine the spaces.

Our iron casting works should comprise every form of iron machinery that could be utilized in this western country, and afforded at prices that would dismay eastern competitors; not only engines and boilers, but cold rolled shafting, and pullies of every size, hangers to suit; presses and dies to cut sheet metal patterns of every thickness, and stamp out pressed metal goods of every description; machinery to work as clay and pottery presses, plungers, shakers, agitators, pressure pumps, and every appliance for turning out glass and color paints.

Nowhere throughout the most fertile districts of the world does a dairy country exist so thoroughly equipped by natural conditions of grasses, water springs, cool nights, bright sunny days the year round, and better grazing facilities than exist in the Colorado series of valleys, from the Yampa Valley, in Routt County, bearing due south, to the line of New Mexico, and into the valley of the Chama River, N. M. The dairy products of the United States are of nearly a billion dollars annual values; and Colorado, for butter and cheese factories, should come towards, if not at the very front at once.

IRRIGATION, BY F. L. DANA.

This brings us to a subject of more than usual importance—that of irrigation. Very little can be added to the article written by the author of this work, and published in the February 4th, 1888, issue of the "Exchange Journal," except the system is still more extended. We quote from it as follows:

According to the Constitution of the State, the waters of the rivers and streams are the property of the public, and while every person has a right, within certain statutory limitations and restrictions, to as much water as he can consume, and not interfere with rights previously acquired by others; yet he has no right, neither can he claim more water, than he can consume.

In the older irrigation districts, the irrigation of fifty acres of land is taken as the standard duty of a continuous flow of one cubic foot of water per second during the irrigation season of 100 days. In other districts traversed by larger canals the standard has been raised to sixty acres per cubic foot per second, which is equal to an annual rainfall of about twelve feet. After two or three years, when the soil becomes thoroughly saturated and settled, the duty of the water grows greater, and, judging from the history of older countries, the continuous flow of one cubic foot of water per second for the irrigating season will be sufficient to irrigate 120 acres. It is almost incredible that water in some of our main canals has a fall of only six inches in one mile, and the carrying capacity of one we have in our mind—the Citizen's canal, near Del Norte, is 1,000 cubic feet per second. The Del Norte canal, probably the largest in the United States, has a carrying capacity of over 2,500 cubic feet per second. It is 65 feet wide at the bottom and 98 feet wide at the top, carries water five and a half feet deep, and for some distance has a fall of 30 feet per mile. This canal is 56 miles long (main canal); it cost over $300,000, and irrigates over 50,000 acres of land. There were 1,750,000 cubic yards of gravel, rock and earth excavation to form the channel, requiring 3,500 men and 2,000 teams to perform the great task, which was completed in the unprecedented short period of four months. The largest canal in Italy - the Naviglio Grande—is only half as large as the Del Norte canal, cost more than $12,000,000.

By practical experience the cost of construction of canals in Colorado varies from 75 cents to $2 per acre, and makes land, otherwise practically worthless, worth from $50 to $100 per acre; such land, however, is on the market at from $10 to $100 dollars per acre.

The art of irrigation is older than history, and is extensively practiced in every country of the world, and yet in the United States it is scarcely understood, except in Colorado; here we know its beauties and utility. About twenty-five years ago a few persons turned their attention from gold hunting to the more profitable industry of agriculture, and were forced by the scanty fall of rain to adopt the irrigation system, which proved a blessing in disguise. Many of our wealthy citizens laid the foundation for their present millions in the early pioneer days by tilling the soil without contending with drought or failure, and alternately supplicating and imprecating Divine Providence, as Illinois, Iowa, Indiana, and most of the eastern, middle and western states have been doing these many years. A farm of 20 acres in Colorado "under ditch" is as capable of sustaining a family as 160 acres in Illinois or Indiana; then why do farmers of moderate means remain in a drought-stricken, cyclone-ridden, pestilential and malarial section of the United States, when Colorado offers health, wealth and happiness? A climate unsurpassed by even Italy. A health-giving atmosphere with the zephyrs laden with ozone from the highly electrified pine and spruce covered mountains; protected from the blizzards by the same mountains; a country that for the fifteen years last past had an average annual temperature of 49.5 degrees; average annual wind velocity of 6.3 miles per hour; average annual rainfall, 14.98 inches; average annual number of sunny days, 343, only 32 days in thirteen years, (July 20th, 1872, to February 22d, 1885,) that the sun was not visible, and within that time, from October 30th, 1879, to February 5th, 1881, fifteen months, the sun was not obscured all of one day; average death rate, 10.5 per 1,000 inhabitants, 5 per cent. of the deaths are consumptives who have come here too late for the climate to do anything for them. We have transgressed somewhat our subject in our zeal to picture Colorado's advantage climatically. To recur to our subject. The first efforts at irrigation in Colorado were of necessity very crude and less effective than the improved systems in vogue to-day. About one-fourth of the water of the streams the state is now appropriated, and the system is said to have redeemed of from two to three million acres of land, which means that with the present water supply, we can hope to redeem at least ten million acres of land, and with the proposed reservoir system to be instituted, we can treble the present capacity of our streams. We have in this state lands on the Divides, and adjoining the Foot-hills, and in the Foot-hills that do not require irrigation, the precipitation is sufficient for all purposes, and on our eastern border three successive crops have just been raised without irrigation. This will foot up in the millions of acres in all within our state, either in the rainbelt or capable of irrigation. This state has nearly 25,000,000 acres of such land, which would form an agricultural area nearly as large as the entire agricultural state of Illinois, nearly one-half of which is capable of sustaining a population, per acre, several times in the excess of the acreage of Illinois, and the rest at least as much, and it is fair to presume that the time is near approaching when Colorado will be more populous than Illinois, even viewed from an agricultural standpoint. Added to that, its mountains of gold, silver, copper, lead, zinc, iron and coal, natural gas and oil, which will require a million of population to develop, and furnish a home market for the agriculturist who inhabits the land which produces most abundantly. The soil is naturally warm, being rich sand and gravel, and with the assistance of a small amount of water, grows in equal or greater abundance any crop or fruits that can be raised in any state in the Union, except those states bordering on the Gulf of Mexico, or Southern California.

The following is an estimate of the number of miles of ditches constructed in Colorado, and of the number of acres irrigated thereby; this estimate is made from the reports of Water Commissioners of Water District 2, 3, 4, 5 and 8. These reports were made at the request of the State Engineer, for the purpose of securing data from which to determine the duty of water, and will be required of all the Water Commissioners of the State next year. Five out of nine Districts in Division 1, report as follows:

District No. 2, miles of ditches 126.25; acres irrigated 43,998.
" " 3. " " 330.5; " " 107,045.
" " 4. " " 235.75; " " 69,908.
" " 5. " " 225.5; " " 86,655.
" " 8. " " 121.5; " " 32,010.

Estimated in Division No. 1, 1,532 miles of ditches, 506,000 acres.

Estimated for the state, 3,000 miles of ditches, and 2,000,000 acres being irrigated.

From reports of Prof. Blount, of the State Agricultural College, we quote some of the experiments made during 1887, on the state farm, which farm is probably kept in better order than the average farms in the state, and allowance should be made therefor:

Buckwheat, average 33 bushels per acre; barley, 31 varieties, averaging 30 to 60 bushels per acre; oats, 47 varieties, range from 15 up to 101 bushels per acre; wheat, 12 varieties, averaging from 16 to 32 bushels per acre; all vegetables grow here in the greatest abundance, likewise all small and large fruits not tropical. No record of fruits or vegetables appear in Prof. Blount's December report.

It is safe to say, however, that fruits and vegetables of every variety, except tropical, are raised here in as great abundance as anywhere in the United States. Colorado vegetables command a premium wherever marketed. Not one-tenth of the fruit used in the state has been raised here; prices are exceedingly good, and the fruit and berry culture is profitable, and will be continued until the home market is supplied.

The states immediately east of Colorado are as much interested in this subject of irrigation as is Colorado,* not because they should use the irrigation system, but it has been practically demonstrated that eastern Colorado has benefited from the irrigating system in use nearer the mountains; it comes from moisture in the air, caused by the evaporation made possible by the water—4,320,000,000 cubic feet in 24 hours—being spread over millions of acres of ground. Nearly 40 per cent of that vast volume of water is evaporated, and comes down on Eastern Colorado, Western Kansas and Nebraska in the shape of rain, which nature distributes in such an equitable manner as to make fertile millions of acres of land, hitherto known as the arid desert

---

*See Major Powell's Report in Appendix, for page see Index.

region. The west half of Kansas and Nebraska can thank Colorado for their fertility, and their comparative exemption from drought. The extension of the Colorado irrigating system by the proposed reservoirs will not only exempt Kansas and Nebraska from drought, but will exempt the Lower Mississippi and Mississippi Valley States from the damaging and dangerous floods known as the June rise in the rivers. The June rise in the Missouri and Mississippi is due wholly to the melting snows in the mountain regions coming down at that time, and no provision being made to store it. The United States Government* should appropriate the necessary money to successfully control the torrents of the mountains, to spread a bounteous blessing over the arid region of the United States, and avert the calamities usual in the Lower Mississippi during the June rise of the Father of Waters. It would appear that from our estimates, that during 100 days (the irrigating season) of the summer, there is carried to our eastern borders, by means of clouds formed from the evaporation usual during that period, from the irrigation section of Colorado, about 1,728,000,000 cubic feet of water per day, or the enormous amount of 172,800,000,000 cubic feet in 100 days, sufficient water to be equal to a rainfall of 36 inches per annum, covering an area of 4,000,000 acres. With the present water supply, if properly controlled and cared for during the remaining period of 265 days of the year (the volume of water being nearly twice as great out of the irrigating season as in it) would increase the irrigated section by 330 per cent., or about 10,000,000 acres in total; that would then increase the amount of water evaporated equal to four times the present amount, or the amount of water possible to have evaporated from the waters of the state by the storage system would amount to the incredible sum of 691,200,000,000 cubic feet, or sufficient water to equal an annual rainfall of 36 inches spread over 16,000,000 acres. The amount is hardly comprehensible, and to simplify the figures, it would amount to a column of water in height of one and three-fifth miles, covering one section of land of 640 acres.

The extension of the irrigation system in Colorado may be somewhat gauged by the number of plats of new ditches filed with the State Engineer since July 17th, 1887, being 210 in six months, or 33 per month. That is a greater number than was filed from the early settlement of the state to July last. The present year promises nearly as great extensions,† and the good work is expected to continue until every drop of water of the state has been made to perform its duty in the development of this great state. In the San Luis Valley there is said to be 50,000 acres of the best prairie land under ditch that is awaiting the homesteader and pre-emptor, and many thousands of acres that is not under ditch at present, but can be brought under by the construc-

---

*See Major Powell's Report in Appendix, for page see Index.

†During 1888 the number of new ditches filed amounted to 611, at a rate of 51 per month, exceeding our prediction of a month ago.

tion of other canals. The Colorado Land and Loan Company own the two great ditches that irrigate this vast fertile valley, containing nearly 7,000 square miles. They own some 80,000 acres, a large portion being cultivated, that they offer for sale at from $5 to $10 per acre, and charge for water for either their lands or homestead properties under their ditch $1 per acre per annum, which is equal to an insurance of the most abundant crops. What farmer in Illinois or any other Eastern state would not give $5 per acre per annum to be insured a large crop each year. All crops raised in Colorado have a home market. There is not one cereal raised in the state that supplies the home demand and only three vegetables that approaches the demand, these are the potato, cabbage and celery; these three vegetables are shipped to Eastern markets, and are celebrated for their excellent qualities. No celery or cabbage in the United States approaches our product. We ship cabbage loose in the cars as far as St. Louis without injury. Our celery finds its way to the best hostelries in New York City and other Eastern cities.

The Committee of the Real Estate Exchange, appointed to investigate our vegetable and canning facilities and demands, reported that our three factories put up last season 20,000 cases of tomatoes and 25,000 cases of other vegetables, about one-third of the quantity actually sold in Denver. Tomatoes brought seventy-five cents per 100 lbs. Dealers expect to shave that price a little this season, probably to about sixty cents per 100 lbs.; even at that price the producer is well repaid. One person, from one-half acre near Denver, raised the almost incredible amount of 22,000 lbs of tomatoes, at the rate of $330 per acre.

In connection with the foregoing, written over one year before the State Engineer's report, it will be interesting to follow how closely they compare, and for that purpose we introduce here the preface to the last biennial report by State Engineer J. S. Green:

A brief reference to the physical features of Colorado, to her rapid development in irrigation matters, and to the governing doctrine in her irrigation laws, may not be an improper preface to this report.

Situated on both sides of the Continental Divide, and including many ranges of a secondary order, Colorado presents a most diversified surface of mountains, plains and valley lands, aggregating in area some 66,560,000 acres, not five per centum of which is void of vegetation, and more than half of which will, in return for the quickening qualities of water, yield the most abundant harvests.

To secure this water, Colorado rears the summits of her mountains to the clouds, and solicits and receives therefrom the rain and snow from which she feeds the great rivers, which, grouping their sources in the center of her boundaries, course thence to the north and south, the east and west, inviting in every direction that union with the soil which it is the province of man to effect and profit by.

In the early territorial days it was the Mexican population of the south which purchased from the thirsty soil its birthright for a little water. This water was conveyed to the land in small channels, irregular in section, fall and alignment. These channels were seldom carried above the highest level of the low bottom lands immediately adjoining the streams, and usually wound around the toe of the slope of the high adjacent lands. From these humble constructions, with but a few square feet of cross-section, step by step, with the advent into the state of each increment of energy, skilled labor and wealth, Colorado has seen her irrigating canals multiply in numbers, and with more and more perfection of construction, develop into great channels, some of which carry a body of water 70 feet wide and 6 feet deep, far out onto the rich mesa lands.

Since that period when the pioneers found within the confines of Colorado, but a few miles of irrigating ditches, and, at the most, but several thousand acres of cultivated lands, three decades are drawing to a close; but such has been the progress of irrigation development in the state during that period, that water in 4,000 miles of ditches, holding sway over 2,000,000 of acres of lands, is accounted to its credit.

That energy which has accomplished so much seems undiminished in strength and purpose, and to aim at no less an achievement than the economic use of all of the waters of the state in the irrigation of lands. How much land can then be irrigated? is an unsolved problem. There enter into the consideration thereof so many unknown quantities and variable functions, that it is carried beyond the sphere of calculation. The only solution of the problem would seem to be a practical one; yet year by year, as irrigation statistics are gathered and assimilated, the estimates of the area of land which can eventually be brought under cultivation will the more nearly approach the truth. As perhaps of interest in themselves, as well as indicative that the supply of water in Colorado is sufficient, if made to supplement properly the rain-fall, to bring under cultivation no inconsiderable portion of the lands of the state, the following facts are presented, prefaced by the statement, however, that though drawn from the best sources of information attainable, they can only, with one or two exceptions, be considered as close approximations to the truth, and are only called facts by courtesy. As the waters falling west of the Continental Divide cannot, to any considerable extent, be brought to the east thereof, the portions of the state separated by the Divide, offer separate problems for consideration.

On the west of the Continental Divide it is found:

That the area of mountain lands is......................16,360,000 acres.
That the mean annual precipitation over that area is...........33 inches.
That the area of plateaus and rolling and valley lands is...9,400,000 acres.
That the mean annual precipitation over that area is.........10.70 inches.

That the total area is..................................25,760,000 acres.
That the mean annual precipitation would average for that area..25 inches.

On the east of the Continental Divide it is found:

That the area of mountain lands is.....................10,200,000 acres.
That the mean annual precipitation over that area is............30 inches.
That the area of plains and rolling and valley lands is.....30,600,000 acres.
That the mean annual precipitation over that area is............15 inches.
That the total area is..................................40,800,000 acres.
That the mean annual precipitation would average for that area.18.7 inches.

Let it be considered in connection with the areas east of the Continental Divide, and with the precipitation thereover, that the limit of remunerative farming, without irrigation, is drawn at an annual precipitation of 22 inches; that the quantity of water passing through the canons of the Cache la Poudre River, as measured by this department in the year 1884, was equivalent to a precipitation of 13.367 inches over the entire water-shed of that stream above its canon; that the total precipitation over that water-shed, though not exactly known for that year, was about 33.4 inches; that about 40 per centum, then, of the snow and rain-fall over the water-shed of the Cache la Poudre River above the canon, flowed through the canon of that stream and was available for irrigation direct, or for storage for irrigation; that the application of this deduction to the precipitation over the entire area of the mountain lands east of the Continental Divide would indicate that about 40 per centum of the mean annual precipitation over that area would be the portion available for supplementing the rain and snowfall on the irrigable lands east of the Divide, and that this would, if it could all be utilized and evenly distributed, afford with the rain-fall a mean annual depth of water of 27 inches over 10,200,000 acres of plains and valley land.

But it is evident on the one hand that the water of the streams could not, by reason of the contour of the country, be quite equally distributed; that a considerable portion of the water drawn from the streams for direct irrigation, as well as that stored in reservoirs, is lost by evaporation and seepage before it is placed upon the land, while a portion of the water in the streams themselves is by the same cause dissipated. On the other hand, it should be borne in mind that much of the water drawn from the streams near their sources, or canons, and carried in ditches and distributed to the land, returns to the streams directly, or by percolation, and can be drawn therefrom again by ditches diverting water below, and thus portions of the water of a stream be used for irrigation several, perhaps many times; that much of the observed loss in reservoirs, through seepage, returns to the water courses and may be diverted therefrom; that while the annual rain-fall estimated as necessary to the profitable raising of crops without irrigation falls at haphazzard times, irrigation works enable the cultivator of the soil to apply water to his crops at the times when they most need it; that less water, on some lands and with some crops at any rate, is needed for irrigation after the first few years of application of water thereto, and that the rain-fall on that belt of the plains near the base of the mountains furnishes some water to the streams, not accounted for in their estimated discharge at their canons, which can be used on the lower lands to the east.

These considerations are not repeated in connection with the western portion of Colorado. A glance at the statements given and relating to that portion of the state indicates that the ratio of mountains to the plateau and valley lands is much greater there than is the case east of the Divide, and that the water supply there, notwithstanding the light rain-fall on the plateaus and in the valleys is greater, both actually and in proportion to the needs thereof, than in the eastern portion of Colorado. While this brief review of the natural conditions governing irrigation development in Colorado shows that any attempt to foretell accurately the area of the land in the state which may be brought under irrigation must be fruitless, a conclusion rendered more apparent when it is recognized that the annual precipitation, both in the mountains and on the plains, varies greatly; it, nevertheless, plainly supports the confidence that the achievement aimed at by her people will make of Colorado a great agricultural commonwealth.

But, however energetic her people may have been, however skillful in construction and fruitful in resources, it was in the legislative halls, and the court rooms that they fostered best Colorado's wonderful development in irrigation enterprises. This is not to be considered, however, as indicating that the irrigating laws of the state are by any means perfect, or complete, or that the actions of the courts have been universally satisfactory. Indeed, more matters of importance in connection with this art of irrigation are now demanding attention at the hands of the law makers of Colorado than has been the case at any previous period. But the demand is now for a systematic arrangement of the laws, the extension thereof, and the modification of those enactments which are not clearly consistent with the fundamental doctrines of the courts governing the use of water for irrigation in the State.

The result of the agitation of the subject of irrigation about one year ago was a reservoir convention in Denver in March, 1888, at which the subject was discussed and resolutions passed, which were the direct cause of the National Government taking hold of the subject. Major Powell was directed by Congress to view proposed sites for reservoirs in the Rocky Mountain region and report to that body the practicability, etc., of the same. His report appears in the appendix (see index).

Col. Richard J Hinton, under the direction of the Commissioner of Agriculture, Norman J. Coleman, compiled a mass of information regarding "Irrigation in the United States," which was printed in

THE GREAT WEST. 73

Fishing on the Rio Grande.

pamphlet form at the Government Printing Office in 1887 and distributed throughout the arid region. The book is out of print and not obtainable from the department; it is a valuable treatise upon the subject, and should be reproduced with correct data to the present time. We look for Major Powell to get out a very exhaustive report upon the subject, probably in time to submit at the next session of Congress, and, in the Government's good time, be available to the hungry public, in book form, some time within the following year. Western Senators and Congressmen should insist upon an unlimited number of copies of that report being published for general information. The public in general are entirely ignorant of what irrigation is, its benefits, its utility and its delights. Why not delightful? We have seen old crusty farmers in Illinois, in drought years, who would have been delighted if they could have opened a flood-gate from an irrigating ditch and saved their withering crops and parched meadows. Yes, we believe they would have stopped shaking with ague long enough to have smiled at their independence of old Prob. or the clerk of the weather.

Irrigation is not so expensive as is generally believed. The average cost to construct canals in Colorado is about $1.50 per acre of ground thus reclaimed. The annual cost of putting the water on the land is about $2 per acre, which includes needed repairs of ditch and cost of water; therefore a farmer in Illinois who raises about one good crop in three, owing to either drought or flood could afford to give away his Illinois farm to secure one in Colorado. Let us compare Illinois' yield and prices in farmer's hands with Colorado, the following taken from United States reports for crops of 1886:

	ILLINOIS.		COLORADO.	
Product.	Bushels per Acre.	Price per Bushel.	Bushels per Acre.	Price per Bushel.
Indian Corn	24.5	$ .31	31.5	$ .50
Wheat	13.7	.69	19.8	.70
Rye	12.	.57	22.	.72
Oats	31.8	.26	33.	.42
Barley	23.	.52	28.1	.62

About one-half of the agricultural area included in above averages of Colorado yield per acre is without irrigation. Irrigated fields average a yield of from 50 to 100 per cent. greater than the above table, and would bring the balance much greater in Colorado's favor; by the table, however, the average gain by farming in Colorado over Illinois, is shown to be 5 bushels per acre, at an average value of 50 cents per bushel; $2.50 and 14 cents per bushel on the amount of product, which averages 21 bushels per acre, making a difference in price in favor of Colorado of $2.94, to be added to the $2.50, makes approximately $5.00 per acre per annum in favor of the Colorado farmer in yield and price; in addition, he has absolute certainty of a crop each year, with only $2.00 per acre to charge up against Colorado for cost of irrigation, leaving a net gain of $3.00 per acre per annum, besides the healthiest climate in the world to live in.

The land can be obtained at government price and terms in many instances, in others it may be purchased, all rights attached, at $10 per acre. No fear of the home market being over-stocked; the mining and industrial interests are rapidly increasing, and the health-seeking population is rapidly improving, all much out of proportion to the increase of farms and farmers.

Grain, provisions, fruit and berries are mainly shipped in from other states; even hay, chickens and eggs are largely imported.

Denver is the best market for all the above farm products of any city in America of less than 200,000 population; for statistics in support of which we cite you to the article on Denver, later on in this work.

Col. Hinton, in his report before referred to, estimates the arid region of the United States to be 1,000,000 square miles, one-third of the entire area of the United States, exclusive of Alaska, one-half of which is mountainous, and incapable of being cultivated, owing to its altitude, or nearly perpendicular sides. This vast area, however, receives more than its proportionate share of annual precipitation by natural humidity, twice to three times, and the water only requires to be properly stored and distributed to furnish an abundance to reclaim the other 500,000 square miles. The mountain region is valuable for grazing, coal and precious metals, which, in value of annual production, exceeds the same area in agriculture, and is capable of employing a much larger population.

Long's Peak, from Estes Park, Colo., on line of Union Pacific Railway.

AGRICULTURE.

COLORADO'S agricultural possibilities have never been fully tested, as far, however, as experiments have been made success has exceeded expectations, as we presently show. In 1886, Colorado had in field crops 332,018 acres. The article on irrigation which preceded this, gives the area of irrigated lands at this time to be 2,000,000 acres. Colorado crops in 1886 were as follows: 29,778 acres, producing 938,000 bushels of corn, valued at $469,000; 122,152 acres, producing 2,419,000 bushels of wheat, valued at $1,693,300; 1,909 acres, producing 42,000 bushels of rye, valued at $30,240; 48,207 acres, producing 1,591,000 bushels of oats, valued at $668,220; 6,876 acres, producing 193,000 bushels of barley, valued at $119,660; 8,096 acres, producing 631,000 bushels of potatoes, valued at $359,670; and 115,000 tons of hay, valued at $1,127,000, making a total of 332,018 acres, producing in value $4,467,090; or each acre yielding in value $13.45, a greater yield per acre than any state in the Union; Ohio ranking next, with a yield per acre amounting to $11.40.

Colorado consumes largely in excess of her agricultural product, and has furnished a splendid market for the surplus product of Western Nebraska and Kansas; and with the millions of acres awaiting the plow in Colorado, with full water rights, we cannot see why this state will not attract a large farming population. The farm and mineral lands of the state are so equitably distributed that each support the other, and never will the state be an exporter of anything except gold, silver, lead, copper, zinc, iron, coal and oil; the workers in which must be supplied with food and raiment by the farmer.

We now turn to Colorado's live stock industry. January 1st, 1888, the state contained 127,483 head of horses, valued at $7,437,086; 8,247 head of mules, valued at $759,697; 63,023 head of milch cows, valued at $2,345,086; 1,049,353 head of oxen and other cattle, valued at $20,918,327; 1,137,686 head of sheep, valued at $2,257,169; and 23,149 head of hogs, valued at $153,103; a total of 2,409,211 head of live stock, valued at $33,810,468; which, added to the agricultural output, makes a grand total of farm products, January 1st, 1888, aggregating $38,337,558; add to this the metal, coal and oil output - metals, gold, silver, lead and copper, $34,500,000; iron, $2,000,000; coal, $5,000,000; oil, $500,000, and we have a grand total of produced wealth from native material, per annum aggregating $80,337,558.

From the late returns of the assessor, the total assessed valuation of the state May 1st, 1888, amounted to $169,000,000, which represents but one-third of the actual value; therefore, Colorado one year ago contained $507,000,000 of wealth, which has undoubtedly increased 20 per cent during the past year. Every dollar of that vast sum has either been dug out of the mountains, or has been made from the large herds that range the Colorado plains, or extracted from the soil by the sturdy husbandman.

Colorado's action in the movement for deep harbors on the Texas Gulf coast is the most disinterested of any western state, since she never hopes to have grain or provisions to export; home consumption will absorb all Colorado's grain product, the only export of value to the state is gold and silver. The Government purchases all of the gold in Denver. The silver, of course, is very valuable compared with weight, hence the bullion is all expressed east, to be absorbed in the arts, or in the United States mint, freight charges being of small consideration.

Deep Harbors on the Texas Gulf, however, will have the effect to build Denver up in the wholesale business, to rival Kansas City and Omaha, and generally benefit the whole state.

The late Colorado General Assembly, through the influence and perseverance of Senator Adair Wilson, appropriated $2,500 to assist in paying the expenses of the Deep Harbor Committee. No other legislature contributed a dollar, not even Texas, where the people should be most interested.

The Colorado Committee on Deep Harbors is composed of exceptionally strong men, Ex-Governor John Evans being at the head; associated with him we find Ex-Governor Alva Adams; State Senator Adair Wilson; Hon. C. C. Davis, of Leadville; and Hon. W. S. Jackson, of Colorado Springs.

IMPORTANT CITIES OF COLORADO.

Denver, population, 130,000; Pueblo, 30,000; Leadville, 20,000; Colorado Springs, 12,000; Trinidad, 11,000; Aspen, 8,000; Boulder, 5,000; and numerous others of less than 5,000 inhabitants, but of considerable commercial importance, among which we mention Golden, Idaho Springs, Georgetown, Glenwood Springs, Greeley, Longmont, Fort Collins, Grand Junction, Fort Morgan, Akron, La Junta, Las Animas, Lamar, Walsenburg, Canon City, Salida, Buena Vista, Gunnison, Montrose, Ouray, Silverton, Telluride, Alamosa and Durango.

STATE FINANCES.

A fitting close to our article on Colorado is an exhibit of the state finances, and we quote from the late reports of the State Auditor and Secretary of State:

AUDITOR'S REPORT.

"From the last biennial report of the Auditor of State, the finances of the state are clearly epitomized, showing the total receipts and disbursements for two years, ending November 30th, 1888, to have been: receipts, $2,280,179.85 which, with the cash on hand December 1st, 1886, $481,885.64, and cash invested in state warrants on that date, $352,617.08, make a total of $3,114,682.57. The total disbursements were $1,721,830.31, which with cash invested in state warrants, $575,047.92, and cash balance in treasury, $817,804.34, make a total of $3,114,682.57. The receipts by biennial terms from the admission of the state to the close of 1888, were as follows:

```
1877-78.................................................$  307,893.53
1879-80.................................................   625,617.08
1881-82.................................................   953,286.60
1883-84................................................. 1,483,468.00
1885-86................................................. 1,837,395.24
1887-88................................................. 2,280,179.85
```

At last we have an intelligent and straight forward analysis of the state debt, and an explanation of the causes of its magnitude, which as a matter of fact is surprising to the tax-payer not much accustomed to investigating the disposition made of the public funds, and it will also be discovered that much of the indebtedness is due to the operation of imperfect laws, otherwise the license permitted by loosely worded statutes, perhaps designed to be liberally and not literally construed.

Auditor Kingsley, after making a brief reference to the statement of his predecessor, published in advance of the decision of the Supreme Court to the effect that only four mills on the dollar could be levied by the State Board of Equalization for all purposes, whereby that official proceeded on the theory that the general fund was entitled to a four mill tax, says the state debt November 30th, 1888, aggregated $952,544.41, and only consisted of outstanding warrants drawn by direction of the legislature in its several appropriations against the general revenue fund, and bearing 6 per cent; certificates of indebtedness issued by direction of the Governor and Attorney General, bearing 6 per cent interest, and loco weed certificates unredeemed. In detail as follows:

```
Outstanding interest-bearing warrants......................  $839,824.17
Certificates of indebtedness ................................    86,879.10
Loco weed certificates ....................................    31,363.00
                                                             -----------
      Total............ .................................   $958,066.27
Less cash available ........................................     5,511.86

State debt November 30th, 1888 ............................   $952,554.41
```

As against this rather respectable debt for a state twelve years old, we have an offset in available delinquent taxes of $435,160.38, leaving the debt in excess of revenue, November 30th, 1888, at $517,394.03.

ABSTRACT OF ASSESSMENT FOR YEARS 1887 AND 1888.

	1887.		1888.	
	NUMBER.	VALUATION.	NUMBER.	VALUATION.
Acres of land	6,697,915	$ 17,035,180.88	9,343,530	$ 20,896,028.50
Improvements on lands	......	16,762,937.13	......	11,155,210.50
Miles of railroad and value	2,054	25,412,039.02	3,730	31,240,602.11
Average value of merchandise	......	6,565,688.00	......	7,062,647.00
Amount of capital employed in manufactures	......	555,783.00	......	707,541.00
Town and city lots	......	48,431,436.50	......	60,722,365.00
Horses	151,084	5,157,430.00	170,056	5,611,699.00
Mules	7,637	465,379.00	10,452	523,886.00
Asses	2,327	20,233.00	1,002	9,340.00
Cattle	900,912	11,469,326.00	911,989	10,202,877.00
Sheep	705,592	802,877.00	747,679	751,377.00
Swine	15,181	46,288.50	16,236	50,165.00
Goats	11,008	11,012.00	10,408	10,617.00
All other animals	4,312	27,902.00	3,967	29,531.00
Musical instruments	4,523	388,121.50	5,085	426,708.00
Clocks and watches	11,565	205,765.00	13,253	215,820.00
Jewelry, gold and silver pate	......	58,349.00	......	66,303.00
Amount of money and credits	......	2,722,909.89	......	2,570,057.00
Carriages and vehicles	26,071	991,993.00	28,612	880,663.00
Household property	......	656,183.00	......	781,909.00
All other property	......	2,337,714.97	......	2,653,990.20
Bank stock and other shares	......	1,329,136.00	......	1,469,260.00
Mines	......	......	......	1,083,540.00
Grand total valuation of state	......	$144,323,684.37	......	$168,812,246.93

The state valuation, as shown by the assessment rolls, has been as follows:

1877	$ 43,453,946.66
1878	43,072,648.26
1879	58,315,380.30
1880	73,698,746.29
1881	96,135,305.48
1882	104,440,683.57
1883	110,759,756.21
1884	115,675,014.51
1885	115,420,193.90
1886	124,269,710.06
1887	141,323,684.37
1888	168,812,246.93

EXTRACT FROM REPORT OF SECRETARY OF STATE.

The revenue of the state from this office have been for the last two fiscal years nearly three times as much as for any two previous years in the history of Colorado. The receipts derived from this office, commencing with the admission of the state up to the time I came into office, amounted to $52,259.60. During my term of office the revenue

Entering Boulder Canon, Colo., on line of Union Pacific Railway

for the two years, ending November 30th, 1888, has amounted to $70,652.12. The amount is sufficient to pay the salaries of Secretary of State, his Deputy, and the salaries of the Governor and his Secretary, Treasurer of State and his Deputy, Auditor of State and his Deputy, Attorney General, School Superintendent and their Clerks; in short, it pays the full salaries of the Executive Department and their Deputies for the two years.

There are in the state 924 corporations for pecuniary gain, embracing 218 for mining and milling ores, 147 ditch and canal companies, and 559 miscellaneous associations. The capital stock of these various corporations amounts to $373,742,485 divided as follows:

Mining and Milling Corporations	$ 181,938,000
Ditch and Canal Corporations	22,474,995
Miscellaneous Corporations	269,329,490
	$373,742,485

CLIMATE.

THE climate of Colorado is varied, owing to altitude and shelter of the mountains and ranges in winter, from mild in low altitudes sheltered by mountains, to extremely severe in high altitudes unprotected. The actual difference within a hundred miles in temperature in winter, is frequently 60 degrees. The telegrams to eastern papers from Colorado often quote the temperature at from 40 to 50 degrees below zero. This is taken from some exposed point, probably 10,000 feet above sea level, the distinction being rarely noted, and throughout the east Colorado is looked upon as a frigid climate in winter, when the reverse is the case. In the valleys and along the foot-hills the thermometer rarely falls below zero, and in summer rarely rises above 90 degrees. In our article on Denver, and on Colorado Springs following, we give more of a detail regarding climate, which may be considered as a fair average for the state. The following table of altitudes will give the reader an idea of the difference of temperature, at the same time of observation:

ALTITUDES ABOVE THE SEA.

	FEET.		FEET.
Argentine Pass	13,000	Middle Park	8,000
Breckenridge Pass	11,800	Mt. Lincoln	14,183
Canon City	4,700	Ouray	6,000
Colorado Springs	5,915	Pagosa Springs	6,800
Denver	5,364	Pike's Peak	14,336
Fort Garland	9,764	Pueblo	4,400
Georgetown	8,466	Sangre de Cristo	9,395
Gray's Peak	14,596	Sierro Blanco Peak	14,402
Greeley	4,779	South Park	9,342
Leadville	10,025	Uncompahgre Mountains	14,540
Long's Peak	14,300	Veta Pass	9,339
Manitou	6,124		

CHAPTER XIV.

PUEBLO, COLORADO.

GEOGRAPHICAL.

PUEBLO is the capital of Pueblo County, situated upon the Arkansas River, 500 miles west of Kansas City and 120 miles southeast of Denver, connected with Kansas City by three direct rail routes—the Atchison, Topeka & Santa Fe; Missouri Pacific and Chicago; Rock Island & Pacific. Connected with Denver by the Denver & Rio Grande; Denver, Texas & Fort Worth; Atchison, Topeka & Santa Fe; Missouri Pacific, and Chicago, Rock Island & Pacific railroads. It is admirably situated for a great distributing point, which accounts for its amazingly great increase of wholesale and jobbing business in the past year, which is referred to later on in this chapter.

HISTORICAL.

Pueblo (Spanish), meaning originally "people," was applied in the early conquests of America by the Spaniards to the people, who lived chiefly in villages or cities, and thereby became confounded with the cities themselves, and, later, became the accepted term for a village in which people resided, and, in modern times, has been applied to particular villages or cities, as in the case of this busy, enterprising city that we now present to our readers, which is rapidly gaining the appellation of the "Pittsburg of the West," richly deserving the same, from its manifold manufacturing and smelting industries, of which we shall have more to say later on in this chapter.

The Spanish conquerors of New Mexico did not establish settlements north of Santa Fe; hence the settlement of the Arkansas valley did not begin until after this territory had been acquired by the United States from Mexico in 1850, with the exception of Bent's Fort, established in 1826 by Bent, St. Vrain & Co., at a point in Bent County, on the Arkansas River, which Col. Bent himself destroyed in 1852 by fire and explosion, refusing to sell it to the United States Government for $12,000, when his price was $16,000.

In 1853 he erected another fort forty miles east, which he afterwards leased to the Government, and which was by them named Fort Wise.

In 1806 Captain Pike started out upon an exploring expedition. Proceeding up the Arkansas to where Pueblo now stands, he turned aside and followed up the Fountain to the foot of the mountain peak

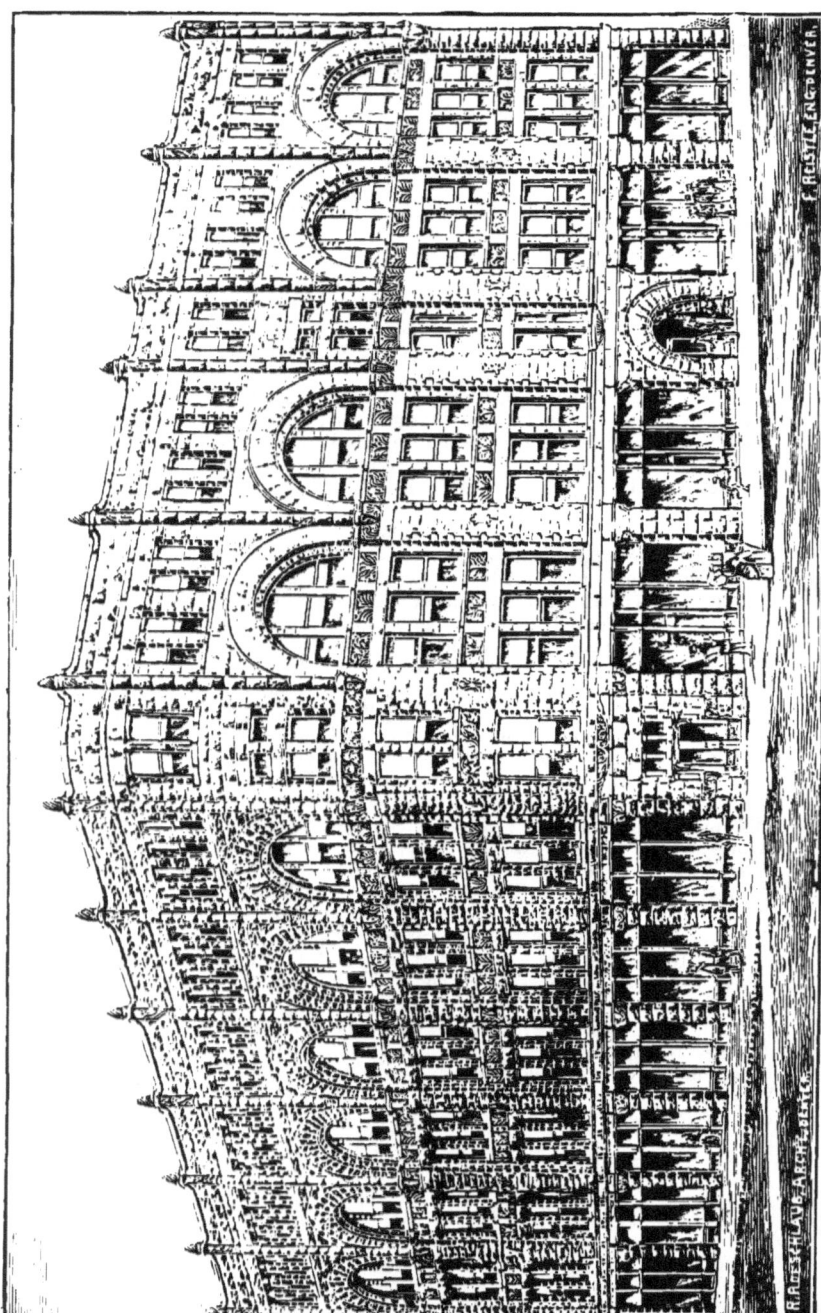

Central Block Pueblo—(Thurlow-Hutton)—Williams & Mallaby, Agents, Real Estate, Loans and Insurance.

which has since borne his name. At that early day it is said Captain Pike realized and expressed himself regarding the importance of the site of Pueblo as a stratagetic point for future commerce.

The next great explorer who passed this particular spot was Fremont, the Pathfinder, who followed in the footsteps of Pike to Pike's Peak in the year 1843. Fremont, however, proceeded further, passing through the Ute Pass, over Fremont Pass and on to California. This latter great explorer did not fail to note the importance of Pueblo as a future seat of commerce.

Probably the first settlement of Pueblo was about 1850, by the establishment of a trading post or fort, rudely constructed of adobe, and cottonwood pickets, called Fort Nepesta, the Ute name for the Arkansas River, at a place near where the Santa Fe depot now stands. A small Mexican settlement had been established by Charles Antobees, an old hunter and trapper, near the mouth of the St. Charles. Agriculture was attempted upon a small scale, and with fair success.

In 1854 the Ute Indian insurrection completely annihilated the small settlement, and no permanent habitations were re-established until about 1858, when the Pike's Peak gold excitement revived the hopes of the early settlers. About this time adventurers began to come in great numbers to Colorado; among the number were Si. Smith, Otto Winneka, Frank Dorris and George LeBaum, who, when they reached the junction of the Fountain with the Arkansas, turned aside from their search for gold and camped at a point about the north line of Shaw's addition to the present city. Wisely they concluded that the most profitable branch of mining was to furnish supplies to the gold hunters and make exchanges with the natives. They therefore concluded to start a town and call it Fountain City. No sooner thought of than executed. They were soon joined by Wm. H. Green, of Green Bay, Wisconsin, George Peck, Robert Middleton, Anthony Thomas, William Kroenig and George McDougal. About this time came two men, Cooper and Wing, from Missouri, bringing a small stock of goods, and with them were two surveyors, Shaffer and Brown, who made a survey and plat of the town site. Robert Middleton's wife accompanied him, and was the first white woman of the settlement. The Arapahoe Indians (about eighty lodges) camped alongside of the whites in the winter of 1858, trading in furs, dressed skins, etc. The following spring a ditch was taken out from the Fountain for the purpose of irrigation. The successful raising of crops in the Arkansas dates from that year, 1859. It was in this year that a rival town was started on the west side of the Fountain, and called Pueblo, established by Dr. Belt, Dr. Catterson, Wesley Catterson, Si. Warren, Ed. Cozzens, Jack Wright and Albert Bereau. The same year Hon. George M. Chilcott, since United States Senator from Colorado, and O. H. P. Baxter came to Colorado, removing to Pueblo in the fall of 1860. Jack Wright, a brother-in-law of Ed. Cozzens, built the first house in

Pueblo, followed soon after by another, erected by Aaron Sims, another brother-in-law of Ed. Cozzens. Dr. Catterson built a house in the rear of where now stands Jenner's store. Thus was a fair start made toward building up the great metropolis that Pueblo is to-day.

A notorious character by the name of Jack Allen, from Fort Wise, believing that a town expecting to become a city, must be duly christened, proceeded to move his "gin mill" from that place to Pueblo. He was the first person to establish a whisky shop in Pueblo; he named it "The Taos Lightning Factory," and began to dispense "good liker" to the settlement and to the poor aborigines. How he compounded his liquids always remained a mystery to the Puebloites. One thing certain, it was fire water, and would paralyze the most hardened frontiersman and lay out an Indian in double quick order. Fountain City soon decayed under the greater civilizing influences exerted by Jack Allen, and finally became a portion of the city of Pueblo.

Colonel Boone built a frame tenement house on Santa Fe avenue soon after the town was fairly started, and opened a store therein. Not long thereafter he was called away from Pueblo on business, leaving Dr. Catterson to keep the store. Tradition has it that he not only kept the store, but the money as well, and that, upon the breaking out of the war, the colonel's riches took to themselves wings and flew with Dr. Catterson to "Dixey." Like all western towns, Pueblo had its baptism of blood ere it became a settled community; the terrors of which it is not our purpose to relate. After the flight of Dr. Catterson, Pueblo was without a store for nearly one year; at the end of that time John A. Thatcher, now one of Pueblo's wealthiest merchants, arrived at the foot of Santa Fe avenue from Denver with a small load of store goods, which he had bought on credit. He soon established himself in a 10x10 log cabin, very shortly disposing of all his stock. He returned to Denver and brought back a more pretentious stock. From that small beginning he gradually worked himself up to be the leading merchant in Colorado.

Messrs. Baxter and Thatcher erected in 1864 a grist mill, which was the first noted event in the progressive history of Pueblo. The first hotel was kept by Aaron Sims, who was also the first postmaster. From the erection of the Baxter-Thatcher mill and the close of the Indian war of that year, Pueblo progressed quite rapidly. In 1868 St. Peter's Episcopal Church was built, (the first in Pueblo), followed soon after by the Methodist, Presbyterian and Catholic societies;

THE FIRST NEWSPAPER.

Probably the most important event in the early history of Pueblo was the establishment of the Pueblo *Chieftain*, which made its first appearance June 1st, 1868. The paper was edited by Gov. George A. Hinsdale (since deceased) and Judge Wilber F. Stone; published

Eastern Slope, Marshall Pass, on line of D. & R. G. Ry.

by Dr. Beshear and Sam. McBride. The first issue contained a notice of the death of the famous scout, Kit Carson, at Bogg's Ranch, then in Pueblo County, together with resolutions of respect passed by a club of his friends in Pueblo. (The progress of the *Chieftain* will be fully set forth further on in this work.)

Pueblo then commenced to make rapid strides, and in 1870 became an incorporated town, with a full complement of officers, Louis Conley being the first president of the Board of Trustees.

In 1872, the Denver & Rio Grande Railway was completed to Pueblo, and marked the next great epoch in the progress of the place. The advent of the first railroad was appropriately celebrated, and the town rapidly changed to a city, and necessitated the change in 1873 from town to city government. The year 1874 witnessed the construction of the Holly system of waterworks, and in 1875 the second railroad was completed to Pueblo,—the Pueblo & Arkansas Valley road connecting with the Atchison, Topeka & Santa Fe.

ARKANSAS VALLEY.

IT has been well said, that "what the Mississippi and Missouri valleys are to the Northwest; what the Amazon is to South America; what the Nile is to Egypt, so is the great Arkansas valley to the middle West." It is the great natural highway across the continent to which travel and commerce are yearly more and more resorting. The valley of this great river is in no part of the world surpassed in fertility, from its very source in the Rocky Mountains to its debouchment in Arkansas. Almost throughout its entire extent, over 2,000 miles, corn and the smaller cereals attain a perfection and yield an abundance very rarely equalled. If corn is king, the Arkansas valley, almost to the base of the mountains, is the most prized of the royal demesnes. Over millions of yet uncultivated acres unnumbered herds and flocks grow fat on the nutritious natural grasses, which need no curing for the winter season—a perennial supply for the year around. It is a region in which thrive luxuriantly all the fruits and varied products of the temperate zones. The climate is healthful, and farms are almost ready made to hand, requiring only an upturned soil to yield abundantly. Between the mountains and the eastern limit of Colorado there are more than fifteen millions of acres drained by the Arkansas and its tributaries. A comparison shows that this vast territory more than equals in extent the combined acres of Massachusetts, Connecticut, Maryland, Delaware and Rhode Island. A large proportion of this great domain is susceptible of irrigation; and yet, with its inconceivably rich resources, immense stretches of land stand idle under the sun, waiting for the industrious millions that will even-

JUDGE W. J. KERR.

W. J. Kerr, secretary of the Stanley Drill Power Company, was born in Newry, Ireland, June 28th, 1849. His father, Rev. John Kerr, was an eminent and widely known Presbyterian orator and divine. W. J. Kerr received his education in Dublin, Ireland; studied law under Chief Justice Sidney Brass, of Illinois, and afterwards engaged in the practice of law in Mt. Vernon, Illinois, and Garnett, Kansas. He came to Pueblo in 1880, and has established such a reputation as a Democratic politician and orator as ranks him among the foremost men of our country.

tually turn these productive acres into flourishing farms, or live in comfort in future towns and villages. Of a very large part of these acres the government is still the owner, but is rapidly disposing of them to homesteaders and pre-emptors. Immense tracts are being provided by capitalists with irrigating ditches, the source of return for their investment being in the sale of perpetual water rights to settlers.

Who can predict the possibilities of development in soil and production and growth of population in this portion of the great Arkansas valley within the next score of years? And then, too, it is true that the resources embraced within the limits of this valley in its mountain division, have not been much more than touched; its mineral wealth, hidden in rocky fastnesses, has only been scratched upon the surface. Wealth of gold and silver, iron, lead and copper, of coal and petroleum, of building stones and clays. Within the confines of this valley are Leadville, ranking among the greatest mining centers of the world, Trinidad, with its unlimited supplies of coal and iron, Canon City and Florence in the midst of great fields of petroleum.

Resting in the very heart of this valley of boundless wealth is Pueblo, on both sides of the Arkansas, where it is joined by the Fontaine qui Bouille. Referring to the

ORIGIN AND GROWTH

of the city, an Eastern writer finds that "prosperity comes to Pueblo as water runs down hill." In the remote past the attraction of gravitation made the ground upon which the present city is built a meeting place for bands of primeval Indians and roving Spaniards, and, later, for scouts, soldiers and overland traders. In the present generation the same force has built there a commercial city and started within it the wheels of industrial progress. The overland traveler bound West made the spot his camping ground, because there he met his friends who had followed the source of the Fontaine qui Bouille down from Pike's Peak to the Arkansas valley, and those who had struck across country from La Veta Pass, or had drifted eastward from the neighborhood of the Royal Gorge. That unwritten law of frontier logic which designates the confluences of streams as meeting points for migratory settlers, was at Pueblo as plainly carried out as that more tangible modern rule, which says that manufacturing must be so placed that raw material shall come to them on the down grade.

CLIMATE.

HEALTH IS THE GREATEST WEALTH.

SO much has been said and written about the climate of Colorado, and Pueblo in particular, that most people, even in the remote East, are well informed on the subject of our superior advantages in this respect. The climate of Pueblo is noted for its delightful autumns and mild, sunny winters, while its springs are pleasant and its summers warm by day and cool by night. Situated at an altitude of about 4,500 feet above the sea level, and in the Pueblo basin, it is, of all the plain cities, the best protected from the winds, which occasionally sweep over the vast prairies of Eastern Colorado, Kansas and Nebraska, while during the winter season the temperature of this basin is much higher than that of the surrounding and more elevated plateaus. Pueblo is essentially a winter resort, and possesses the best features of a dry, mild winter climate to be found upon the western slope of the Rocky Mountains. To a person accustomed to the damp, foggy, cloudy winter months of the South and East, with their accompanying mud, slush and chill, or to the rigorous winters of the North, with icy fetter and snowy mantle, the climate of Pueblo and this section of Colorado presents a most vivid contrast. There is scarce one day out of the 365 during some parts of which it is not a pleasure to be out of doors, for the sun shines clear and warm, the ground is dry and the air bracing, stimulating and invigorating. An occasional wintry storm brings the only clouds, snow or cold, lasting from one to three days, to remind one of the season, after which the bright sun glows warm in the sky, the snow disappears from the ground as if by magic, and mild weather again prevails. Winter does not begin until Christmas or New Year's, and the few storms which ensue occur during the following six weeks. In the severe winter of 1884–5 there were but thirteen cold days; of 1885-6 but eight such days in which during a part of the twenty-four hours the thermometer registered zero or below; in the winter of 1886-7 there were only two days of cold, and in the winter of 1887-8 but seven cold days. To show the effect of the sun upon the atmosphere, when no storm was present, the temperature at 2 p. m. during each of the cold months often registered 60 to 70 degrees F. in the shade. The dryness of the atmosphere is most remarkable and salutary, the average relative humidity being .46 or equivalent to 1.91 grains of vapor in the cubic foot of air. Contrasting this condition with that of other health resorts, we find at Santa Barbara, California, a humidity of .60, and grains of vapor 4.23; at Jacksonville, Florida, a humidity of .69, and grains of vapor 5.60. The constant sunshine is well shown by the small number of cloudy days in which four-fifths or more of the sky is overcast. During 1887 there were of cloudy days, 57; of fair days, 118; of clear days, 189.

Out of door work of all kinds, such as ploughing, building, etc., can be engaged in at all times of the year without any delay on account of bad weather.

To persons in search of a climate in which is to be found the greatest number of pleasant sunny days, and the very fewest disagreeable ones; to those who love sunshine and a clear, pure atmosphere; to all who are fond of an out-of-door life, none will be found superior to that of Pueblo. People in health thrive here, and those seeking health are more apt to find it in Pueblo than in more remote but less favored places. This climate is particularly recommended for pulmonary complaints of all kinds, and the most severe cases of asthma, hay fever, etc., are promptly relieved and quickly cured at Pueblo.

PUEBLO'S WONDERFUL HEALTH ATTRACTIONS.

Probably the most wonderful attraction possessed by this aspiring city is the Clark's Magnetic Mineral Springs. The flow was first tapped January 1st, 1880, by drilling, at a depth of 1,402 feet. The daily flow averages 4,000 barrels. The water is highly magnetized; a knife blade held in the water for a few moments will, after being withdrawn, readily lift a pin by magnetic force. The temperature of the water remains, as at first, at 80 degrees Fahrenheit. This celebrated spring, situated in the City of Pueblo, about four blocks from the Union Depot and six blocks from the business center of the city, has recently been improved by the erection of a large and elegant bath house, fitted up with all the latest improvements for bathing. The Terrace House, opposite the bath house, has also been newly furnished, papered and refitted, for the accommodation of its patrons. There are also other first-class hotel accommodations convenient to the bath house, which, with the marvelous curative properties of the water, low altitude and fine climate, make this the most desirable health resort in the West. The water used in bathing and drinking flows direct from the spring, and, so far as the medication of waters can favorably affect the bath for which they are used, these baths have the strongest claim to confidence, inasmuch as no other waters in the United States that are used for bathing and drinking are more highly impregnated with mineral salts and acids. Persons bathing in this water, previous to doing so, should be intelligently instructed, under a proper knowledge of their case, as to the precise temperature of the bath and the length of time they remain in it. A trial of this water, in a multitude of cases, has demonstrated the fact, that, however insensible their properties or unknown combinations, they are able to overcome many of the very worst forms of disease. These waters have acquired a national reputation for curing Bright's disease of the kidneys and diabetes. Kidney affections in all stages and forms have been treated here with uniform success. Sufferers should send to the Clark Magnetic Mineral Spring Company for circulars, etc.

Pueblo also has several other artesian wells of less strength, but all of a mineral character, and each said to be a specific for some form or other of disease. The Clark Spring, however, continues in greatest favor, and retains the early reputation acquired for the cure of rheumatism in all forms, kidney diseases, liver complaints, etc. Over 100 cases of Bright's disease have been cured, twenty of whom came from England. A qualitative analysis of the water gives the following constituents: Sulphuretted hydrogen, iron (form titanic acid), bicarbonate of lime, sulphate of soda, sulphate of magnesia, manganese, potassium (trace), sulphuric acid, arsenious acid. One remarkable peculiarity about the water is that knives are readily magnetized by holding them in the water.

COAL AND OIL.

Pueblo has in favor of manufacture 1,000,000 acres of coal land, within a radius of sixty miles, all a down hill haul, the quality of which is unsurpassed in America for steam, heating, furnace or smelting uses. The average cost of coal is $2.25 per ton at the mines, or $3.50 to $5 per ton at Pueblo. The grade of coal known as "mining" or "pea" coal, for manufacturing purposes, sells at Pueblo for $1 to $1.50 per ton. Petroleum fields, producing 1,000 barrels per day, situated thirty miles from the city, is another important factor in the development of manufactures in and about Pueblo. Already a strong concern has been incorporated to pipe oil from the newly discovered field of Oil Creek (about ten miles further away than the present developed fields) to Pueblo, a distance of forty miles. The company is known as the Pueblo Oil and Development Company; capital, $1,000,000. The officers are: H. D. Mory, president and treasurer, Pueblo; N. R. Turchell, of Canon City, first vice president; H. D. Sickles, of New York, second vice president; J. S. C. Bee, secretary, Pueblo, and L. W. Smith, general manager, Pueblo. This company own or control about 4,000 acres of oil land. Wells are being drilled, and will be in operation September 15th next. The pipe line is also being constructed, and the vast system will be in operation before the snow flies. The purpose of the company is to pipe the crude oil to Pueblo, where it will be refined, the refuse to be used in manufactures for fuel. The plan is entirely practical, the fall being about 1,500 feet in forty miles. Undoubtedly they will meet with strong opposition from the great Standard Oil monopoly. We are informed, however, that this company have several millions of dollars back of them with which to meet that arch fiend, and will run them a pretty hard race for the business west of the Mississippi River.

Pueblo people are scarcely aware of their vast natural advantages, which accounts for their enterprise in securing the attention of the manufacturing world. Too often a city with such immense resources, places too much dependence upon their natural advantages, and, consequently, a less fortunately situated city gets all the sinews which make cities great, while the city trusting in its natural advantages remains at a standstill, until some genius shall have arisen and awakened the people to a true sense of the importance of pushing the natural advantages. Eastern capital is shy, and will only invest in places where local capitalists are willing to show their faith in their city.

FREMONT PASS.—Altitude 11,500 Feet.
On line of Denver and Rio Grande Railway

RAILROAD ADVANTAGES.

"Pueblo is the key to the railroad situation in the West," said Jay Gould in an interview in Denver, when he was looking for a terminal point in Colorado for the Missouri Pacific Railway, which was completed to Pueblo in December, 1887. This western extension opened a new territory in Kansas and Eastern Colorado, now so rapidly settling up; it shortened the distance between Pueblo and Kansas City, gave direct passenger connection with St. Louis, and, more than all, healthy competition in many towns and cities in Kansas, from which farm and dairy products are shipped into Colorado to supply the demands of those engaged in mining and manufacturing industries. When it is considered that 6,518 miles of railway are operated by this system, and over a thousand prosperous towns and cities placed in direct communication with Pueblo, the value of the Missouri Pacific to this city may be appreciated.

The first trunk line to enter Southern Colorado was the Atchison, Topeka & Santa Fe Railway, which follows the Arkansas River through a region now improved by many productive farms and thriving villages and cities. This vast system of 7,374 miles, which has been for years the main artery for commerce in Kansas, and connects Pueblo with every trade center in that state, has, by its recent extensions east of the Missouri River, given Pueblo through trains into Chicago. The main offices of the western division are located in Pueblo. A branch of this line extends west to Canon City and the coal beds owned by the company. The coal fields of Trinidad are reached by this line by La Junta. The Denver & Santa Fe road, extending from Pueblo to Denver, is also operated by this same company.

The Chicago, Kansas & Nebraska (Rock Island route) was completed to Colorado Springs in November last, and its trains enter Pueblo over the track of the Denver & Rio Grande Railway, of which company it has secured that right. This extension opens up a new territory in Northern Kansas and Eastern Colorado, besides facilitating the intercourse between Colorado and the States of Nebraska, Iowa, Minnesota and Northern Illinois. This road was the first in the state to introduce the vestibule cars on regular trains.

The immediate object of the Missouri Pacific and Rock Island roads in building into the state is to gain access to the extensive coal beds of Southern Colorado, of which Pueblo is the acknowledged center and source of supply for the entire western portions of Kansas and Southern Nebraska, as well as to share in carrying eastward the products of the manufactories now established, and those to come at no distant date.

The ultimate purpose of these powerful trunk lines is to secure passage by natural and easy grades through the mountains to the

Pacific coast. It has often been asserted by railroad managers that "Pueblo stands at the only natural gateway to the Rocky Mountains in Colorado," by which route freight can be carried at rates which cannot be met with profit by roads operating over tortuous routes, steep grades and road beds expensive to keep in repair.

When Pueblo was brought within easy distance of New Orleans and Galveston by means of the "Panhandle" route, another great commercial advantage was gained. The Denver, Texas & Fort Worth Railway, operating 804 miles, was completed in the month of April, 1887, placing Pueblo but little more than 1,000 miles from tide water and the cheap rates of ocean commerce. Merchandise arrives in Pueblo via steamer to Galveston and over this air line in twelve to fifteen days. Texas and Colorado are rapidly building up an extensive trade in the exchange of field and orchard products for Colorado coal and iron. The most wonderful tide of emigration which is setting in towards the vast territory reached by these four trunk lines will find Pueblo the supply depot for coal and manufactured products.

The Denver & Rio Grande Railway, now the greatest narrow gauge system in the world, was called the "Baby Road" when a small locomotive drew a few cars into Pueblo in 1872. The road was extended west to the base of the mountains at Canon City. It was extended south to the coal fields of El Moro, and over Veta Pass to Fort Garland in San Luis Park. Then it rested. But when the rush began to the rich fields of ore about Leadville, the "Baby Road" became a little giant. It blasted a narrow trail through the granite-walled canon of the Arkansas, where heretofore no man had ever ventured, and it rapidly made its way to the "Carbonate Camp." With the discovery of other rich mining districts, new mines were established over mountain ranges, through canons and along narrow edges, high up on the sides of mountain walls, to carry to the miner the supplies he should need, and to take away the rich ores or products of the reduction works. To reach some of these camps, the feats of engineering skill were the marvel of the scientific world. The Denver & Rio Grande now operates 1,800 miles of narrow gauge track. It is widening its main lines to standard gauge by the laying of a third rail. The small locomotives of earlier days are now replaced by the latest pattern of consolidated "moguls," both narrow and standard gauge; the freight and passenger cars are enlarged to standard size; in short, in equipment this road is the peer of any in the country. Broad gauge trains run between Pueblo and Denver, Pueblo and Canon City, and Pueblo and Trinidad, and will soon be running west to Leadville. A large portion of the distance between Pueblo and Denver is covered by a double track to accommodate the volume of traffic.

Pueblo is the center of this great system of broad and narrow gauge tracks, which penetrate by water grades the mountain fastness and bring down hill the products of the mines to be smelted in this natural depot point. One hundred camps in this state are reached by this road alone, while in some sixty others it competes for business with other roads. From Pueblo a branch extends south to the coal fields of Las Animas County, to the rich agricultural lands in San Luis valley and to "Silver San Juan." Westward it extends to Leadville, Aspen and Glenwood Springs; down the valleys of the Gunnison and the Grand, and across the plateau country to Salt Lake City and Ogden, Utah, while numerous branches reach out and up to productive mines. This road offers to the miner, the ranchman, the lumberman, the stockman, the fruit grower, a ready market for the products of their toil; it aids to develop the rich valleys and stores of mineral wealth.

Not only in a commercial sense is it a benefit to the whole state—it offers to the tourist easy access to the grandest mountain scenery in the world. From the windows of a Pullman he may view with wonder on canon, pass and gorge; in a day, "ride from summer to winter." By extensive and expensive means of advertising, this road attracts thousands each year to Colorado, many of whom, while enjoying the attractions of the "Scenic Route of the World," are led to investigate the resources of the country traversed, and who finally become citizens of the state.

The Colorado Midland, while not running trains into Pueblo, indirectly adds to the railroad advantages of this point by giving needed competition into the mountains by means of a traffic arrangement with the Denver & Santa Fe road.

This road is splendidly equipped and ably managed. It was the first standard gauge line to break through the mountains of Colorado to the rich mineral field on the western slope. Rich coal deposits are found along the line, valuable agricultural and pastural lands have been opened up, and the tourist has much to amaze and delight him in a tour over this route. From Manitou Springs to Glenwood Springs the ride is one continued succession of surprises. Canon and plain and tunnel and gorge alternately are presented to the unwearying eye. The great expanse of South Park is seen in broad mid-day, the rich mining camps of Leadville and Aspen are reached in comfort at nightfall. The company is extending its line down Rifle Creek and beyond New Castle, ultimately to reach Salt Lake City.

PROJECTED LINES.

There are signs of new roads for Pueblo, and already rumors of the arrival of more trunk lines from the East are freely circulated. The Missouri Pacific will build to its coal beds some fifty miles southwest of Pueblo. The Fort Worth will build an independent line from Pueblo to Trinidad, its lease with the D. & R. G. being only a temporary arrangement. The Pueblo, Gunnison & Pacific is an organization of local capitalists, who have surveyed a line into the San Luis valley, and find a most practicable route. Some of the trunk lines seeking to penetrate the mountains will build this line. As a railway center Pueblo has no equal in the West; in a few years its supremacy as a commercial center will be as firmly established, as it is now the best smelting point in the West.

A new Union Depot is arranged for, to cost $400,000, and before this article is in print, work will have been begun upon it, and, ere a year rolls around, this magnificent edifice will be completed.

PUEBLO'S BUILDINGS.

A recent canvass discloses the fact, that, at this time, buildings are being constructed in Pueblo that, when completed (and all will be by January 1st, 1890), they will cost a little over $2,000,000; other buildings for 1889 completed before this canvass, will swell the sum total of building for 1889 to exceeding $3,000,000.

Pueblo is at present receiving a large amount of Eastern capital for investment, as is evidenced by the Thurlow-Hutton or Central block and the Swift block, costing respectively $400,000 and $150,000. The Central block is a large five-story stone structure, covering 135x 139 feet of ground; the building is to be used as a store and office block. The Denver & Rio Grande division headquarters will be located there. Messrs. Williams and Mallaby, the popular real estate and insurance firm, are agents for the block, and we are informed by them that the building will be one of the best finished buildings in Colorado, having three elevators, steam heat, electric lights and all other modern improvements. While not as tall as some Denver buildings, the floor space will be greater than any building in the state; we produce a cut elsewhere of this handsome building, which will give our readers a fair idea of its massive proportions.

The Swift block is almost completed, and will be occupied by Paul Wilson, Pueblo's leading dry goods merchant. The building is four stories in height, built of stone, brick and iron, a very handsome and solid building, and one in which Pueblo takes great pride.

The Opera House is about one-half completed and the work being pushed as rapidly as men and money can accomplish the work; when completed it will be the finest theater building west of Chicago, and will be to Pueblo what the Tabor Grand has always been to Denver, insuring her citizens first class attractions. This building is being erected on local capital, as is also the great Mineral Palace, which is destined to be the greatest public attraction of America. The officers are well known western men of high standing, and regarded as "pushers." More of this palace in a future issue.

The Grand Hotel block is one of the substantial buildings of the city. It would require an entire volume to enumerate all of the substantial business blocks of the city, and we therefore direct your attention to the business of the city, the most important of which is the banking business, to which we give precedence.

PUEBLO BANKS AND BANKING,

PUEBLO is justly proud of her banking institutions. There are four national banks and two private banks, all sound financial institutions, having ample capital and a large surplus. Another national bank is organizing and will be ready for business soon. There is no single business in any city that is as accurate a barometer as the banking business, and with the history of the banking system of Pueblo is closely identified the progress of the city; each have made marvelous strides, and entitle Pueblo to rank as the second city west of the Missouri River. When the —— National Bank shall open its doors, Pueblo will be only two national banks behind Denver, a place it has held for some time. Denver having just added a new bank, keeps the balance the same.

The history of banking in Pueblo might be said to date from 1868, at which time Thatcher Brothers, who were largely engaged in merchandising in Pueblo, commenced to receive deposits and issue drafts for the benefit of their customers; they did not, however, start an exclusive banking business until July, 1871, at which time they started

THE FIRST NATIONAL BANK OF PUEBLO,

incorporated with $50,000 capital. J. A. Thatcher was first president of the bank and M. D. Thatcher, cashier. Similar relations continued to exist until 1888, when J. A. Thatcher retired from the presidency of the bank, and M. D. Thatcher was chosen president and Robert F. Lytle, cashier. The prominent position held by this bank in the confidence of the people of Pueblo and the West generally, is due to the amplitude of its resources, the conservative methods of its management, and the substantial character of the gentlemen having its destinies in charge as officers. The facilities of the bank for the transaction of every description of banking business are unsurpassed. Every department of a legitimate banking business is carried on, and the bank carries the accounts of individuals, firms and corporations, to whom it affords the best facilities consistent with correct banking principles. The safe and conservative management of this bank by the Thatcher Brothers and Mr. Lytle has placed it in the front rank of commercial institutions, a point only obtained after years of strict and practical attention to the details of the business and fidelity in dealing with business men. The capital of the bank has been increased to $100,000, and a surplus fund has accumulated, until it has reached the handsome sum of $350,000; the working capital of the bank is therefore $450,000.

Early in 1873 the banking business had increased so rapidly, keeping pace with the city, that additional facilities became necessary. It was then that Jeff. Reynolds and associates, came to the front with a private bank, and continued thus until 1876,

STOCKGROWERS' NATIONAL BANK.

The history of this sound financial institution goes back to the year 1873, at which time it was organized as a private bank, and in 1876 it was incorporated under the National Banking Act, with a capital stock of $250,000, of which $50,000 was paid up. From a small beginning the bank has steadily worked up to a first class business, and has accumulated $60,000 in surplus and profits, in addition to dividends paid to its stockholders. Mr. George H. Hobson, president, succeeded Colonel M. H. Fitch some years ago, having previously been vice president. The other officers are: John D. Miller, vice president, and A. V. Bradford, cashier, who, with Robert Grant and M. A. Rhodes, form the board of directors. This list presents an array of names which entitles this bank to the most favorable consideration, and commands the confidence of the business community. The business of the bank is of a general character, including deposits, discounts, loans and collections in all parts of the country.

The success of the Stockgrowers' National Bank has been as marked as the rapid growth of the city, and to-day the institution stands as the peer of any financial institution in the state. The management is as liberal as is consistent with good and safe banking, commanding the confidence of depositors and borrowers to a marked degree.

The next addition to the banking circles of Pueblo was the organization of the

WESTERN NATIONAL BANK OF PUEBLO

in 1881, by W. L. Graham and associates. Organized with a capital of $50,000, which was rapidly augmented, until to-day capital and surplus amount to $130,000, and deposits amounting to $450,000. The phenomenal success of this institution is due almost entirely to W. L. Graham, the president, and to Charles E. Saxton, the cashier, both competent bankers, conservative and reliable. This institution does a general banking business, receives deposits and loans money on good security, purchases bonds and issues foreign and domestic exchanges, makes collections, etc., etc. Messrs. Graham and Saxton are well known citizens of Pueblo, recognized as public spirited and very honorable men.

The South Pueblo National Bank was opened the same day as the Western National, and continued under that style until February, 1889, when the name was changed to the Central National Bank. The officers are: D. L. Holden, president; H. L. Holden, acting cashier. Capital paid in, $50,000; surplus, $12,000; undivided profits, $7,230. The bank is doing a very fair business.

The Bank of Pueblo (not incorporated) is owned by Frederick Rohrer, who is also cashier; A. J. McQuaid assistant cashier. This bank began business April 10th, 1882, and has enjoyed the confidence of the people, and has transacted a large general banking business, to the entire satisfaction of its customers. The bank issues drafts, letters of credit, etc., upon all large cities of America and Europe.

MANUFACTURES.

PUEBLO presents unequalled advantages for manufactures of almost every class and kind. Already some mammoth establishments are here—one, the Colorado Coal and Iron Company, is one of the largest in America.

COLORADO COAL AND IRON COMPANY.

The Colorado Coal and Iron Company owns 100,000 acres of land, consisting of coal, iron, fire clay and limestone deposits, in various parts of the state, and of agricultural and pastural lands located mainly in the Arkansas valley between and around Pueblo and Canon City. It also owns the town sites of South Pueblo and Bessemer, though a large portion of the former is now held by residents of that portion of the city. This company has ten coal mines opened on its land in various parts of the state from which it is mining at present about one million tons per year. The coal varies in quality from dry domestic to coking and gas coal. The company has two coking plants, one at El Moro, the other at Crested Butte, of 375 ovens, and produces a quality of coke equal to that of Connellsville, Penn. It has at Bessemer, adjoining Pueblo, an iron and steel works, consisting of two blast furnaces of a combined capacity of 200 tons, a Bessemer converting works, steel rail mill, nail mill, puddling works, merchant bar mill, pipe foundry and machine shops.

It has adjacent to the city of Pueblo 65,000 acres of land, which it proposes to irrigate by means of a large canal taken out of the Arkansas River, and which requires only a water supply to make it the finest agricultural land in the state. This land is capable of supporting a population which will be dependent on Pueblo for trading and market. This trade alone will make a volume of business amounting to $1,000,000 a year for Pueblo merchants, and will increase the population in and around Pueblo by at least 10,000. This canal, surveys of which have already been made, will probably be completed during the coming year.

The iron works of this company have proved that Colorado can successfully manufacture Bessemer steel and merchantable iron. For the making of the former, Colorado possesses all the varieties of ores necessary even to manganic ore for the making of speigel. The iron mines of the Colorado Coal and Iron Company are located at Calumet, near Salida, at Hot Springs, near Villa Grove, near Gunnison and at Ashcroft. A large trade in nails, merchant bar iron and iron pipes for city mains has already been established. During the past year the Colorado Coal and Iron Company has had in its employ a large force of men, and has paid in wages $1,250,000.

During 1888 the output of the company's works at Bessemer was: Pig iron of all kinds, including speigel, 20,800 tons; steel rails, 8,040 tons; merchant bar iron, 5,300 tons; cast iron water pipe, 1,340 tons; nails, 45,080 kegs; railroad spikes, 1,330 kegs. The output of the company's coal mines was about 1,000,000 tons, valued at the mines at $2,250,000.

SMELTERS.

It is, in fact and theory, the chief smelting point in the West. Beginning with the year 1889, it has more furnaces than any other town in the state, and its output will rapidly increase in volume. It has three smelting plants for the treatment of ores containing gold, silver and lead. The oldest, the Pueblo Smelting and Refining Company, began operations in Pueblo in the year 1878. Its works and grounds now cover an area of forty acres. For 1888 its output was as follows:

Lead, 8,230 tons, value	$ 717,656 00
Silver, 2,089,705 ozs., value	1,953,874 18
Gold, 10,324 ozs., value	213,397 08
Copper, 105,645 ozs., value	* 17,959 65
Total	$2,902,886 91

At these mammoth works bullion is produced from the ores, and from this is separated and refined gold, silver, lead and copper. In the lead refinery, besides pig and antimonial lead, lead pipe and bar lead are made.

The average number of men employed during 1888 was 359. Total wages paid, $307,446.

This company, composed mainly of Boston capitalists, has been erecting, at a vast expense, a mammoth copper smelting works, for the purpose of extracting merchantable copper from western ores, and it will be in operation early in the present year. At least $250,000 have been expended in the construction of this plant.

The Colorado Smelting Company, with four furnaces, produces only lead bullion carrying gold and silver. This plant is noted among mining men for the extreme neatness and system shown about the works. Its output for 1888 was: Silver, 1,027,500 ozs.; gold, 4,858 ozs.; lead, 8,330 tons. The average number of men employed, 140; total wages paid, $117,530.65.

The Philadelphia Smelting and Refining Company started its furnaces for the first time just at the close of the year. Mr. Ed. R. Holden, president of the company, has conducted smelters in Leadville and Denver, but found that Pueblo had the most advantages for cheap smelting; so, associating with him the Messrs. Guddenheim, of Philadelphia, the company decided upon Pueblo. Being the last built, this smelting plant is complete in its facilities for treating ores, containing all the labor-saving devices known to the smelting world. The estimated cost of the buildings and machinery is $300,000. Fully 300 men have been employed about the works for several months. The capital stock of this company has recently been increased to $1,225,000 paid in, and the capacity of the works will be at once doubled by the addition of six more blast and twelve more roasting furnaces. In May the building of a refinery will be commenced. This will be furnished with all the latest improved appliances. When this is completed, by autumn, the Philadelphia will be the largest and most complete works of its kind in the world.

Colorado Smelting Company at Pueblo.

In connection with the smelting business are the two public sampling companies.

The Pueblo Public Sampling Works was in continued operation during the entire year, doing a steadily increasing business.

The Central Ore Sampling Company completed its works late in December, and are already doing an excellent business.

With the increased facilities for smelting ores, the value of Pueblo as a public ore market increases. When miners can save from one to two dollars on a ton of ore in freight charges alone, they will not be anxious to ship elsewhere, provided Pueblo can use their ores.

PUBLIC STREET RAILWAYS.

The Pueblo Street Railway Company grows apace with the city, and furnishes excellent accommodations. The company now have laid thirteen and one-half miles of track, over which are run fourteen cars. They have in their barns on Union avenue twenty-one cars in all, and four more will be added to those running. These additions will be put on the Victoria avenue route and extend to the Insane Asylum from Elizabeth street. On their pay roll are the names of fifty men on an average, drivers receiving $55 per month. The aggregate paid out each month to employees will touch $2,000. In the barns they keep eighty-one horses. To feed these, $600 is paid out monthly for feed. This food supply is all purchased in Pueblo and is chopped in the barn. It is the intention of the company to soon commence laying the additional track to that already down, which, of course, will press additional cars into service.

The first car leaves the barn at 6 a. m., and the last one comes in at 11:09 at night. Between the above hours the aggregate distance traveled by the cars daily is 1,300 miles; so it will be seen they are not very idle. The company's property has a frontage on Union avenue of fifty feet, running straight through the block to Main street. On this are built the fine commodious barns, car houses, feed bins, blacksmith and repair shops, etc. They do their own repairing, horseshoeing, etc., having competent men in charge of each department. Thus it will be seen that the Pueblo Street Railway Company is quite an important acquisition to this city's many enterprises, and causes a large sum of money to be circulated monthly.

BUSINESS CONVENIENCES.

The Colorado Telephone Company has an exchange here, with 200 subscribers. Telephone communication is established between Pueblo and Canon City and all intermediate points, and northward to Denver, a distance of 120 miles. The service is excellent.

The Western Union Telegraph Company has two city offices, where five employees are kept constantly at work receiving and sending messages.

The Pueblo Gas and Electric Light Company supply the city with gas and with two kinds of electric light—the Thompson-Houston arc and the Heisler incandescent. The former light is used by the city to illuminate the principal streets. The Pueblo Light, Heat and Power Company supply the Westinghouse system of incandescent light to a large number of consumers.

The City Water Works supply all that portion of the city north of the river at low rates. The source of supply is the Arkansas River.

The South Pueblo Water Company have an exclusive franchise in all the territory south of the river.

SCHOOLS.

THE public schools of Pueblo will compare favorably with those of the older cities in the East in the earnestness of the pupils and in methods of instruction. There are two school districts in the city, one on each side of the river. In district No. 1, on the north side, the affairs are managed by a board of five directors, who select a superintendent, and, with his advice, select the teachers. The course of study represents eight years' work in the primary grades and four years in the High School. In the primary grades it embraces, besides

Central High School on the Mesa.

the fundamental studies, drawing and special work in English literature from memory exercise, to the analysis of classic literature of the best English and American writers. The High School course includes higher mathematics, the natural sciences, Latin and literature studies throughout the course. Honest work is done. In this district the school buildings are three in number—the Centennial, containing eight rooms, with 400 sittings; the Hinsdale, having six rooms and 324 sittings, and the Fontaine, with four rooms and 190 sittings. They are of modern design, constructed on the most improved plans to secure comfort and health. Nineteen teachers are employed. The present enrollment is about 900, including seventy in the High School. The district owns a reference library of 400 volumes.

The present crowded condition of the schools has warned the directors to prepare for the increasing demands, and during the past year they purchased three desirable sites for the erection of more buildings.

District No. 20, on the south side, is in a very prosperous condition. It has four buildings—the Central High School, built of pink lava stone, containing seven rooms, with 400 sittings, and three buildings for primary grades, containing eight rooms, with 470 sittings. Seventeen teachers are employed, besides the city superintendent and

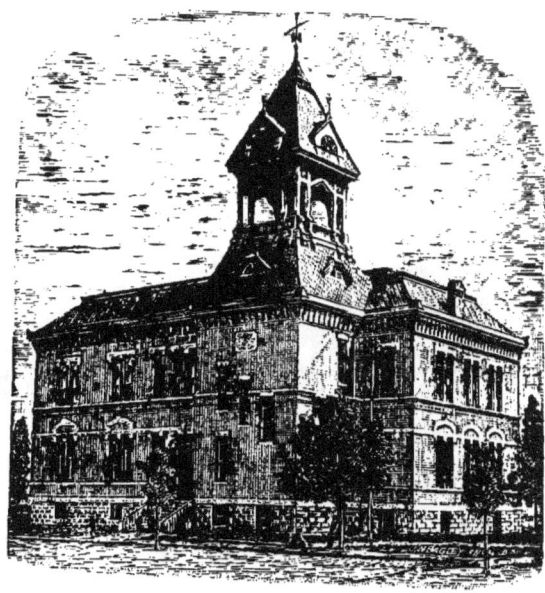

Hinsdale School, North Side.

his assistant. In these schools considerable attention has been paid to kindergarten work in the primary grades, the design being to work largely into the manual training instruction. During the past year the directors spent about $3,000 in purchasing reference books, supplies and appliances of various kinds.

In private and special schools, Pueblo is fortunate. The Sisters of Loretto conduct a most excellent school for young misses. Besides rudimentary instruction, the more graceful accomplishments of music and painting are taught. Being a boarding school, all the comforts of the home are secured.

In connection with St. Patrick's Church, a free day school is conducted for children of both sexes.

One wing of the Southern Methodist College is completed and was fitted out late in the fall of 1888. A competent corps of instructors were secured, and the school started off in good style.

Besides these, there are private classes in painting, in vocal and instrumental music, taught by competent artists.

LORETTO ACADEMY, PUEBLO.

FOR YOUNG LADIES.

This well conducted academy, under the charge of the Sisters of Loretto, and is one of the institutions of Pueblo of  which the citizens are justly proud. The academy was founded in 1877, and began with a limited number of pupils. The institution, however, has made rapid strides, and had, at the end of the spring term, 150 pupils and ten teachers. Special attention is given to music; in that art this institution has earned an enviable reputation. Board, tuition and washing, per session, $100. Tuition on piano, with use of instrument, per session, $30. For full particulars and catalogue, address the

MOTHER SUPERIOR, Pueblo, Colo.

CHURCHES.

Pueblo is well supplied with churches, there being seventeen in number, as follows: Baptist, two; Catholic, three; Christian, one; Congregational, two; Episcopal, three; Methodist, four, and Presbyterian, two.

SOCIAL LIFE IN PUEBLO.

THE leading feature noticeable in western life is the sociability of the people. There is a heartiness in the street salutations, a frankness in conversation in parlor, church and in all places where the people congregate, which attracts the attention of an eastern man. In this the people of eastern states are amazingly ignorant. Most amusing questions are asked of visitors from western cities as to the class of people living in the West, their habits, manners and customs.

Colorado draws citizens from every state in the Union, from nearly every country of Europe. Educated and cultured people of the New England and Middle Atlantic states seek in Colorado renewed health, or to find here better opportunities for business. Many of the best families of the South are represented in our towns and country districts. Graduates of Harvard, Yale, Cornell and Ann Arbor are seeking in Colorado to build up a good name and a snug competence. The news stands sell the leading magazines and journals of the country. Popular books, the leading topics of the day, are as ably discussed here as in any old community.

Because Pueblo depends mainly on its manufactures and commercial business for support, no one need suppose that, in point of culture and intelligence, the city is far behind its neighbors. In the factories are students of the problems of the day, men who can talk intelligibly on subjects of culture and of the fine arts. Social clubs for mutual improvement are in fine condition; clubs where men meet to debate on topics covering a wide range; ladies meet in afternoons to read on special lines of literature, science or art. Young people have their social times. Representatives of the leading art firms of New York and Boston find purchasers in Pueblo of rare etchings or choice art treasures. In music, we have cultivated voices and fine performers on the piano. Instructors of well attested skill find large classes anxious to improve their knowledge. In the domain of art, Pueblo is justly proud of its well known landscape painter, Mr. Joseph Hitchins, whose studio is visited by hundreds of strangers each week to find therein masterpieces of art.

In the line of amusements, the amateur entertainments given for charitable and benevolent purposes display an amount of talent surprising for a city of the size of Pueblo. Sweet charity is not forgotten in this busy city. The Ladies' Benevolent Union, unique in its system of work, accomplishes in a year a vast amount of good, relieving suffering, clothing the needy, saving from misery many a wayward one. This association is supported by voluntary contributions, and its published monthly reports show how firmly it is established in the hearts of our citizens. Other organizations for benevolent purposes do much good. The Sisters of St. Mary have a neat, well-kept hospital, where many a young man, far from home, has been as well cared for as though he were at home.

Not the least of the pleasant social features of Pueblo, are the number of home entertainments given each winter. The home life can be readily imagined in a drive about the city. It is a constant surprise to the tourist to note the beauty of the well-kept lawns, the flowers in the windows, the sounds of mirth and joy from happy voices.

SECRET AND BENEVOLENT SOCIETIES.

Pueblo is well supplied with secret and benevolent societies: Of the Masonic order, there are seven; Odd Fellows, eight; Knights of Pythias, three; Knights of Honor, one; Ancient Order of United Workmen, four; Good Templars, one; besides which there are several military organizations and working men's associations.

PUEBLO CITY GOVERNMENT.

THE city government is conducted by a mayor and fourteen aldermen. Until three years ago there were three separate city governments—North Pueblo, Central Pueblo and South Pueblo. The manifest advantage of three distinct corporations, with streets only dividing them, caused the people in 1886 to vote almost unanimously for consolidation, the result being a strong government and an influential city. The differences of the past have all been settled, and the united cities are working for the common interest with the result of more than doubling the population in three years, and to-day Pueblo points with pride to her 30,000 industrious, happy and contented people. Population is steadily increasing, and in 1890 it is confidently believed that Pueblo will contain at least 50,000 human beings.

Last year witnessed the completion of three excellent bridges, substantial levees and sewer pipes laid, streets leveled and graded, and a city hall, to cost $50,000, begun (now completed).

The police department consists of a marshal, a night captain and thirteen policemen, whose salaries aggregate $26,000 a year. The arrests average 160 a month, and the receipts from fines about $700 per month. Of the arrests about sixty-five are from drunkenness, fifty-five for violation of ordinances, and the remainder minor offenses. There has in the past year been but few serious crimes committed, and the community is as orderly as any city of its size in the country.

The fire department consists of a volunteer and a paid department (the latter just inaugurated). The volunteer department is equipped with seven hose carts and one hook-and-ladder truck; while the paid department is equipped with one of the latest improved fire engines and patent extension hook-and-ladder outfit and trucks and

City Hall, Pueblo.

two hose carts, employing ten as fine horses as any department in the West can boast of. The first fire engine is named the "A. T. Stewart, No. 1," in honor of Alderman Stewart. The extension hook-and-ladder truck is named "A. A. Grome, No. 1," in honor of Mayor Grome. Aldermen Lamkin, Caffray and Lloyd compose the fire committee of the council, and to their untiring energy and discretion the city of Pueblo owes its present excellent fire equipment.

Hon. Andrew A. Grome, the mayor of this progressive city, is favorably known as a reliable and progressive business man of Pueblo; he was born in Bavaria, Germany, in 1856, and came to the United States with his parents when he was eight years of age. The first settlement of his parents was at Cincinnati. At the early age of twelve he came westward as far as Kansas and went to work in a brewery. In 1870, appreciating the fact that an education was necessary for prime success in this country, he attended college in St. Vincent's, Pennsylvania, for two years. Returning to Cincinnati, he determined to acquire "the art preservative of all arts," and entered a printing office, and came out of it a full fledged printer. But his health had succumbed to the confinement of the trade, and in 1876 he started upon an extensive tour of travel through Louisiana, Arkansas and Texas, settling himself for some time at Texarkana. But in 1878 he again started upon a traveling tour, visiting the United States of Colombia, South America, and subsequently Aspinwall, where he remained for a time, and then visited Carthagena, Baranquilla and Costa Rica. Returning to Panama, he set sail for New York, fully satisfied with travel in South and Central America. Leaving New York he again sought the West and came to Wichita, Kansas, where he arrived in the spring of 1879. In the fall of the same year he came to Pueblo, and here his wanderings came to an end, for he found in that city all the elements of prosperity and future growth that he desired. Here he planted his stakes and entered into active business relations, becoming the local agent of the Denver Brewing Company. He is succeeding admirably as a business man, and is deservedly popular among his fellow citizens. He was elected a member of the board of trustees of Central Pueblo in 1882, afterwards city clerk, justice of the peace and police magistrate. After the consolidation of the three divisions of the city, he was twice elected to serve as alderman of the second ward. Mr. Grome served as president of the council last year. Last spring he was elected mayor of the city. On every hand Mayor Grome receives the applause of the citizens for his just administration and business-like methods in despatching the business of the city. From personal observance we can say, Mayor Grome makes one of the best presiding officers we have ever seen. He is a young man less than 33 years of age (the youngest mayor of any large city in America), and we are certain to see Mr. Grome one of the foremost men of Colorado.

T. S. SMYTHE, CITY CLERK,

Native of Ireland; came to America in 1863, to Colorado in 1868, to Pueblo in 1870. Engaged in grocery business until about six years ago, when he embarked in the cattle business in Arizona, returning to Pueblo about two years ago. Has served as city clerk since July, 1888—first under Mayor Royal and at present under Mayor Grome. Mr. Smythe makes an efficient officer, and is an affable gentleman.

W. P. GARTLEY, CITY TREASURER,

Was born near Saltsburg, Pennsylvania, in the year 1859. Came to Colorado in 1877; engaged in the railroad business until about three years ago, when he was employed by McCord, Bragdon & Co., wholesale grocers, as shipping clerk. Was elected city treasurer in the spring of 1888, and was re-elected in the spring of 1889. Mr. Gartley enjoys the confidence of the citizens of Pueblo to a marked degree, and is prominently spoken of as a probable candidate for the position of county treasurer in the approaching election.

A. T. STEWART.

Alderman Stewart came to Pueblo in 1876. In the early days he was the blacksmith for the Barlow & Sanderson stage line. In 1877 Mr. Stewart opened up a shop on Union avenue, where he plied his trade with great profit until 1885. In addition to his blacksmith trade, Mr. Stewart carried a large stock of wagons and carriages, and during his business career he earned an enviable reputation among his fellow townsmen as a shrewd financier and expert workmen. In the spring of 1886 he was elected alderman from the third ward, and has been re-elected at each successive election. Was chairman of the finance committee during Royal's administration and was reappointed at the beginning of Grome's term. The council have lately secured a new fire engine (their first), and, out of compliment to Alderman Stewart, the council voted unanimously to name the first steamer, the "A. T. Stewart, No. 1."

GEORGE F. WEST.

Alderman West was born in Simpson County, Kentucky. Came to Colorado in the spring of 1880, in company with his brother, John T. West, and engaged in mining for the La Plata Mining and Smelting Company at Leadville. Mr. West has been more or less actively engaged in mining ever since that date, having extensive interests at White Pine Camp, Gunnison County. He came to Pueblo in December, 1885, and engaged in the furniture business, in which he has built up a large trade, and to-day carries a very choice stock of goods in a spacious store on Union avenue. In April, 1889, he was elected alderman from the fifth ward. It is a notable fact that, while that ward polls a Republican majority, Mr. West, being a staunch Democrat, was elected, with a majority of two to one.

J. H. ELSPASS.

Mr. Elspass is the alderman from the third ward; born in Detroit, Michigan; came to Pueblo in the summer of 1877, and was engaged with the Atchison, Topeka & Santa Fe Railway as locomotive engineer until May, 1888, at which time he was compelled to resign, on account of poor health. He then engaged in the manufacture of cigars, and made some extensive real estate deals, which have resulted very favorably. As a manufacturer of cigars, he is regarded in the lead, his brands being among the best offered in the market. In April, 1889, he was chosen alderman from the third ward, which usually polls a Democratic majority of over 200. Mr. Elspass, a staunch Republican as he is, secured a majority over one of the most popular Democrats in that ward.

CHARLES H. LAMKIN.

Mr. Lamkin, the alderman from the fifth ward, was born in Washington County, Arkansas; came to Pueblo in the summer of 1872 and engaged in contracting and building, continuing the same for twelve years. In April, 1873, he was elected a member of the board of trustees of the Town of South Pueblo, serving one term. He was re-elected in 1876 and in 1880, and in the spring of 1888 was elected alderman from the fifth ward of the united cities of South Pueblo, Central Pueblo and Pueblo. In 1883 was appointed county commissioner by Governor Grant, serving one term. In 1884 he was appointed chief of the fire department. He was appointed deputy collector of internal revenue in 1887. Owing to his perfect familiarity with the fire department, he was made chairman of the fire and water committee of the council, which important committee has just secured a first class fire equipment, which includes a fire engine of the latest improved pattern, a patent extension hook-and-ladder truck and two hose carriages. With Mr. Lamkin on this committee is associated Aldermen Thomas P. Lloyd and -- Caffray, two very efficient men.

THOMAS P. LLOYD.

Mr. Lloyd, alderman from the second ward, was born in New Haven, Connecticut; came to Pueblo May 11, 1882, and engaged in the manufacture of cigars, in which line he has successfully engaged ever since. His manufactory is centrally located, and he enjoys a leading position in both the wholesale and retail tobacco trade of the city. He employs eight cigar makers, who are said to be expert in the manufacture of fine goods. In April last he was elected alderman from the second ward, a Republican stronghold, by a majority of ninety-four, which, considering Mr. Lloyd's pronounced Democracy, is certainly a great compliment.

Mayor A. A. GROME, Pueblo.

THOMAS P. LLOYD,
Alderman.

W. P. GARTLEY,
City Treasurer, Pueblo.

GEORGE F. WEST,
Alderman.

T. S. SMYTHE,
City Clerk, Pueb'o.

JOHN NORRIS,
Senior Member of the Real Estate firm of Norris & Struble, Pueblo, Colo.

Alderman A. T. STEWART,
After whom Pueblo's first fire engine was named.

HOTELS.

THE Fariss Hotel is the most popular hotel in Pueblo, commanding as it does the largest patronage, and, as a moderate priced hotel, it is excelled by none in America. Prices, $1.50 to $2 per day, which, with its central location, makes it the home of the commercial, health or pleasure tourist. One grand feature in connection with this hotel is the artesian well, which flows 750 barrels per day of magnetic mineral water, which, upon analysis by Messrs. Von Schulz & Low, chemists and assayers, of Denver, Colo., showed the following results:

Sodium chloride	2.42 grains per gallon.
Sodium sulphate	41.92 " " "
Calcium sulphate	3.43 " " "
Calcium carbonate	6.28 " " "
Magnesium carbonate	6.16 " " "
Ferrous carbonate	0.91 " " "

The well has two outdoor discharge pipes and a large number in the bathing house, which is attached to the hotel. The bath house is so arranged as to supply hot or cold tub baths and plunge bath. The plunge is a large artificial pool, 60 feet long by 30 feet wide, and, in depth, 4 feet at one end and 8 feet at the other. The temperature of the water as it flows from the well, summer and winter, is 77 degrees. J. R. Fariss, the genial proprietor, is a model host, taking great pains to see that his guests are well cared for. The hotel is one block from the Atchison, Topeka & Santa Fe Railway depot. Cars pass the house every five minutes, communicating with every portion of the city of Pueblo and the Union Depot. The hotel contains more than 100 rooms, which are nearly always filled. Mr. Fariss now has under advisement plans for doubling the present capacity of his house. Mr. Fariss' friends are urging him to do so, that he may be able to accommodate all who apply. The growing fame of his mineral bath will soon force him to build a house of 400 or 500 rooms.

PUEBLO JOURNALS.

PUEBLO has three very good daily papers—the *Chieftain*, a morning paper, being the only one possessed of the Associated Press franchise; the *Pueblo Press* and the *Pueblo Star* are the evening papers. Thus it will be seen Pueblo has a fair start in the journalistic field. Beside the dailies, Pueblo has several weekly and monthly papers of more or less note, and the *Review and Standard*, a semi-weekly paper, that will, it is said, ere long blossom out into a morning daily, to compete with the long-time-ago established *Chieftain*.

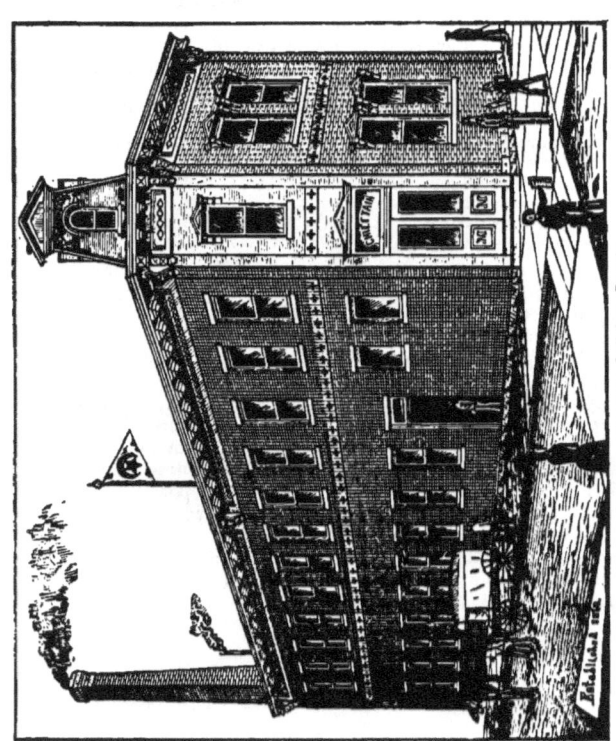

The Daily Chieftain Building, Pueblo.

THE CHIEFTAIN.

This large and influential journal was established in 1868 by Dr. M. Beshear and Sam. McBride, with Governor George A. Hinsdale (since deceased) and Judge Wilber F. Stone (now of Denver) as editors. The first issue contained a notice of the death of the famous scout, Kit Carson, at Bogg's Ranch, then in Pueblo County, together with resolutions of respect passed by a club of his friends in Pueblo. In June, 1869, Captain J. J. Lambert, who was then in the regular army, came into possession of the weekly *Chieftain*, and placed his brother, N. N. Lambert, in charge, who had the management of the paper till 1873, when Captain J. J. Lambert resigned his position in the army and assumed full charge. The same year a daily edition was started, which has steadily gained in popularity, until to-day it has a circulation of from 2,500 to 3,000. The first daily *Chieftain* printed was a five-column folio, the Sunday issue containing from twelve to sixteen pages. To-day the paper is of regular size, six-column folio, and is the oldest daily in the state, except the *Rocky Mountain News*. When the weekly *Chieftain* was started there were but three other papers published in the state, two of which very soon after suspended publication. The *Chieftain* was the only paper published in the state south of Denver, and at present has a circulation of 2,000. It is considered the principal weekly paper in the state, and enjoys a large circulation in Europe, besides being read in every state in the Union. The weekly *Chieftain* is known as the *Colorado Chieftain*, under which name it was started. It is the oldest weekly outside of the *Rocky Mountain News*. Captain J. J. Lambert is the president and manager; John C. Latshaw, secretary, and G. G. Withers, editor. Mr. Withers has been connected with the paper for twenty years. He started as printer's devil in 1869 and worked in all the various departments up to twelve years ago, when he was appointed editor, which position he has since held with increasing popularity.

In 1880 Captain Lambert erected the *Chieftain* building, a large imposing structure, on Fourth street, which the citizens of Pueblo are justly proud of. Captain J. J. Lambert, to whom great credit is due for his untiring efforts in establishing such a readable sheet, served through the war as captain of the 9th Iowa Cavalry. He enlisted in Dubuque, Iowa, where he was raised; he also served as lieutenant in the 5th United States Infantry. In 1874 J. J. Lambert and his brother, N. N. Lambert, started the Del Norte *Prospector*.

THE DAILY PUEBLO PRESS.

This excellent afternoon paper is published daily by the Press Publishing Company (incorporated). This company was started in May, 1886, by Colonel John C. Moore (a brilliant journalist) and John A. Hill, who were practically owners of the paper up to November, 1888, at which time Colonel Moore, who had been editor, retired from

Residence of J. J. Lambert, Pueblo.

the paper at that time. W. B. McKinney, who had been business manager almost from the starting of the paper, became Colonel Moore's successor as editor, and was also promoted to the position of general manager. The officers of the company are: B. M. Wilson, president; A. W. Arrington, secretary, and A. T. Hasslock, business manager. The *Press* started out under favorable circumstances, and has steadily gained in influence and in business. When started, it was a six-column folio, soon one column was added; finally, in March last the demands justified a greater change, and the paper was increased to a quarto, with six columns. The paper is newsy and spicy, and enjoys a good circulation, averaging about 2,200 daily, there being over 500 regular subscribers to the paper in Utah alone, which is an amount probably not equalled by any other paper in the state. The *Press* contains special telegraphic news of the state and the daily local news. General Manager McKinney is about to conclude arrangements to get the United Press Association despatches; when he does the *Press* will take a long step in advance.

MANUFACTORIES AND BUSINESS FIRMS.

The following is a list of the kinds and number of lines of business represented in the City of Pueblo:

Kind of Business.	No.	Capital Invested.
Manufacturers:		
Brooms	1	$ 500
Smelters and Sampling Works	5	2,500,000
Cigars	8	10,800
Crackers and Confectioners	1	35,000
Bakeries	5	7,500
Trunks	1	500
Combination Fencing	1	2,000
Foundries (iron)	2	30,000
" (brass)	1	500
Barb Wire	1	30,000
Bottling Works	1	5,000
Brick	9	50,000
Dry Goods, W. and R	1	75,000
Dry and Fancy Goods, Ret.	8	160,000
Millinery and Notions, "	10	7,000
Drugs, Ret	11	60,000
Leather and Findings, Whol.	1	9,000
Saddlery, W. and R.	1	12,000
" Ret.	2	7,000
Groceries, Exclusive Whol.	2	300,000
" W. and R.	3	100,000
" Ret.	35	70,000
Liquors, Whol.	6	47,000
" W. and R.	1	3,000
" Ret.	85	60,000
Furniture and Carpets, W. and R.	2	75,000
Carpets and Drapery, Ret.	1	1,500

Kind of Business.	No.	Capital Invested.
Hardware, W. and R.	2	55,000
" Ret.	6	40,000
Music	3	10,000
Jewelry	12	67,000
Meats, Whol.	2	8,000
Meat Markets	13	15,000
Photographers	5	10,000
Tannery	1	300
Produce and Commission	11	55,000
Marble	1	1,000
Second Hand Goods	9	25,000
Printers and Newspapers	15	51,000
Restaurants	26	15,000
Cigars and Tobaccos, W. and R.	3	4,000
" " Ret.	8	10,000
Wall Paper, Paints, etc., W. and R.	4	27,000
Lumber and Planing Mills	6	300,000
Hats and Furnishing Goods	1	5,000
Teas and Coffee	1	3,000
Blacksmiths	10	5,000
Barbers' Supplies	1	5,000
General Stores	2	20,000
Plumbers	3	6,000
Fruit and Confectioners	11	5,400
Clothing and Gents' Furnishing, W. and R	1	50,000
" " " " Ret.	9	150,000
Boots and Shoes and Makers	25	60,000
Pawnbrokers	4	6,500
Books and Stationery	2	30,000
Department Store	1	35,000
Livery	11	40,000
Undertakers	3	7,000
Ice	5	25,000
Tailors	9	12,000
Woodenware, Whol	1	20,000
Hay, Grain and Feed	7	40,000
Coal, Lime and Cement	6	—
Transfers and Express	22	20,000
Theatres	3	—
Contractors and Builders	50	—
Real Estate	50	—
Hotels, First Class, and Boarding	28	—
Gas and Electric Light	2	350,000
Towel Supply Company	1	1,000
Water Company	2	300,000
Brewery Agents	6	—
Guns and Ammunition	1	5,000
Auction	1	3,000
Merchandise Brokers	3	3,000
Hides and Pelts	3	5,000
Queensware	2	25,000
Sewing Machines	4	2,000
Laundries	3	10,000
Dye House	1	500
Bridge Builders	1	—
Florists	5	5,000
Dairies	3	2,000
Cheese, Canned Goods and Fish	1	1,000
Cornice Maker	1	1,500
Scales	1	500
Stove Repairs	1	200
Upholsterer	2	500

Kind of Business.	No.	Capital Invested.
Barbers	18	7,000
Junk	2	5,000
Railroad Contractors	6	
Assayers	2	2,500
Painters	12	5,000
Novelty Works	1	800
Game, Oysters and Fish	1	1,000
Abstractors	5	
Architects	10	
Artists	10	

BIRD'S EYE VIEW OF SALIDA, COLO.
Division Headquarters of the Denver and Rio Grande Railway

H. D. MOREY,

President of Pueblo Oil and Development Company and principal of the real estate firm of H. D. Morey & Co., who are large dealers in Pueblo realty.

MONTE VISTA,

RIO GRANDE COUNTY, COLORADO.

THIS beautiful and prosperous city is situated in the very heart of the far-famed San Luis Valley, and is destined to be the metropolis of that fertile valley. This charming little city was platted in the spring of 1884 by the Travelers' Insurance Company, which company have, by their enterprise, constructed large canals and made of this valley one of the most fertile in the world. For two or three years the place was scarcely known, but, by a liberal and effectual system of advertising the great advantages of this spot as a trading center, they have succeeded in turning the attention of thousands to this spot, and to-day they boast of a $46,000 hotel, a $12,000 public school building, and have lately secured the location of the State Soldiers' Home, which was provided for by the late Legislature. Within the city limits are sixty artesian wells, flowing strong, steady streams of pure water, each of a capacity of one barrel per minute and one of a much larger flow, the pressure from these wells being strong enough to force the water thirty feet in the air. The water has a slight per cent. of sulphate of iron, which is not at all unpleasant to the taste, and is regarded a very valuable tonic. The altitude is about 7,600 feet above sea level, so high that it would be uninhabitable were it not entirely surrounded by high wind breaking mountains, which, with the extremely light, dry air and perpetual sunshine, gives it an exceptional combination of conditions pertaining to both northern and southern latitudes, yet wholly unknown to either, to-wit: a cool-all-the-year climate, the highest summer temperature in a good house being 84 degrees, with winters so mild, that an ordinarily clothed person can read comfortably in the sun on a south fronting veranda, while extremes of heat and cold (winter nights are cold) are 20 degrees less appreciable than at sea level. Ordinarily there is but little snow and scarcely any winter winds. With no hail storms to damage crops, no tornadoes, no cyclones, no drouths, no grasshoppers, no chinch bugs, and very few other insects, no possible malaria, with summer nights so cool as to require two blankets for sleeping purposes, it is unsurpassed as a health resort, being peculiarly adapted to asthmatics and consumptives, curing nearly all who in time make it their permanent home, besides being an extra desirable residence locality. The mountain scenery is magnificent; the Rio Grande River furnishes the best of trout fishing; the wagon roads, like those of Los Angeles County, become more compact and smooth the more they are traveled, while comfort and health is in excess of that in any portion of California. The surrounding country is full of coal, oil and gas. Very rich mines are being developed (ore running from $1,000 to $2,000 per ton) in the mountains southwest of Monte Vista, which is located in the midst of 300,000 acres of the richest irrigable land, with abundance of water to supply it. Monte Vista is a new, growing, enterprising prohibition town, has a superior class of citizens, and is beginning to assume city airs. It is rapidly becoming an extra desirable residence locality. It has a first-class roller process flouring mill, fifteen stores, two banks, a planing mill, three lumber yards, three weekly papers, three livery stables, large public library, an $8,000 school-house, seven church organizations, a secular Sunday society, secret societies, military company, cornet band, etc. This little city contains a live progressive population of 1,500, which is being daily increased with the health, pleasure and business seeker.

Mr. H. H. Marsh has platted a fine tract of land adjoining the eastern boundary of the city and has named it Grand View addition to Monte Vista. Mr. Marsh is erecting some substantial residences on his addition, which he has for sale on easy terms or for rent to tourists or health seekers, furnished or unfurnished, and at reasonable rates.

The Hotel Blanca, recently completed at a cost of $46,000, exclusive of furniture, is now handsomely furnished and opened for the reception of guests. O. E. Troth, the genial proprietor, announces reduced rates for time guests—regular rates, $3 per day. It is a first-class hotel in every respect, and is of ample proportions to accommodate a large number of guests. Mrs. Troth, the wife of the proprietor of this excellent Hotel Blanca, has written many excellent pieces of poetry upon the Rocky Mountains, one of which we are pleased to acknowledge receipt of, and we gladly give it space:

The Hotel Blanca, Monte Vista.

Written for THE GREAT WEST.

DEDICATED TO THE "SUNNY SAN LUIS."

There is not in the wide world a picture so grand
As the beautiful Rockies in this Occident land.
The Greek Hesiod on Mt. Halicon stood,
But we gain inspiration from Pike's Peak and Mt. Hood,
And old Blanca, the highest, the king great and bold,
With his cold heart of stone and veins of pure gold,
Where the muses for ages have found quiet retreat,
Nestle close in his shadow, where bright waters meet.
Grand Sangre de Cristo, the blood of the Christ,
Like fair vestal virgins, arrayed in pure white,
A panorama sublime it presents to the eye,
With the glintings of gold when the sunset is nigh.
Its deep Alpine gorges, made in fierce volcanic fires,
See high piled toward Heaven, grand domes and lofty spires;
And sometimes methinks the hunters of the Holy Grail have sought
Here to find the chalice that the blood of Christ had caught,
And ever up through the stillness comes, tender and low,
The murmuring refrain of bright Rio Grande's flow;
Past mountains and gorges, past forest and glade,
How grandly it courses in sunlight and shade;
There are beauty and freshness, and splendor untold,
As it flows through valley in ripples of gold,
And I think, when its banks of fresh verdure are seen,
Of Eden's still waters and pastures of green.
Laboring up Veta's side the grandest pass we find,
And tiaras of flower gems its lofty brow entwined.
Upward still and heavenward, through sun's bright, dazzling glow,
Where vapory clouds enwrap the brow of Blanca's crest of snow.
Near dwelt the dusky forest child, where lands lay low and drear,
Wild barren tracts for miles and miles, all brown and sear,
Then came the tide of empire, with quick invention rife,
Watering all the barren wild—new verdure sprang to life;
Bright flowers luxuriant rise where silver waters flow,
And many thousands make their homes where fruits and cereals grow.

CLARA TRUTH.

TOLTEC GORGE
On line of Denver & Rio Grande Rai'way

CANON CITY.

CANON CITY is situated in one of the loveliest valleys in the state; sheltered in winter from rude blasts and protected in summer by the same overtowering fastnesses from the heat of the sun. Its population is about 4,000 inhabitants. Nature has been lavish of her means in this delightfully tempered valley, for it possesses the finest vein of bituminous coal in the western country and only equaled by a single vein in Pennsylvania. She is not merely rich in her inexhaustible coal supply, but also abounds in a varied supply of building stone, fire and potter's clay, variegated marble, oil and gold and silver mines within the borders of the country.

Canon City stands at an elevation of 5,287 feet above sea level. The dryness of this entire section, the thinness of the air, the freedom from moisture and immunity from high winds, in connection with almost constant sunshine, make the climatic features of this city unrivaled. The city is delightfully provided with pleasant thoroughfares, shaded from the rays of the sun by rows of large trees, which line both sides of the principal streets. The Arkansas River flows through the city and has a fall of forty feet to the mile, sufficient to run a number of large factories on its banks. A large flouring mill is operated by this valuable water power. Aside from the advantages of this uniform flow of water, coal is cheap, being mined within the city limits. The city is well provided with good public schools, excellent churches, a public library, a telephone system, electric light plant, splendid police and fire departments, and, in short, all the varied paraphernalia of a progressive, prosperous city. The city has two good hotels—the McClure House and St. Cloud—both excellent hostelries, which rank among the first in the state.

Conspicuous among the business men of Canon City is the firm of Harding Brothers, composed of T. M. Harding and L. L. Harding. These gentlemen have done much during their residence in Canon to bring it to its present prosperous condition. They have a large and commodious store, which is utilized for the display of their immense stock of goods, which embraces a full line of hardware, stoves, house furnishing goods, cutlery, etc. The firm is also largely engaged in real estate, and are among the most active in that business. They are engaged in every branch of the business, but make a specialty of their own property, which consists of a large addition of nearly 700 acres lying directly northeast of the city, in which there are many fine lots at exceedingly low prices. The Messrs. Harding Brothers have spared neither money nor labor in making their addition the most attractive portion of the city as a residence location.

Mount of the Holy Cross,
On the line of the Denver and Rio Grande Railway.

In long-forgotten Springs, when He who taught,
  Amid the olive groves of Syrian hills—
Wayfaring by the blossom-bordered rills,
From sparrow, fig-tree, vine—a lesson caught—
He marked pure lillies which the sun had
    wrought,
  In crucible whence molten gold distils.
"Consider these," He said, yet shadow fills—
As of the coming Cross—His prophet-thought;
  It soon should deepen o'er the flower-full land,
But when with passion past He death defied,
  With living lilies was the dark cross spanned.
The lilies bloom upon the prairie wide,
  A stainless cross is reared by Nature's hand,
And plain and height alike keep Easter-tide.
                    M. V. DONAGHE.

Mother Grundy, Clear Creek Canon, Colo
On line of Union Pacific Railway.

CHAPTER XV.

UTAH—1847 TO 1889.

UTAH TERRITORY was established in 1850 out of the northeast third of the Mexican cession in 1848 to the United States, and included all of its present limits, nearly all of that which afterwards became the State of Nevada, and about one-half of the area now embraced within the State of Colorado.

The territory was named after the famous Ute tribe of Indians that inhabited that region at the time of its acquisition by the National Government. The Mormons had, however, been led into the Salt Lake valley by Brigham Young, in July, the year before, and that little band constituted the only white settlement in the territory, and were the actual discoverers and explorers of the territory.

In 1850, when the territory was organized by act of Congress, Brigham Young was appointed its Governor, and Salt Lake becoming the seat of the Territorial Government, began to assume the proportions and aspects of a city. The Mormons rebelled in 1857 against the National Government, which rebellion was only quelled by the speedy dispatch of Federal troops to the territory. They established a post (Fort Douglas), which overlooked the city, and was so arranged as to be able to destroy the city in a very short time, and by that constant menace the Government has since been able to check any extensive resistance, which, however, has not been anticipated for many years, and the fort is now used more as a park than a menace of war. The discovery of gold caused many gentiles to flock to the territory, until now it is believed the Mormons are in the minority in the two principal cities of the territory—Salt Lake and Ogden.

In 1861, Congress passed an act establishing the Territories of Nevada and Colorado, which cut the limits of Utah down, and in 1866 an additional strip was detached from Utah, and added to the then organized State of Nevada, which left the territory with its present boundaries, comprising 84,970 square miles.

Utah is an immense basin, elevated about 4,000 to 5,000 feet above the level of the sea, surrounded by high mountains 7,500 to 13,500 feet. There are no considerable rivers in the territory. The Green, Grand and Colorado rivers flow across the southeast corner of the state; the Santa Clara, across the southwest corner; other rivers all flowing into the Great Salt Lake. This great valley is formed by the Rocky Mountains on the east, and Sierra Nevadas on the west.

Minor ranges extend north and south at various intervals of 15 to 50 miles. The Wahsatch range, near the center of the territory, forms the only considerable mountains in Utah. Some of the peaks of this range are at an altitude of 12,000 to 12,500 feet.

Numerous hot and cold mineral springs and salt lakes are found throughout the territory, none of them except the Great Salt Lake, being of more than local notoriety. The majority of the valuable springs are either on the banks or near this lake. The rocks are mostly primitive, and the mountains are rich in granite, jasper, syenite, porphyry, etc., showing everywhere evidences of volcanic action. Good building stone of all kinds and character abounds within easy reach of Salt Lake City, and other important cities of the territory. Gold, silver, lead, copper and zinc are found in the Wahsatch mountains in quite considerable quantities. The output of the territory for 1888 of those metals amounted to $7,557,241. Coal has been found of fair quality and quantity in Utah, sufficient for local use, and after developing further, may prove to be one of Utah's principal elements of wealth. Asphaltum and gilsonite are found in almost unlimited quantities, suitable for paving, painting, etc., and will add largely to the general wealth of this favored territory. Pine and fir constitute the native timber; other trees grow when planted and cared for. Utah abounds in all kinds of wild game, and her streams are alive with fish of many varieties, such as salmon trout, mountain trout, perch, pike and bass. The climate resembles Colorado, severe in high altitudes, and mild in the valleys, described more particularly in the article which follows on Salt Lake.

Utah, like Colorado, depends almost entirely upon irrigation for the utilization of its rich soil for the cultivation of field crops. The territory is quite well provided with railway facilities, and has direct connection with San Francisco, Portland, Denver and Omaha.

In 1886 Utah cultivated crops as follows: 13,330 acres producing 267,000 bushels of corn, valued at $160,200; 101,704 acres producing 1,541,000 bushels of wheat, valued at $955,420; 2,264 acres producing 32,000 bushels of rye, valued at $17,600; 28,794 acres producing 858,000 bushels of oats, valued at $343,200; 20,417 acres producing 470,000 bushels of barley, valued at $230,300; 11,509 acres producing 978,000 bushels of potatoes, valued at $352,080; 124,848 acres producing 159,120 tons of hay, valued at $1,113,840 total value of field crops, $3,172,640.

Utah contained January 1st, 1888, the following farm animals: 120,692 head of horses, valued at $4,906,026; 3,686 head of mules, valued at $201,668; 49,878 head of milch cows, valued at $1,259,420; 435,000 head of oxen and other cattle, valued at $7,292,733; 1,335,000 head of sheep, valued at $2,594,172; 40,118 head of hogs, valued at $286,846 total, 1,984,374 head of live stock, valued at $16,540,865, which, added to the value of field crops, makes a farm value Jan. 1st, 1888, of $19,713,505.

Utah has stood manfully side by side with Colorado in the deep harbor movement. Hon. Elliott Willden, of Beaver, Utah, has been very active as vice president of the permanent committee and head of the Utah delegation. He attended the Denver convention last fall, and with Charles T. Storey, of the same place, also a member of the committee, attended the Dallas, Texas, meeting October 17th last, and, with the entire committee, made a tour of the state. Without other assistance than his own means, he has expended time and money in aid of the enterprise. The Legislature of Utah, which meets next January, will, without doubt, appropriate some money to keep up that territory's share of the expense of agitation. Utah, by proposed railroad routes, will be brought almost as near to the Gulf as Colorado is. The important cities of Utah are Salt Lake (the capital), Ogden and Provo.

DELEGATE CAINE ON IRRIGATION.

The following letter by Delegate Caine, of Utah, on the subject of irrigation appears in Col. Richard J. Hinton's report, referred to heretofore, and by Col. Hinton regarded as good and reliable; therefore we insert it almost entire, and it will answer as a standard of the entire so-called arid region:

"Whatever conditions future developments may bring about, the present water supply in Utah Territory is surface; it depends entirely upon the fall of snow in the winter, and, to a slight degree, upon the rainfall during the fall and spring months. As a natural consequence, the character of the water supply is found in mountain streams. The fall of snow in the mountains is incomparably greater than in the valleys, and it lasts much longer, for the reason that the cold is much severer.

"The snow packs in the ravines until it is almost as hard and solid as stones; the solidifying is materially assisted by what are termed "January thaws," the result of a marked relaxation in the severity of the weather, which generally occurs during the month of January. This temporary relaxation is invariably followed by a renewal of the rigor of winter, when the snow, that has settled and become packed by the thaw, freezes, until it is almost a solid mass of ice. This snow is the source of all streams in Utah save the little running water that comes through rains.

"The volume of these streams depends entirely upon the season of the year. During the winter months the supply is very small, for the reason that the quantity of snow is at its minimum, and the cold has a tendency to stay the flow. With the disappearance of winter and the increased warmth of the sun, the snow begins to melt; the volume of water increases and continues to grow until tiny and puny streams are swollen into torrents, sometimes causing great damage from the overflowing of their banks. The water supply attains its maximum height between the 10th and 20th of the month of June. This statement may be given the force that attaches to a rule almost, if not entirely, without exception. The solidifying and freezing of the snow in winter, as above stated, makes certain the tenure of the water supply that would otherwise be both uncertain and disastrous; it prevents the too rapid melting which would result in absolutely uncontrollable torrents for a period, and thus makes the streams available for agricultural purposes.

"The experience of Utah farmers as to the best methods for increasing and preserving the water supply would be valuable only to people surrounded by a similar country with like elemental conditions existing. The only means of increasing the water supply is, so far as existing knowledge throws any light upon the subject, confined to the introduction of genuine artesian wells. Experiments sufficiently thorough to clearly demonstrate the success that would attend the digging or boring of such wells in Utah have not been made. The best opinions, however, are that the geological conditions existing in Utah are peculiarly favorable to their introduction and successful development.

"The territory, or rather its habitable portion, is composed of valleys, mountains and canons, with some lakes. The melting snow on mountain and in valley, which fails to find its way into some of the streams, must sink and collect somewhere, and there is a well-founded belief, which could easily be verified, that beneath these valleys are subterranean lakes that would feed, with a never-failing supply of water, innumerable artesian wells. To increase the supply by other means would be to increase the fall of snow, a thing humanity is not yet prepared to base a calculation upon. Preserving methods are, however, more practicable, and nature has done her best to make that task as light as possible. The outlet for all streams is into the valleys. The streams come from the canons high above the valleys, and the supply can be preserved or saved by the construction of reservoirs or dams. In case the latter method was adopted, it would simply be necessary to select the most suitable place in season, and place a dam across the ravine.

"The work would be more or less expensive, as the stream was large or small, and the canon wide or narrow, but in every canon suitable points abound, and as the future development and continued prosperity of Utah largely depend upon her permanent and increased water supply, her people will be forced to resort to damming the streams within their natural confines in the ravines. This idea carried out, would save the water that yearly runs to waste, the word 'waste' being used here with the knowledge that every drop of water is invaluable in a country where agriculture depends upon irrigation, it is absolutely impossible to form even an estimate, and for several reasons; first, the volume of the stream differs every day in the year, and one year from another; second, it would require a measurement of the streams and a knowledge of the amount consumed in irrigation, which would increase with increased distributing canals and ditches. It may be safe to state, however, that if complete and thorough methods of saving were introduced, all the land in the territory, if it could be reached, could be well and thoroughly irrigated; this, too, without resorting to artesian wells, so vast is the amount of water that runs to waste during the winter, spring, and early summer months.

"As heretofore stated, the increase and decrease in the water supply depends entirely upon the fall of snow in winter, and, to an important degree, upon the fall of rain in the fall, spring, and early summer months. A very noteworthy fact, attested on the best authority, is that for a period of years there has been a steady increase in the water supply. It has been thought by many that the claims of increased water has been more imaginary than real. The claim, however, has been verified by measurements made in Great Salt Lake, which is the reservoir for many of the largest mountain streams, including the Jordan, which is the outlet for Utah Lake, the Bear river, the Ogden, Weber, Logan and Blacksmith Fork, and innumerable smaller streams.

"The lake has a shore line of 350 miles, and since 1856 the water has increased 14 feet in depth; and the Great Salt Lake, depending as it does entirely upon the inflowing mountain streams, and that amount of water which is not consumed by agricultural utilization, shows beyond question that there has been a marked increase in the water supply.

"This rise in the body of the water of the lake has taken place, it must be remembered, during a period when there was a rapid increase in the demand for water for agricultural purposes.

"The increase in the water supply in Utah since its settlement by Mormon pioneers, in 1847, has been not less than 75 per cent., and might be honestly put at 100 per cent.

"Whatever changes may have taken place in the grasses in Utah, are artificial. The native mountain 'bunch grass' has become so well known for its remarkably nutritious character, that rather than change it, the desire of the people of Utah, or those growing stock, would be to propagate it.

"Where irrigation has been applied for a few years, there has been a perceptible decrease in the amount of water necessary to properly irrigate the land. The decrease is placed at about 25 per cent. The census returns give the most available information as to the extent of irrigable lands.

"The value of such land depends entirely upon its location, not only in a territory, but in a precinct or county, and upon the character of the soil, which often differs materially from land adjoining it, and enjoying the same water advantages. In earlier days all persons interested in the digging of a canal would turn out and keep on working, under the direction of a person chosen by themselves. Later laws were passed on the subject, and will be found by reference to the statutes of the territory, which will give the fullest attainable information as to water rights and conditions in the territory.

"Grants, of course, are given to municipal and canal corporations, counties and districts, but these also are set forth in the statutes.

"The most important undertaking of the class under consideration yet accomplished in the territory was the construction of a canal to supply Salt Lake City with water. The city was bonded for the purpose, and the canal was commenced in December of 1879 and finished in the fall of 1881.

"Its length is something over twenty miles, and its source is the Jordan River, a short distance below the point where Utah Lake has its outlet into the Jordan. The canal is twenty feet wide at the bottom, the depth being six feet, sufficient to carry four feet of water.

"The city was authorized to borrow $250,000 on its bonds for the construction of the canal. The expenditures in detail were: For excavation, $130,832.77; for dams, flumes, bridges and culverts, $30,036.17; for lumber for flumes in the city, the distance being one and one-quarter miles of redwood flumes, $24,844.56; for right-of-way, $39,253.97; for recording deeds, etc., $6,757.65. In cities the municipal corporations control the water, water-masters being appointed to regulate the division of the same.

CHAPTER XVI.

NEW MEXICO—1540 TO 1889.

THE territory of New Mexico was constructed in the year 1850 from the southeast third of the first cession from Mexico, containing all of that area now embraced within the Territories of Arizona and New Mexico, which lies north of the Gila, and west of the Rio Grande rivers. In 1853 a second cession was made by Mexico to the United States, known as the Gadsden Purchase, which, in 1854, was annexed to the Territory of New Mexico, extending the southern boundary line of that territory to its present limit, some 50 to 100 miles farther south; at the same time the eastern limits were extended across the Rio Grande river, and took in that unauthorized territory known as the Texas cession of 1850. Seven years later, Colorado Territory was organized and took quite a large portion from New Mexico's northeast corner.

In 1863, the Territory of Arizona was organized, and reduced the territory still further, leaving it, however, with its magnificent dimensions, with an area of 122,580 square miles. The only rivers of note to which New Mexico is entitled are the Rio Grande, which rises in Colorado, flows south through the territory, dividing it nearly equally into east and west divisions. This river is not navigable within the territory, is valuable for stock and agricultural purposes mainly; and the Pecos river, a branch of the Rio Grande, which rises a little north of the center of the territory, flows southeast into Texas, and finally to a junction with the Rio Grande about latitude 30 N., and logitude 25 W. A branch of the Colorado rises in the extreme northwest corner, and the Gila has its source in the southwestern part of the territory. Much of the territory is well adapted to agriculture, by means of irrigation, which system has been in vogue since the first discovery of the territory and settlement in 1540 and 1582, and had been practiced by the aborigines for all time as far as we are able to learn from the Pueblo Indians who were found there, and whose decendants are yet to be found within the confines of New Mexico.

About the time that De Soto was coasting along Florida, looking for the mouth of the Mississippi River, Don Antonio de Mendoza, Viceroy in Mexico under the King of Spain, fired with a desire to gain favor with his sovereign, and add territory to the crown, conceived the idea of fitting out an expedition to push northward and explore, hoping thereby to discover rich gold fields which were reputed in that direction, the reports having been brought in by two or three survivors of Narvaez' expedition into Florida in the year 1528, who, in a wonderful manner, had made their way overland, from Florida to Mexico, having traversed almost the width of the continent, and wandered through a portion of this coveted territory to the north. Chief of these survivors was one Alvar Nuñez, who had been treasurer to the expedition. In relating their experiences, he told the Viceroy, Mendoza, that great riches must abound in the mountains to the north, as the natives were a very rich people, living in large cities, and having an abundance of gold and silver. This information was corroborated by Indians that Mendoza had captured and made slaves of.

Notwithstanding Mendoza's desire to obtain this rich country for his sovereign, he hesitated attempting a conquest of such a rich and no doubt powerful people, his armed force being too small to cope with the foe he expected to meet; he, therefore, wisely concluded to send out a scouting or exploring party in the simplest possible garb, accompanied by a man of peace. The Viceroy took a poor bare-footed friar from his cell, by name, Marco de Niza, of the Franciscan Order of Priests; gave him Alva Nuñez as a guide, and with a few natives, sent him out to explore the great unknown region beyond the northern mountains.

After reaching the most northerly point explored by the Spaniards, Culiacan, the wise friar, sent ahead the captive Indians, with messages of peace and goodwill to the distrustful natives. These promises of peace were received in good faith by a great many of the natives, who came down from their mountain hiding places to meet the good friar, who, with kind words and small presents and with promises to not capture and enslave them, as the Spaniards had done before them, he succeeded in gaining their favor, and, in return, they told the Spaniards to come and go as they chose. These natives returned to their homes and spread the news of the treaty of peace among their brethren. The friar and his small party then continued their journey northward and, it is believed, reached the Cibola (the name applied to the unknown region), or Zuni (as known to-day). The friar brought back information which to-day reads like a fairy story, and we omit it.

The next attempt to explore this territory was not until 1581, at which time the Church took the responsibility of fitting out an expedition to explore the country and convert the natives, believing conversion to be the most successful method of conquering the country and solving the secrets of this mysterious land. Two Franciscan friars were consequently started out from the Spanish settlement of New Biscay; they proceeded northward by the Rio Grande valley. For more than a year nothing was heard of them, and a rescuing party was dispatched; traces were found of the two pious men, but they failed to find them. This party, however, accomplished that which the two friars had started out to do, viz.: made a successful exploration of the country. They followed the course taken by the Franciscan monks along the valley of the Rio Grande River. As they progressed northward they encountered populous towns on every hand, which improved as they proceeded, until they found themselves in the midst of a land of thrift and plenty, where the art of spinning, weaving and dyeing was practiced by the natives in a very skillful manner with the very crudest of machinery. The topography of the country resembled Old Mexico so much, that these explorers gave it the name of New Mexico, and, therefore, the history of New Mexico really dates from 1582-3, although its discovery dates back to 1540-1.

Acoma* was probably the greatest town visited during this expedition (Old Fort Wingate is situated forty miles north of Acoma). The town was built upon the flat top of a high cliff, accessible only by means of steps hewn out of the solid rock, forming an impregnable fortress. Large cisterns were hewn out of the solid rock to store their water supply. They grew corn quite extensively, their fields being at some distance from the town, owing to the barrenness immediately surrounding their home on the cliff, and also that the ground might be irrigated by a neighboring stream. The Pueblos, therefore, were among America's first farmers to use the system of irrigation to supply the want of water, this section being dry and almost barren from lack of natural precipitation. The expedition turned westward from the valley of the Rio Grande and entered the land of Zuni. No particular discoveries were made, except here and there they found Spanish crosses erected by one of the former exploring parties, and they were told by the natives of a great lake, situated at a great distance, where a people dwelt who were very rich and wore bracelets and earrings of gold. The little band divided, some desiring to continue explorations with a view to finding this great lake, a small number desiring to return to New Biscay and report their discoveries, which they did. The leader, with a few men, continued his way forward, everywhere receiving good treatment from the natives, they regarding him and his followers as superior beings, caressing and feasting them while they remained in the country.

Without finding the great lake or the strange people who resided thereabouts, they returned to Old Mexico by the valley of the Pecos River, which they named "River of Oxen," because of the great herds of bison they encountered feeding along the valley. The reports by these returned explorers incited the people of Mexico to fit out an armed expedition with a view to conquering the Pueblos. The expedition was placed in charge of Juan de Onate, who invaded New

---

* Space does not permit an extensive description of Acoma. We refer you to "Three Years in Arizona and New Mexico," by S. W. Cozzens, for a full description of the Pueblo race of people, and assure you it will prove both interesting and valuable.—DANA.

Mexico in about the year 1585 (no official data obtainable). The San Miguel mission was erected in 1587 at Santa Fe, and gives sufficient basis to warrant us in assuming 1585 as the correct date). Onate went armed with the viceroy's commission as governor of the territory to be conquered. Accompanying this expedition was a number of Franciscan friars, bent upon converting the Indians as fast as conquered, to accomplish which they erected missions in the towns as fast as subdued.

Onate proceeded rapidly up the Rio Grande, conquering as he went, until finally he reached the point where Santa Fe now is and there began to erect his capital. The seat of government was firmly established at Santa Fe, and Onate and his successors ruled the native population with a severe hand. Inside of fifty years the Catholic clergy had succeeded in establishing fifty missions, and Spanish rule had reached its greatest prosperity. For forty years more, little, if any, progress was made; the Indians, especially the Apaches and Navajoes, had become restless and for years had kept up an incessant warfare upon the Spaniards.

In 1680 the native population arose *en masse*, determined to remain slaves no longer, and, after a severe struggle, they succeeded in driving the invaders from the country with great slaughter. The remnant of the fugitives halted when they had fled as far down the Rio Grande as the present boundary line between Texas and Old Mexico, and there founded a town, which continues to bear the name of El Paso del Norte (meaning "the gateway to the north.") It was nearly fifteen years before the Spaniards recovered from their repulse in New Mexico, and not until about 1695 did they attempt a second invasion of the coveted territory. It required nearly five years to restore the lost power over the Pueblos. This time their stay was permanent, and they remained masters of New Mexico, successfully weathering the successive revolutions in Old Mexico, up to the treaty with the United States in 1848, when Mexico ceded it away, and the United States became its possessor. Since that time considerable progress has been made in New Mexico, and we now find her knocking at the doors of Congress for admission to the Union as a state, and we unhesitatingly say she possesses most of the qualifications necessary to enter upon the duties of local self-government.

New Mexico is traversed from north to south, near its center by the Rocky Mountain Range, with peaks occasionally reaching up to an elevation of 14,000 to 14,500 feet. Less important ranges diversify the western portion, peaks sometimes reaching an elevation of 11,000 feet. The northeast corner of the state is taken up by the Ratoon mountains, which reach an elevation of 10,000 feet. The larger part of the east half is plains, used extensively for grazing the immense herds of cattle that are owned in that territory.

A ROUND-UP SCENE IN NEW MEXICO.

The climate is cold in the elevated portions, and mild and dry in the valleys and on the plains, but everywhere healthy. Very little rain falls, and irrigation is resorted to, in some localities on a very large scale, and they are thereby enabled to rank well as an agricultural territory. Gold, silver, lead, copper and zinc are found in considerable abundance in various portions of the territory. The largest mica mine in America is in New Mexico near the Colorado line, and is owned and worked by Denver capitalists. Coal is believed to be in abundance in the territory, although no considerable find has yet been reported.

The principal cities in the territory are Santa Fe, the capital, and next to St. Augustine, Florida, it is the oldest city in the United States. It contains the oldest house and oldest church building in the United States, both being built of adobe, (a sun-dried brick), the former in 1540, the latter in 1587; Taos, Albuquerque, and Las Vegas.

In 1886 the territory produced from 48,625 acres, 973,000 bushels of corn, valued at $681,100; from 80,566 acres, 921,000 bushels of wheat, valued at $644,000; from 15,078 acres, 528,000 bushels of oats, valued at $253,440; from 3,303 acres, 63,000 bushels of barley, valued at $53,550; from 1,050 acres, 101,000 bushels of potatoes, valued at $111,100; from 27,300 acres, 24,570 tons of hay, valued at $356,265; making the total value of field crops amount to $2,100,155. The territory contained, January 1st, 1888, farm animals as follows: 51,336 head of horses and mules, valued at $2,059,272; 19,394 head of milch cows, valued at $460,608; 1,257,597 head of oxen and other cattle, valued at $18,911,121; 3,623,168 head of sheep, valued at $3,953,239; 19,941 head of hogs, valued at $112,466; a total of 4,971,436 head of live stock, valued at $25,496,706, which, added to the average annual field product, makes a grand total of $27,596,861.

New Mexico, next to Texas, will reap the benefits of the establishment of deep harbors on the Texas Gulf coast, owing to her proximity, and the necessity of almost the entire northwest, to traverse her territory to reach the Gulf.

New Mexico is ably represented on the Inter-State Deep Harbor Committee, by such representative citizens as Hon. W. W. Griffin, of Santa Fe; Hon. Frank C. Plume, of Taos, and Hon. Numa Raymond, of Las Cruces.

CHAPTER XVII.

WASHINGTON TERRITORY—1845 TO 1889.

WASHINGTON TERRITORY was first permanently settled by Americans at Tumwater, in 1845, although explored by Lewis and Clarke as early as 1805, under the direction of the United States Government. Originally it was a portion of Oregon Territory, and when it was erected into a separate territory in 1853, it comprised all of its present dimensions, and included a portion of what is now Idaho and Montana Territories. When Oregon was admitted into the Union as a state in 1859, the remainder of Idaho and nearly all of Wyoming, being detached from Oregon, was added to Washington Territory. In 1863 and 1864 Idaho and Montana Territories were organized with their present dimensions, and what is now Wyoming was annexed to Dakota Territory, which was organized in 1861. Washington was then left with its present magnificent dimensions, comprising 69,180 square miles, divided by the Columbia River, and Cascade mountains, into three grand divisions— Eastern, Central, and Western Washington. The Eastern is mainly agricultural, the Central agricultural and stock raising, some precious metal mining in the Cascade mountains, likewise anthracite and bituminous coal is found in the Central division. The Western division is mainly made up of valuable forests, with a small per cent. of agriculture.

The territory is well supplied with bays and sounds, affording most excellent shipping facilities. The Columbia river, which forms a portion of the southern boundary, supplies ocean-ship navigation almost up to the Cascade mountains. Puget Sound extends south into the heart of the Western division, and abounds in excellent harbors. Olympia, the capital, is situated on the extreme southern point of this indentation, while the excellent shipping points, Tacoma and Seattle, are situated farther north, on the same branch of Puget Sound.

The diversity of natural resources of Washington have attracted a large immigration to the territory, which has had the effect to force the National Government to recognize the territory's demands for statehood, and an Enabling Act was passed at the last session of Congress, providing for the admission of the State of Washington.

Washington is entitled to the second place in agricultural possibilities of all the territories, Dakota only being superior.

In 1887, Washington produced from 3,375 acres, 88,000 bushels of corn, valued at $66,000; from 445,490 acres, 7,560,000 bushels of wheat, valued at $5,005,200; from 1,412 acres, 21,000 bushels of rye, valued at $13,650; from 88,393 acres, 3,126,000 bushels of oats, valued at $1,406,700; from 29,055 acres, 872,000 bushels of barley, valued at $601,080; from 10,943 acres, 1,258,000 bushels of potatoes, valued at $679,320; from 163,894 acres, 194,763 tons of hay, valued at $1,460,728; total value of crops for 1887, $9,293,273.

January 1st, 1888, Washington contained 97,365 head of horses and mules, valued at $6,055,226; 65,523 head of milch cows, valued at $2,181,916; 300,676 head of oxen and other cattle, valued at $7,060,177; 549,885 head of sheep, valued at $1,068,976; 91,054 head of hogs, valued at $455,997—total, 1,104,503 head of live stock, worth $16,822,332, which, added to the crop product of the year previous, makes a grand total value of farm products on hand January 1st, 1888, of $26,115,605.

Fruit is being grown quite extensively in the territory, and is destined to prove a very valuable feature in the agricultural productions of the coming state.

Washington is well provided with railroads, in addition to the extensive navigation facilities, and contains many growing and prospectively large cities.

The climate of Washington varies from mild and damp near the coast to moderate in the valleys and extremely cold in the mountains.

THE CLIMATE OF WASHINGTON TERRITORY AS TAKEN FROM SIGNAL SERVICE REPORTS.

"Last July the Senate passed resolutions directing the transmission of reports prepared under the direction of the chief signal officer upon the climate and climatic conditions of Oregon and Washington Territory. These reports, together with illustrative charts and a letter from General Greeley, have just been published, and, in view of the emigration to the far Northwest, will be found to be of general interest. The rainfall on the Pacific Coast is the heaviest in the United States, ranging from 70 to 170 inches annually, but this enormous fall covers only 6 per cent. of the area of Oregon and Washington Territory. On the other hand, the area where less than 10 inches fall is less than 5 per cent. of the whole. Wheat can be grown in nine-tenths of these two states without irrigation. Owing to equable rainfall, agricultural operations are more fruitful with the small rainfall than in some sections of other states with a considerable larger precipitation. Remarkably equable temperature conditions also obtain, the entire range of mean annual temperature over this territory being but $8\frac{1}{2}$ degrees—from $45\frac{1}{2}$ at Fort Colville, in Northeastern Washington Territory, to 54 degrees at Ashland, Oregon. In 300 miles of latitude along the coast the range of temperature in the summer time is only $3\frac{1}{2}$ degrees—from 56 at Port Angeles, Washington, to $59\frac{1}{2}$ at Fort Stevens, Oregon. During the winter months the mean temperature of more than half of these states is above the freezing point, and, on the coast, ranges between 40 and 45 degrees. Gen. Greeley says:

"'To summarise, Oregon and Washington Territory are favored with a climate of unusual mildness and equability. While the immediate coast regions have very heavy rainfalls, yet such rain occurs during the winter months of December to February, and in all cases the wet season gives place gradually to the dry season, during July and August. While the preponderating amount of rain falls during the winter, yet the spring, early summer and late fall are marked by moderate rains at not infrequent intervals. These climatic conditions favor, to a marked extent, the growth of most cereals, and other important staples.'"—*Minneapolis Tribune*, April 4, 1889.

Washington is well provided with schools and churches, and society averages very well with eastern communities.

CHAPTER XVIII.

DAKOTA—1682 TO 1889.

DAKOTA TERRITORY was originally included within the Louisiana Purchase, and comes within the limits of discovery which attaches to that portion of America claimed by La Salle for the French Crown in 1682; however, Dakota was not actually explored until nearly 100 years later, when the Hudson Bay Fur Company traversed the eastern portion from north to south with their long trains of Red River carts, each cart hauled by a single ox hitched in shafts. The Red River cart was a two-wheeled concern, manufactured entirely from wood and raw hide. It was a very clumsy affair, high, broad wheels, rough frame, and a high rack to accommodate the load of dried furs, which were carted down as far as Dubuque, Iowa, to be forwarded from thence by water to England. It is said that these trains were often made up of 5,000 carts in a string. One round trip a year was all that was expected of the train going south in the spring, laden with furs, through Dakota, and returning in the fall laden with supplies, through Minnesota. The latter was the shorter route, but impassable in the spring, owing to the low swampy character of much of the route through Minnesota, the route being through the bottom lands of the Red River of the North.

Not until the famous voyage of Lewis and Clarke up the Missouri River to its source, and from thence to the Pacific, in 1805, was Dakota explored with any view of settlement; nearly half a century then elapsed before any settlements were effected.

Dakota was first a portion of Minnesota Territory, until 1854, when it was covered by the Territory of Nebraska up to 1861, then it was organized as a territory, with its present boundaries. In 1864 the territory was enlarged by the addition of what is now Wyoming, the next change occurring in 1868, when the Territory of Wyoming was organized, reducing Dakota to its original and present size, which is magnificent in proportions, containing 149,100 square miles. Complying with the expressed will of the people of Dakota, the last Congress enacted that Dakota should be admitted into the Union as two states—North Dakota, and South Dakota—the dividing line, being the 46th parallel of latitude, which division gives about an equal area to each. Dakota has increased in population and wealth at a more rapid pace within the past ten years, than any other territory has in the entire history of the United States. The population in 1880 was very little over 100,000, whereas to-day there are upwards of 600,000 inhabitants.

The surface of Dakota is an elevated plateau; average altitude about 1,700 feet. There are no mountains in the state, the nearest approach to which are the famous Black Hills, in the extreme southwestern corner of the territory. There are numerous streams throughout the territory, the largest, the Missouri River, which extends from the northwest corner to the southeast corner, being navigable throughout. The Red River of the North is the only other navigable stream; it flows north from Lake Travis along the eastern border and empties into Lake Winnipeg, in Manitoba, and is navigable for 200 miles in Dakota.

The eastern portion of Dakota is famous for its many large lakes, the largest, Minne Wakan, or "Devil's Lake," covering nearly 300,000 acres, and is very deep; it affords navigation to one large steamer, the Minnie H., and two smaller ones, the Arrow and the government steam launch. Considerable traffic in freight and passengers is accommodated by these steamboats, aided by a large fleet of sail boats, which ply between the several important points on the lake during the summer season. Devil's Lake is becoming famous as a summer resort, the most frequent spot on the lake being "Dana's Grove," founded by the author of this work. The other lakes worthy of mention are Stump Lake and Freshwater Lake, near Devil's Lake, Thompson, Long, Travis, Big Stone, Turtle, Wood, Tchanikanah and Pembina.

The climate of Dakota might be termed very rigorous, the winters being severe and very long, the thermometer often registering from 40 to 50 degrees below zero. Notwithstanding the low temperature, the winters are not severe, owing to the dry atmosphere.

The summers are delightful, the days being very long. Crops mature in a surprisingly short time. Dakota raises more wheat and oats than any other territory, and, including the entire United States, ranks sixth in wheat and twelfth in the production of oats.

The seasons are too short for successful corn raising, except in the southern half, notwithstanding which fact, Dakota outranks in that cereal all of the territories and ranks twenty-second in the entire United States.

Dakota produced in 1886, from 662,625 acres, 15,805,000 bushels of corn, valued at $5,847,850; from 2,675,350 acres, 30,704,000 bushels of wheat, valued at $15,966,080; from 5,145 acres, 67,000 bushels of rye, valued at $28,140; from 825,600 acres, 20,651,000 bushels of oats, valued at $6,195,300; from 56,000 acres, 1,232,000 bushels of barley, valued at $468,160; from 46,800 acres, 3,042,000 bushels of potatoes, valued at $1,764,360; from 275,000 acres, 385,-000 tons of hay, valued at $1,636,250—total value of crops in 1886, $31,906,140.

Dakota contained, January 1st, 1888, 247,459 head of horses, valued at $18,858,156; 12,323 head of mules, valued at $1,206,340; 223,418 head of milch cows, valued at $4,841,468; 767,800 head of head of oxen and other cattle, valued at $16,687,171; 269,019 head of sheep, valued at $700,526; 533,970 head of hogs, valued at $3,173,918 -total, 2,053,989 head of live stock, worth $45,467,579, which, added to the agricultural product of the previous year, makes a grand total value of farm product January 1st, 1888, amounting to $77,373,719.

Dakota produces no coal worth mentioning, except an inferior quality that is found in unlimited quantities west of Bismark, on the line of the Northern Pacific Railway, and the same quality found in the Turtle mountains in the extreme northern portion of the territory. Timber grows only on the banks of the streams, or on the margins of the lakes of the territory, and that not in merchantable quantities or quality, valuable mainly for domestic use.

Gold and tin are found in large quantities in the Black Hills, which enables Dakota to rank about fourth as a gold producer. Bismark is the capital of this, and one of the several quite pretentious cities in Dakota, Fargo, Grand Forks, Devil's Lake and Jamestown being the other prominent centers of population of North Dakota; Pierc, Mitchell, Huron, Sioux Falls, Aberdeen, Redfield, Chamberlain, Watertown and Yorkton are the principal cities in South Dakota.

The States of North Dakota and South Dakota will be admitted into the Union, by the President's proclamation before January 1st, 1890.

Dakota is vitally interested in the subject of deep harbors on the Texas Gulf coast, owing to her large agricultural resources, and should join without delay the movement inaugurated for the purpose of urging the importance of the matter upon Congress, which was inaugurated in Denver last fall at the Inter-State Deep Harbor Convention.

CHAPTER XIX.

IDAHO TERRITORY—1805 TO 1889.

IDAHO was first explored in 1805 by Lewis & Clarke, who were sent out by the United States Government to explore the Missouri River to its source, to cross over to the Pacific Ocean and complete the chain which ultimately bound the Pacific with the Atlantic states and completed the bond of union that has made this nation the greatest on earth.

The explorations of Messrs. Lewis and Clarke were a complete success and furnished the Government at Washington with the only valid title to this, until then, unexplored region. Idaho was at one time a portion of Oregon, then of Washington, and only became a separate division in 1863, when territorial organization was provided by act of Congress. The territory then included a portion of the present territory of Wyoming, which was detached in 1869, leaving the territory with its present boundary lines, British America on the north.

Idaho extends from 42 deg. to 49 deg. of latitude; has the British Possessions on the north, Montana and Wyoming on the east, Utah and Nevada on the south, and Oregon and Washington on the west. The length of the territory is 410 miles, and its width, from 257 miles in the extreme south, to 60 miles at its northern limit. Its area is 55,228,160 acres; of this 18,400,000 acres are classed as mountainous, 15,000,000 acres agricultural lands, 7,000,000 acres forests, 25,000,000 acres grazing lands, and some 600,000 acres lakes. Its vast mineral belts are included in the mountain area, as are also most of its forests.

Stretching along its eastern edge, and separating Idaho from Montana and Wyoming, are the rugged mountains of the Bitter Root, Rocky and Wahsatch ranges, the Bitter Root occupying the northern, the Rocky the central, and the Wahsatch the southern links in this boundary. The "spurs" of these ranges, especially of the Wahsatch, extend well over into Idaho, and they contain some of the territory's best mineral belts. Their highest peaks reach altitudes ranging from 9,000 to 13,000 feet. On the south and southwest are the Owyhee Mountains, which form an important link in the great divide between the waters of the Columbia and those of the Humboldt. The Sawtooth, Salmon River, Wood River and Boise are among the prominent mountain ranges in Central Idaho. On the west are the Blue Mountains of Oregon and Washington. Idaho is, therefore, practically mountain-locked, although from the south, southeast and west there are numerous depressions through which railway and wagon-roads find easy, natural access.

The interior of the territory is a vast plateau varying in altitude from 600 feet above the sea in its lowest valleys, to 10,000 on the top of its highest peaks. The average elevation is from 2,000 to 3,000 feet less than that of Wyoming, Utah, Nevada or Colorado. Its numerous mountain ranges run in a variety of directions, the trend of the principal ones, however, being southeast to northwest. In these interior ranges are the mineral belts which first attracted general attention to the territory.

Alternating and nestling among the mountain ranges are many villages, large and small, affording in the aggregate a vast area of agricultural lands not exceeded in fertility by any in the world. Through these meander a river system well worthy of the extended notice which is given in succeeding pages.

The arable portions of the valleys lie from 600 to 6,000 feet above the sea, and they range in size from 1 to 20 miles in width, and from 20 to 100 miles in length.

Traversing Southern Idaho is the extensive volcanic belt on the basin of Snake River. This basin stretches far into neighboring territories, being 800 miles in length. In Idaho it averages about 50 miles in width. Some of the best valleys traverse it, but it is more noteworthy as the great winter grazing region of this and adjacent territories. Its nutritious herbs and grasses fatten thousands of cattle and sheep annually.

There are no navigable streams in the territory, although many small streams are found which are capable of supplying all of the water necessary to irrigate every foot of the 15,000,000 acres of agricultural lands, and falls of sufficient power to turn the wheels of manufactories sufficient to supply the entire Great West. The climate compares favorably with Colorado, which was fully described in chapter XIII of this work.

The mineral wealth of Idaho is very great; gold and silver are found in nearly all portions of the territory, and the total output of those precious metals to date is well up to $150,000,000, at present averaging about $6,000,000 per annum. Coal has been discovered in the territory, but as yet no commercial use has been made of the find.

Idaho has an abundance of good milling timber, the area of which is reliably estimated at 7,000,000 acres, principally located throughout the central, eastern and northern portions of the territory, and generally convenient to water power.

Nearly one-third of this immense territory is suitable for agriculture, which, by means of irrigation, is made very desirable. Idaho produced, in 1886, from 1,950 acres, 42,000 bushels of corn, valued at

$28,140; from 65,489 acres 1,039,000 bushels of wheat, valued at $748,080; from 1,106 acres, 15,000 bushels of rye, valued at $9,000; from 34,770 acres, 1,078,000 bushels of oats, valued at $592,900; from 12,576 acres, 283,000 bushels of barley, valued at $135,840; from 4,095 acres, 43,000 bushels of potatoes, valued at $245,100; from 112,995 acres, 137,164 tons of hay, valued at $1,371,164; total valuation, $3,130,700.

January 1st, 1888, Idaho contained 104,080 head of horses and mules, valued at $5,228,875; 26,458 head of milch cows, valued at $705,635; 424,316 head of oxen and other cattle, valued at $7,955,925; 312,408 head of sheep, valued at 640,436; 42,150 head of hogs, valued at $252,900; making a total of 909,412 head of live stock, valued at $14,783,771, which, added to the value of crop products, makes a grand total value of farm products January 1st, 1888, of $17,914,471.

There are no considerable cities in Idaho, Boise City, the capital, is probably the most important; Haley and Blackfoot are each prosperous and growing cities.

Idaho has not yet joined the Inter-state movement for deep harbors on the Gulf coast of Texas, but, as it can be demonstrated that she is interested with the Great West in the improvement of such harbor facilities, we do not despair of soon receiving moral and financial support from this territory, as Idaho will ultimately form no unimportant part of the proposed "Western Commercial Congress," described fully elsewhere in this issue.

CHAPTER XX.

ARIZONA—1540 TO 1889.

ARIZONA was first explored by Coronada, a Spanish subject, in 1540; he penetrated this wild and unknown region as far north as the Magollan Mountains and, it is thought, entered New Mexico at the point where the Gila River crosses the boundary line, exploring as far as the source of that river. Evidences of Coronado's visit was found by Spanish explorers in 1583; Spanish crosses erected by him were encountered throughout Southern Arizona and New Mexico.

Arizona is bounded on the north by Utah and Nevada, on the east by New Mexico, west by California, and on the south by Old Mexico.

This territory was originally attached to Mexico during the Spanish rule, and remained a portion of the same throughout the strife and turmoil of that government until it was ceded to the United States in 1848 and 1854. In 1850 it was included within the territory of New Mexico, and was only detached in 1863, when Congress provided for the territorial government of Arizona. The territory was the home of the Aztec race, a no less interesting people than the Pueblos or Zunis of New Mexico. Several tribes of aborigines still inhabit the territory, mostly civilized and engaged in agricultural pursuits. The Aztecs are extinct, however; evidences of that powerful people and their advanced state of semi-civilization are found upon every hand; well preserved mummies are also found, which give to the present generation a fair idea of how that prehistoric race looked. The topography of Arizona is similar to that of New Mexico, slightly more elevated, but as susceptible of a high degree of cultivation by means of irrigation.

The territory contains an area of 113,916 square miles, divided about equally between mountain and plateau, the former reaching an altitude of 12,000 to 14,000 feet, the latter, in the northern portion of the territory, averaging about 7,000 feet elevation, gradually declining toward the south, until, on the southern border, it is scarcely 100 feet above sea level. The streams flow west and south, emptying into the Gulf of California. In their course they have cut their way through the mountain ranges, until often the bed of the stream is thousands of feet below the brink of the canon.

The Colorado River flows through the northwestern part of Arizona, and forms a portion of the western boundary line, and in its course has cut through the solid rock until it has formed what is known as the Grand Canon of the Colorado, larger than which there are none in the world. This canon 400 miles in length, the perpendicular walls being from 1,500 to 4,000 feet high. This is the only navigable stream in the territory, navigable for moderate sized steamers some 400 miles above its mouth. The Gila, the next largest river in Arizona, flows from east to west entirely across the territory, and empties into the Colorado River just before the latter empties into the Gulf of California.

Arizona contains some good gold and silver mines, and is beginning to rank well as a precious metal producer. The territory is sparsely settled, and the natural resources are practically undeveloped, in fact, much of the territory is yet unexplored or prospected.

Agriculture has received very little attention from the white settlers, the little attempted being principally by the natives with rude implements and without system.

In 1886, the territory contained but 75,790 acres of cultivated land, producing crops valued at $1,168,356. In live stock it averages well up with many of the other territories.

January 1st, 1886, the territory contains 12,149 head of horses and mules, valued at $638,587; 16,298 head of milch cows, valued at $606,286; 420,000 head of oxen and other cattle, valued at $7,560,000; 658,561 head of sheep, valued at $1,152,482; 16,444 head of hogs, valued at $94,536; total 1,123,452 head of live stock, valued at $10,051,891, which added to the value of the crop product, equals $11,220,247, total value of farm product January, 1888.

Arizona joins in the movement for deep harbors on the Texas Gulf coast, was represented in the late Inter-State Deep Harbor Convention held at Denver by Hon. C. W. Lechner, and Hon. A. Leonard, of Phoenix, and Lewis Wolfley, (now Governor of Arizona), Tucson.

CHAPTER XXI.

MONTANA—1805 TO 1889.

MONTANA TERRITORY was first explored in 1805, by Lewis and Clarke, under the direction of Thomas Jefferson, then President, of the United States. Until 1854 it was included in that vast region of the United States known as the unorganized or Northwest Territory. In 1854 territorial rule was provided for, and Montana was then a portion of the territory of Nebraska, continuing thus until 1864, when Congress established the territory of Montana, with the present area, and supplied a government similar to the present form.

At the last session of Congress provision was made for Montana to become a state, and active preparations are now in progress to conform to the new order of things. The area of this magnificent territory is 146,048 square miles, or 93,491,200 acres. It is bounded on the north by British America, west by Idaho, south by Wyoming, and east by Dakota. The surface is generally mountainous; the Bitter Root and Rocky Mountains are in the west, the Little Rockies, Little Bear, etc., in the east, the Highwood in the North, and the Spoonbill range in the southern portion of the territory. Less than one-fifth of the territory is adapted to agriculture, two-fifths for stock raising, and the balance is valuable for the precious metals there found.

Montana ranks first in the Union as a precious metal producer. The value of the annual output now approaches $40,000,000. A poor quality of coal is found in portions of the territory, sufficient for local consumption, but not valuable as a shipping commodity, owing to its slacking soon after it is exposed to the air. Most of the mountains are covered with a dense growth of pine trees, valuable for lumber and fuel. The territory is well supplied with rivers, the Missouri and Yellowstone Rivers furnishing navigation within the limits of Montana of over 800 miles each during most of the year, and, nearer their source, supplying an unlimited water power, which will ultimately be utilized for manufacturing purposes, etc. There are several other smaller rivers carrying a large volume of water, but whose descent precludes any idea of navigation. The waters from all these streams can be diverted from their natural course and used for irrigation purposes. It is believed that before many years Montana will be cultivating her millions of acres of agricultural lands, and, by means of irrigation, bring the culture of field crops up to the highest state of perfection. Wheat, oats and other small grains are naturally adapted to the soil and climate of this territory, which stands next to Colorado in the yield per acre of these cereals, Colorado being first in the United States.

In 1886, Montana produced from 890 acres, 22,000 bushels of corn, valued at $14,300; from 88,896 acres, 1,509,000 bushels of wheat, valued at $1,131,750; from 56,774 acres, 1,987,000 bushels of oats, valued at $1,095,850; from 3,144 acres, 72,000 bushels of barley, valued at $32,120; from 4,253 acres, 451,000 bushels of potatoes, valued at $405,900; from 139,650 acres, 152,048 tons of hay, valued at $1,596,504; total value of field products $4,274,424.

January 1st, 1888, the territory contained 192,881 head of horses and mules, valued at $9,896,631; 81,132 head of milch cows valued at $884,149; 934,500 head of oxen and other cattle, valued at $17,948,007; 1,265,000 head of sheep, valued at $2,658,398; 22,289 head of hogs, valued at $150,898; a total of 2,445,802 head of live stock, valued at $31,561,083, which, added to the crop value for year previous, makes a grand total value of farm products of Montana, January 1st, 1888, of $35,835,507.

Montana's traffic is now very largely with the south, east and central portions of the Great West, and should exhibit more interest in the grand improvements to commerce contemplated by the action of the great Denver convention, in August, 1888, and perpetuated through the means of a permanent committee appointed at that time known as the Inter-State Deep Harbor Committee.

CHAPTER XXII.

WYOMING—1806 TO 1889.

WYOMING was first explored by Clarke, in 1806. It was upon the occasion of the return of the famous expedition under the charge of Lewis and Clarke, Lewis returning by the route pursued by the explorers, when going west. The year previous, Clarke, with a small party, recrossed the Rocky Mountains at a point considerably south, and encountered the source of the Yellowstone River in Wyoming. He embarked on the waters of that stream and floated down to the juncture of the Yellowstone and Missouri Rivers, and there joined Lewis on his home trip, they returning east via the Missouri River.

Wyoming was in the vast unorganized Northwest Territory until Nebraska Territory was organized in 1854, when it was included within that political organization. Afterwards Wyoming was attached to Washington, then a portion of Utah, Idaho and Dakota, and was only organized as a distinct territory in 1868, and then embraced its present area, 97,883 square miles, bounded by Montana on the north, Dakota and Nebraska on the east, by Colorado and Utah on the south, and on the west by Utah and Idaho.

The following from the Secretary of the Territory, S. D. Shannon, is a brief synopsis of the territory's resources, etc.:

"Wyoming is the youngest of the territories, excepting Alaska, having been organized under an act of Congress, passed July 25th, 1868. It is 365 miles long by 274 miles wide, covering an area greater than all the New England States combined. The general appearance of the country may be described as mountainous, with valleys, bold bluffs, foot hills and broad rolling plains. There are mountains covered with everlasting snows, deep canons and gorges and elevated plateaus or natural parks, like the great Yellowstone National Park. Of the entire area, 62,645,120 acres, more than 10,000,000 are covered with timber, and 15,000,000 acres are capable of being successfully cultivated; but the greater part of Wyoming is adapted to grazing. The mean elevation is about 6,000 feet above the sea level, the extremes ranging from 3,400 feet to 14,000 feet. In most of the valleys, in order to obtain crops, it is necessary to irrigate the land. The soil is of various qualities, but usually a rich loam covers the valleys and plains.

"Farming, however, is carried on only to a limited extent, the chief industry being stock raising. At the present time there are nearly 2,000,000 cattle, 1,000,000 sheep and 100,000 horses and mules, worth in round numbers $50,000,000. There are 5,000 miles of irrigation ditches in Wyoming, by which 2,000,000 acres of land have been reclaimed from their desert character. The Territorial Engineer estimates that fully 4,000,000 acres more can be made productive by the ordinary means of irrigation. If the aid of Congress or the state can be secured in the construction of great storage basins or reservoirs, the area of farming lands can be increased several times their capacity under present conditions. Coal in vast quantities is found in almost every county, varying from four to forty feet in thickness. There are engaged in this industry alone 2,000 miners, the product of whose labor in 1888 amounted to 1,455,220 tons of coal, worth $4,365,720. One-third of this amount was paid in cash to the miners for taking out the coal. Wyoming contains mountains of iron, vast deposits of soda, gypsum, salt, sulphur, copper, lead, tin, mica and other minerals, also, marble, granite, sandstone, mineral paint, fire clay, kaolin, graphite, cinnabar and magnesium. Gold and silver are found in many places. Very extensive oil basins of petroleum exist in Central and Northern Wyoming, and must soon prove of great value. With the exception of coal, hardly any of the mineral wealth of Wyoming can be said to be developed. But the extension of new railroads throughout Wyoming will surely bring great changes in these undeveloped regions and give a wonderful impetus in increasing its wealth.

"According to the census of 1880, Wyoming had a population of 20,789; the present population is variously estimated between 75,000 and 100,000."

Mr. Shannon omits in the above any allusion to the petroleum possibilities of the territory, which industry promises to be Wyoming's most valuable resource. We therefore quote from the territorial geologist's reports (L. D. Ricketts, geologist), as follows:

"Few have any conception of the broad-spread occurrence of oil springs and indications now made known by active prospecting. It is found in numerous escapes in Uinta County near Hilliard and Fossill; in Fremont County, near Lander, in Dutton basin, and on the Stinking Water River; in Carbon County, along the base of the Rattlesnake Mountains, on Salt Creek and the South Powder; in Johnson County, on the South Powder and No Wood Rivers; in Crook County, at various points bordering the foot hills of the Black Hill Range and Bear Lodge Mountains.

"The three wells sunk on the Popoagie, in Rattlesnake district, all struck oil. At this place there is a small oval valley surrounded by abrupt, often precipitous, hills, over which, at various points he found oil and gas escaping. A good flow of oil was encountered in each. These wells, which varied in depth from 350 to nearly 800 feet, were cased and supplied with valves to prevent the oil from escaping, but owing to the great gas pressure a large leakage cannot be prevented—a pressure so great that, upon suddenly opening the valves the oil spurts up like some black watered geyser for 75 feet in the air. After the pipe thus clears itself, the steady flow of the oil is assumed which, it is variously estimated, will aggregate from 600 to 1,000 barrels per twenty-four hours.

"In color this oil is black. When fresh it contains a very large amount of absorbed gas. It will yield both illuminating and lubricating oil of excellent quality when distilled, and a residue which will be used as fuel for steam making just as the residuum from the Colorado refineries is used under the boilers at the Leadville shaft.

Precious metals have not been mined to any considerable extent as yet, the prospects, however, are exceptionally flattering, and at no distant day it is believed Wyoming will rank high in the production of gold and silver.

The agricultural production of 1886 amounted to $1,284,895 from 100,888 acres. January 1st, 1888, the territory contained 1,865,075 head of live stock, valued at $29,420,909, according to the United States reports, the actual returns to the territorial and it or nearly doubles that amount, as is stated in Secretary Shannon's report herein quoted.

Wyoming has evidenced considerable interest in the Inter-state movement for deep harbor facilities on the Gulf coast of Texas, and is excellently represented on the permanent committee, appointed at the Denver Convention, by Hon. Francis E. Warren, now Governor of Wyoming; Hon. Joseph M. Carey, delegate to Congress, and Hon. F. J. Stanton, all of Cheyenne.

CHAPTER XXIII.

ALASKA—1741 TO 1889.

ALASKA was first discovered in 1741 by Russians, and became an important trading and fishing point before the close of the last century. In 1778 Captain Cook, in search of a northwest passage, coasted along Alaska and established the fact, not known before, that Alaska was attached to the North American continent; he also reported having seen large numbers of otters along the coast, which stimulated the Russians to establish fur-trading stations in that faraway land. One company, known as the Russian-American Company, secured a grant to Alaska from the Emperor Paul I. in 1799, for a period of twenty years, and two years later a settlement was permanently established at Sitka. The charter of the company was renewed again and again, and only expired about five years before the United States (in 1867) purchased the country from Russia for the sum of $7,200,000, which, in the light of the present day, seems an insignificant sum for such a valuable and extensive country, although at that time the amount was considered a vast sum, and the Government was censured for the purchase.

Alaska boasts of the highest mountains on the North American continent—Mount St. Elias, 19,400 feet; Mount Wrangle, 20,000 feet. The territory contains an area of 581,000 square miles, laying between the 130th west and 165th east meridian, being 4,500 miles east and west, and between the 55th and 70th degrees of north latitude, being 1,000 miles north and south.

The Aleutian Islands, about 150 in number, with several active volcanoes, form an insular continuation of the North American peninsula of Alaska, in the shape of an arch or bridge, between the American continent and Asia, enclosing the Behring Sea, over which the United States claims control, and which is disputed by England. The subject will probably so complicate our relations with England, as to require considerable diplomacy to steer clear of an open rupture. Should war result with England over the seizure of English ships in Behring Sea, for violations of the regulations established by the United States Government for the protection of the fisheries of Alaska; then will this Government proceed to annex the territory once claimed by the United States and now known as British Columbia, and owned by England since the treaty of 1846. By right, we should own that territory now; it would then give us uninterrupted connection with Alaska and land communication to within twelve miles of Asia, enabling us to accept Russia's proposition to meet us there with a railroad, and thereby form a continuous rail route from New York to St. Petersburg and Paris. Governor William Gilpin, of Colorado, has for years advocated just such a rail connection, and we hope he will live to see the work completed. It only requires about 7,000 miles of road to be built to accomplish the Governor's proposition—4,000 in America and 3,000 in Siberia. In the light of successful engineering in the Rocky Mountains, the task of reaching Behring Strait is entirely feasible; that railroad would open up the great territory of Alaska, which is in size equal to one-seventh of the entire United States. If war should not afford us the pretext to seize British Columbia, then should the United States endeavor to purchase the same from England, or, better still, create a sentiment in British Columbia favorable to annexation and have them make a request of Congress to permit their coming peaceably into the Union.

Alaska is valuable for its immense forests, and salmon, cod, halibut, and seal fisheries, and for precious metals; one mine alone, on Douglass Island, is turning out $200,000 in gold per month; other valuable mines and placer ground are known to exist, but not as yet much prospected. Coal is said to be found in the territory; the last report of Gov. Swineford describes several marvelous veins, varying in thickness from 2 to 15 feet, and quality equal to the famous cannel coal. Some of the islands are said to abound in the finest quality of grass for grazing purposes. It is said some San Francisco parties have frequently shipped large herds of cattle up there, in the spring of the year, to fatten on the native grasses, slaughtering in October for return shipment, any quantity of ice being obtainable for preserving the beef in transit.

Regarding commerce, Gov. Swineford has to say:

"The commerce of Alaska is at present such only as grows out of and is intimately connected with, its fisheries, fur trade and mining interests. Its extent may be inferred from the following carefully estimated statement of the market value of the products of her several industries the present year:

Fur trade	$3,000,000
Gold (bullion and dust)	2,000,000
Fisheries	4,000,000
Lumber and Ivory	100,000
Total	$9,100,000

"The indications are that the output of gold will be trebled, if not quadrupled, the coming year, while there is every prospect that a large amount of capital will be added to that already employed in the fisheries. The fur trade is at its maximum, and aside from the fur-seal industry, may be expected to diminish in volume just in proportion to the development of the other natural resources of the territory.

Alaska is the only novelty left for the tourist and sight-seer in all this great world; every other place of interest has "been done" by the tourist. During the past two years, Alaska has received some attention from pleasure seekers, and the Pacific Coast Steamship Company has placed additional boats upon their Alaska route, and in various ways so improved the service that a trip from San Francisco or Port Townsend to Alaska is but a charming pleasure trip, with every luxury known to ocean or river navigation.

The excursion fare is extremely low, say from San Francisco to Alaska and return, $130, which covers nearly a month's time, about 4,000 miles of transportation, besides meals and sleeping accommodations on board the steamer. From Portland and return, $110. From Tacoma and return, $100. From Port Townsend and return, $95. Excursion tickets are sold only during excursion months, viz: from May to September inclusive.

CHAPTER XXIV.

OKLAHOMA, APRIL 22, 1889.

OKLAHOMA is the smallest and newest territory of the United States, is situated in the midst of the Indian Territory, and contains less than 2,000,000 acres of area. For years a persistant effort has been made to open up for settlement this valuable tract of land, which Captain Payne and thousands of his followers believed was public land without the formal act of Congress, and consequently at short intervals invaded the territory with a view to settlement, and was each time ejected by the United States troops. For several years this invasion and ejection play (sometimes very serious play) was continued and had the effect of turning all eyes to that coveted spot, whose virtues had become magnified into a veritable Eden; the consequence being that, when Congress passed an act permitting the President to proclaim the country open for settlement, there was a grand rush of probably 100,000 people to that territory. The President wisely, or unwisely, fixed a definite day upon which settlers might enter Oklahoma, the effect being to concentrate this immense concourse of people upon the frontier several days in advance of the date fixed. Upon that day, April 22nd, 1889 the whole number, (twice or thrice the number that could possibly get a quarter section of land), made a mad rush for the supposed Eden. In one day the entire area of public land was seized; towns were created, and large cities formed, Guthrie, the capital, sprang from nothing at noon of that day, to be a city of 15,000 people before sunset of the same day. Such an event never before occurred in the history of the world. Probably the greatest lesson taught by this rapid absorption of public lands was, that the public domain is being so rapidly settled upon, that "Uncle Sam is rich enough to give us all a farm," will die with the Nineteenth Century.

APPENDIX.

A SUMMING UP OF THE RESOURCES AND POSSIBILITIES OF THE GREAT WEST.

In the interests of the Texas Deep Harbor movement, the following statistical facts are appended, with careful comparisons and deductions. We have compiled the facts from the latest United States reports, aided by the report of the statistical committee appointed by the Fort Worth Convention in July last, of which Hon John Hancock, of Austin, Texas, was chairman, and Hon. Henry A. Lewis, of Dallas, Texas, was secretary. Mr. Lewis performed his work with care and precision, and where we quote from his compilation we feel that we can recommend its accuracy equal with the United States reports from which we quote. We shall not tire our readers with a long list of figures, but confine ourselves to totals in groups, dividing the United States by the Mississippi River into East and West, and stake our reputation on their being exact as taken from the sources acknowledged

The total area of all the States and Territories west of the Mississippi river, exclusive of Alaska Territory, amounts to 1,840,595 square miles. Alaska cotains 577,390 square miles, but being detatched and not calculated in our estimates to follow, we will not include it in the grand aggregate of area.

East of the Mississippi river the total area is 1,187,859 square miles, or, the West is more than one and one-half times in area that of the East.

West of the Mississippi river in the United States, it is estimated by competent authorities, there are fifteen million human beings—one-fourth of the population of the entire Union. The total appropriations of the United States Government for public buildings, rivers and harbors, roads and canals, light stations and beacons, forts, arsenals and armories, from 1789 to 1886 amounts to the vast sum of $426,-794,810, or $7.11 for each inhabitant, basing population of 1886 at 60,000,000. Of this enormous sum there was expended in the States east of the Mississippi river and including the improvements of that river and tributaries and the State of Louisiana, $292,357,775, and the greater portion of unclassified or miscellaneous appropriations, which amounts to $150,655,219, which would make at a fair estimate $300,000,000 expended for public improvements east of the Mississippi river, or $8.06 per capita.

In the States and Territories west of the river, exclusive of Pacific Coast States, $20,102,372, or $1.54 per capita, based on a population of 13,000,000. In the Pacific Coast States $16,825,491, or $8.41 per capita, based on a population of 2,000,000. It is hardly fair to include the Pacific Coast with the trans-Mississippi States in a comparison with the East, owing to the fact that nearly every dollar of the above Pacific Coast appropriations was expended in harbor improvements and defenses, which concern the East quite as much as the West. If, however, we include the Coast, we have a total appropriation of $36,927,863, or $2.46 per capita. We are entitled in proportion to population to have expended $90,000,000 more by the Government in public improvements, without one cent more being expended in the East, to even us up with that section of the United States. We are at present too weak to enforce our demand for a just proportion of the Nation's favors, but the time is approaching when this vast Western Empire will cut no small figure in National affairs, and, at no distant day, the East will have her sins hurled back upon her by the balance of power wielded by the West. We can almost see the Grand Old Man (who will be to the West what Governor John Evans has been to

Colorado), standing upon the summit of Pike's Peak (that grandest of all mountains), and defying the money bags and monopolists of the East, because he shall then have to support him the majority of the legal voters of the United States, and wealth extracted from the mountains or produced by the fertile plains and valleys, such as the East never dreamed of and the world never saw.

We shall then have evened up on a Nation's favors. We shall have demanded and received appropriations from the National Government to build harbors, erect government buildings, store the surplus water for irrigating purposes, etc., etc. We demand for The Great West $10,000,000 for deep harbors on the Texas-Gulf coast, as much more for the construction of immense reservoirs to store the waters of our mountain streams during the seasons that the torrents rush onward to the sea, unchecked and unappropriated, wasted, and worse than wasted, for it swells the lower rivers until their banks are overflown, devastating the fields, destroying thousands of homes and drowning their occupants—the loss by one season's overflow sufficing to erect reservoirs that would check in its incipiency and for all time the dreadful flood, and one season's crop from the land made fertile by these proposed irrigation storage reservoirs would exceed in value the cost of the reservoir construction, so that to the government we offer an investment that will yield 200 per cent. per annum income. We propose further on to show an income from an investment by the Government in Texas deep harbor ports that will show even greater returns.

In the past history of the Government many millions of dollars have been squandered through appropriations for public improvements—in fact it has been the rule rather than the exception—and our law makers have come to regard such appropriations as so much money wasted, and as a rule the men who are sent to Congress are not business men, and do not know an investment from a donation.

We do not appeal to Congress for a donation. The Great West is not peopled by paupers. We ask and demand of this Government, of which we are no small portion, a just distribution of the Government's appropriations or investments. We want $90,000,000 more money invested in this Western Empire before another dollar is invested in the East. That already wealthy section is to-day enjoying the returns from the millions of the Government money that justly belongs to the West. If the Shylocks of the East imagine this order of things can be tolerated forever, then will a fearful day of reckoning come to them. If the politicians of the East imagine that the West will forever tolerate being snubbed, slighted or cajoled, then will there come a day of reckoning for them such as they never dreamed of; and if the great transportation monopolies imagine that the West will forever submit to their extortion, then will they come to grief.

Even now the light dawns upon us which proclaims the morning of the day of deliverance.

The Denver, Texas and Fort Worth railway has saved the commerce of Denver from being entirely controlled by the whim or caprice of an Eastern railroad president. The D., T. & Ft. W. road opened up to Denver less than one year ago a short highway to the sea, which is being used by all of the Territories to the West and north of us to keep the east and west trunk lines from practicing extortion.

Returning to the statistical, we take up the farm products of the United States and make comparisons.

The year 1886 being about an average year for crops, and official data by the United States not being obtainable later, we will confine our estimate of field crops to that year. In 1886 the United States produced 1,665,441,000 bushels of corn, and shipped out of counties where grown 288,640,900 bushels of that crop. Total exported, 42,000,000 bushels. The States and Territories west of the Mississippi produced 739,149,000 bushels, and shipped out of the counties where grown 170,757,060 bushels, nearly one-half of the corn product; and, nearly two-thirds of the surplus, amounting to more than four times the total corn exported during that year from the United States. The actual amount crossing the Mississippi river from the west is not obtainable, but aggregates about four times the actual export from the United States of the corn product, and should be shipped out of the country via the Gulf route without burdening the Eastern markets.

The wheat product of the United States for 1886 amounted to 457,218,000 bushels. The amount shipped out of the counties where grown was 263,170,110 bushels. Total exports, including flour, 160,600,000 bushels. The States and Territories west of the Mississippi river produced 222,584,000 bushels, about one-half of the etire product of the United States; and shipped out of counties where grown 133,626,521 bushels, more than one-half of the surplus of counties of the United States, and almost equal to the total exports of the United States of that product for that year.

The pork and beef supply of the United States comes mainly from the States west of the Mississippi river. Cotton, sugar-cane and tobacco are likewise principally produced west of the river. January 1st, 1888, the States west of the Mississippi river had 22,614,795 head of oxen and other cattle, exclusive of milch cows, and the entire United States had but 34,378,363 head. The West therefore had nearly two-thirds of the cattle of the United States. The trans-Mississippi States had January 1st, 1888, 20,523,899 hogs; the entire United States had 44,346,525 head. Therefore the West had nearly one-half of the hogs of the United States. Commissioner, now Secretary of Agriculture, Norman J. Colman, in his reports of 1887 states that the average of exports of swine products per annum for twenty-seven years past has been 15 per cent. of the production, or about 4,500,000 hogs. The same authority gives the annual production at 30,000,000 head; the West is then entitled to a credit of producing about 15,000,000 hogs annually, or one per capita. The East produced about 15,000,000 head, or one-third per capita, a little short of the actual consumption. they requiring from the West about 5,000,000 head per annum.

In proportion to population the West stands in production of corn, 50 bushels to each person, while the East stands 20 bushels to each person, or in proportion to population the West is two and one-half times the East. Secretary Coleman estimates that in the United States the proportion of consumption of corn averages 25 bushels per capita. The States east of the Mississippi therefore lack five bushels per capita of supplying local consumption. West of the Mississippi the States produce 25 bushels per capita more than local consumption. Therefore, after supplying the local demands of the East with five bushels per capita, or 225,000,000 bushels, the remainder of surplus amounts to more than four times the total export of the United States.

In wheat the West produced 15 bushels per inhabitant, while the East produced about $3\tfrac{2}{3}$ bushels per inhabitant; or in proportion to population the West produced four times the East. Secretary Coleman estimates that the average consumption of wheat in the United States is $4\tfrac{2}{3}$ bushels per capita as follows:

The estimates of production, as recorded in our reports, average 448,000,000 bushels, in round numbers, for seven years since 1880, not including the present year. The exportation averages nearly 136,000,000 bushels, and with estimates of seed and bread, the entire distribution averages over 447,000,000 bushels. The difference is less than the losses by fire and foundering en route to market. These figures may not be absolute proof of the accuracy of the estimates, because the consumption is estimated. But as no one has furnished evidence to disprove the accuracy of the rate of consumption of $4\tfrac{2}{3}$ bushels per capita, there is no peg in existence upon which to hang a doubt as to the verity of the estimates. As the range of annual production is more than 150,000,000 bushels, and that of exportation as large proportionally, the estimates made in advance of consumption are entirely independent of the ultimate facts of distribution, and are made entirely from the crop records of the year.

As to the per capita rate of consumption, it is almost a bushel less than that of Great Britain; and it corresponds with all data of local distribution that has been found available, especially in New England and the Middle States, which obtain a large portion of their supply from the West. Those States consume five bushels, and the West quite as much, while some of the Southern States require but three or four. The average of $4\frac{2}{3}$ bushels was fixed ten years ago from an exhaustive study of the local facts of distribution, and will be changed only on proof of inaccuracy, or at least a strong presumption fortified by ample facts. It should be remembered that in addition to wheat, about three bushels per head of maize is used for human food, besides oatmeal, rye and buckwheat, making the fullest bread ration of any nation in the world.

If this rate is too high, then the estimates are too high; if too low, they are equally understood. That they are not too high is a reasonable conclusion, from the fact that in 1879 the wheat estimate was two per cent. lower than the census enumeration, and in 1869 it was six per cent. lower, and that all estimates of area and of comparative product tend naturally to be low rather than high, notwithstanding efforts made to prevent under-estimate.

The following table presents the exports and home consumption in comparison with the estimates of production, the latter made months before it is possible to know the extent of the year's contribution to the supply of the European deficiency:

Years.	Production.	For Food.	For Seed.	Exportation.	Total distribution.
	Bushels.	Bushels.	Bushels.	Bushels.	Bushels.
1880	498,549,868	242,046,655	56,563,530	186,321,514	484,971,699
1881	383,280,090	235,249,812	55,215,573	121,892,389	412,357,774
1882	504,185,470	255,500,000	52,770,312	147,811,316	456,081,628
1883	421,086,160	259,500,000	54,688,389	111,534,182	425,717,571
1884	512,765,000	265,000,000	55,266,239	132,570,366	452,836,605
1885	357,112,000	271,000,000	51,474,906	94,505,794	417,040,700
1886	457,218,000	277,000,000	51,524,858	153,804,970	482,333,628
Total	3,134,196,588	1,805,336,467	377,502,607	948,500,532	3,131,339,606
Average	447,742,370	257,905,210	53,928,944	135,500,076	447,334,229

Thus in seven years since 1879 the average of annual estimates is 447,742,320 bushels, and the distribution 447,334,229 bushels. This is marvelous closeness, especially in view of the fluctuating export, ranging from 186,321,514 to 94,505,794 bushels. Thus three-tenths of our wheat has been exported in the last seven years, and the proportion exported of the last crop (one-third) is only exceeded by the unprecedented volume and percentage of the crop of 1880, and only twice exceeded in the history of our wheat exportation."

The West, as will be seen by estimates of the highest authority of the United States on agricultural products, produces $11\frac{1}{3}$ bushels per capita more than local consumption, and the East 1 bushel less than local consumption ; therefore the West must supply the East with its deficit, 45,000,000, and actually supplies all of the export of the wheat product. There is a discrepancy of nearly 30,000,000 between the actual amount of surplus left in the West, after supplying the deficit of the East, which may be accounted for by wheat shipped into the United States from British America in bond and exported in flour. In our calculations we reduce flour to bushels of wheat, and corn meal to bushels of corn. Of corn we have a grand surplus, not accounted for either in export or supplying the Eastern deficit, which, without doubt, feeds the West's surplus of cattle and hogs.

Secretary Colman furnishes us no statistics of cattle consumption or export, and we therefore refrain from comparisons, except that the surplus of the West undoubtedly makes up a deficit in the East equal to nearly the annual production of the States east of the Mississippi and all of the export.

In hog product the average local annual consumption is about one-third of one hog per capita. The East does not produce its quota; therefore the West must supply the deficit, which it does, and its surplus also supplies the export demand.

Cotton is raised entirely in the Southern States, the majority of which lie east of the Mississippi river. However, in the four cotton producing States west of the Mississippi river nearly one-half of the cotton produced annually in the United States is raised, 2,550,000 bales in 1887, out of a total of 6,439,000 bales, Texas alone producing 1,345,000 bales. The cotton raised east of the river is principally manufactured in the United States, the cotton factories, with a single exception, being east of the river; therefore, the amount produced west of the river is nearly all exported. The exports of cotton in 1887 amounted to 4,400,000 bales.

The West supplies the raw material exported, and is justly entitled to direct transportation via the Gulf and is entitled to every harbor facility required. The following table of exports will give the reader a comprehensive view of the point we are making:

	Total Export.	West supplies the East for local consumption	West supplies for Export.
Corn, bushels	42,000,000	225,000,000	42,000,000
or pounds	2,352,000,000	12,500,000,000	2,352,000,000
Wheat, bushels	156,971,949	45,000,000	125,000,000
or pounds	9,418,316,940	2,700,000,000	7,500,000,000
Hogs, head	4,500,000	5,000,000	4,500,000
or pounds	900,000,000	1,000,000,000	900,000,000
Cotton, bales	4,400,000	none	2,000,000
or pounds	2,200,000,000	none	1,000,000,000
Total pounds	14,870,316,940	16,200,000,000	11,752,000,000

Thus it is seen that the West's surplus for export is within about 3,000,000,000 pounds of the total exports of the United States for those products, the actual surplus of the West for export being 5,876,000 tons.

TABLE OF COMPARATIVE DISTANCES TO NEW YORK AND TO THE TEXAS GULF COAST—IN MILES

	To New York.	To the Gulf.
Little Rock, Arkansas	1080 miles.	440 miles.
St. Louis, Missouri	885	720
San Francisco, California	2650	1820
Topeka, Kansas	1135	680
Des Moines, Iowa	1000	830
Lincoln, Nebraska	1185	820
Cheyenne, Wyoming	1600	1020
Bismark, Dakota	1335	1240
St. Paul, Minnesota	1200	1120
Boise City, Idaho	2160	1400
Santa Fe, New Mexico	1735	760
Denver, Colorado	1620	920
Salt Lake City, Utah	1960	1200
Helena, Montana	1920	1495
Oregon City, Oregon	2140	1685
Carson City, Nevada	2380	1185
Tacoma, Wash. Ter.	2550	2000
Tuscon, Arizona	2000	850
Totals	30835	20685

The difference in favor of the Gulf amounts to 10,150 miles from the centers of each of the eighteen States, except Missouri, which favors New York by a couple of hundred miles, or an average mileage in favor of the Gulf of 564 miles from each. By a careful study of the table any person must admit the fairness of the comparison. Then what does it mean? It means that the West pays the railroads for conveying export freight to the seaboard on 5,976,000 tons over 564 miles of road more than would be necessary if there were deep harbor facilities on the Gulf coast of Texas. East of the river a very low rate charged, is one cent per ton per mile on the commodities mentioned, while west of the river it will average three cents per ton per mile; a fair average, taken together, would be two cents per ton per mile, which means that the West pays $11.28 per ton more freight to the seaboard than by a Gulf route. Experience teaches that the charges from Galveston Texas, to Liverpool on cotton is but ½ cent per hundred higher than from New York to Liverpool. For argument's sake we will assume that it costs twenty-eight cents per ton more, instead of ten cents per ton more, and it still leaves $11 per ton in favor of the proposed Gulf route, and which should be saved to the West, in dollars it amounts to $64,636,000 per annum that the Eastern monopolies are grinding out of the West, and, by such methods and usurous rates of interest for the use of their millions used in farm and city improvements, they have kept the West poor.

As will be seen, we ask $10,000,000 for Texas harbors, the annual income of which amounts to $64,636,000, or nearly 650 per cent. upon the investment. Can the Government make a more magnificent investment? We say not, and as we fifteen millions of people are as much and infinitely more to the Government than the handful of capitalists who control the ways of trans-continental transportation, we demand the appropriation or investment by the Government for our relief.

The relief of the Eastern markets of our surplus production will equally benefit Illinois, Wisconsin, Michigan, Indiana, Ohio and Kentucky, the only States east of the Mississippi that actually produce a surplus to ship to Eastern markets. They should stand with us, and with us demand that the West shall be provided with such shipping facilities as shall stop the accustomed glutting of Eastern markets. Let us add interior Mexico, which is fast opening up to the United States a market that promises to be quite as valuable as our trade with Europe. Compare distance to Galveston and New York from ten of the principal cities of Mexico:

APPROXIMATE TABLE OF DISTANCES FROM NEW YORK CITY TO THE FOLLOWING POINTS.	Miles.	APPROXIMATE TABLE OF DISTANCES FROM TEXAS GULF COAST TO THE FOLLOWING POINTS.	Miles.
New York to Chihuahua	2000	Chihuahua to Galveston	600
New York to Ures	2180	Ures, Mexico, to Galveston	840
New York to Culiacan	2240	Culiacan, Mexico, to Galveston	805
New York to Durango	2080	Durango, Mexico, to Galveston	640
New York to San Luis Potoso	2000	San Luis, Potosi, Mex., to Galveston	560
New York to Cerro Gordo	2080	Cerre Gordo, Mexico, to Galveston	580
New York to City of Mexico	1980	City of Mexico, Mex., to Galveston	685
New York to Vera Cruz	2260	Vera Cruz, Mexico, to Galveston	600
New York to Matamoras	1080	Matamoras, Mexico, to Galveston	240
New York to Colivea	2280	Colivea, Mexico, to Galveston	810
	20780		6420

Difference in favor of Galveston or Aransas Pass 14,360 miles, an average of 1436 miles of rail haul saved by improving harbors at the points suggested, or $28.72 per ton for every ton of freight now transported via New York from the Mexican cities mentioned above. We would not be surprised if the total saving to the producer and consumer of this western country would amount to one hundred millions of dollars the first year of the proposed deep harbors.

A new West is forming, and despite the efforts of Wall Street is growing rich, influential and populous. The time is almost here when the West will hold the balance of power of this great government, and in the near future will be in the majority in the nations' councils ; soon the West will receive her just share of the appropriations for public improvements ; soon will the West elect a president, a Western man, and then we may expect to see the National Capitol removed to a more central point less exposed, and the nations' wealth so equitably disbursed as to build up another New York, a rival of that proud city in wealth and population, protected by nature's best fortification—distance, and not by useless fortifications that the modern navies scoff at and safely disarm from distance too great for fort armament to reach. The West is famous throughout for its vast mountains, ranches, herds, crops, railways, etc., and the people for their vastly (to Easterns), enlarged ideas. It is said one Western man can tell stories so large that it requires a dozen Eastern men to believe.

The average citizen of the West is so impressed and enthused by the vastness of everything, that when he really believes and feels all that he says, he is put down by the slow-going and pent-up New Englander as an enthusiast, and his statements are regarded as gross exagerations. We note, however, that the most skeptical Easterner when he comes West becomes more enthusiastic over the possibilities, resources, etc. of the West than the old timers, and they in fact are those who are sounding our praises the loudest. The West develops that in man which is virtuous or vicious in proportion to the largeness of the country, either men are very good or very vicious, increased civilization is fast eliminating the bad, and is evidenced in Denver, the tide is strongly in the opposite direction, and Denver reputation is world-renowned for its schools and churches, in fact Denver could almost claim to be the city of churches, having 66 in number, capable of seating 40,000 persons, nearly the entire population over fifteen years of age.

According to good authorities the West embraces 785,000 square miles of tillable land, 645,000 of grazing lands, nearly one half of which under the proposed system of irrigation will be classed as tillable land ere many years, it is safe, therefore, to estimate the arable lands in the United States. west of the Mississippi River, at a round 1,000,000 square miles, and grazing 430,000; timber 200,000, and 425,000 square miles of waste or useless lands except that which contains mineral, of the latter it is safe to estimate one-fourth is valuable for its precious metals, and as much more for coal and iron, and much of the mineral land has sufficient timber for local demands. The mineral area is far from being waste land, as it produces annually more in value than an equal area in agriculture. The arable area of the East is reduced by local causes to about 700,000 square miles, every acre of tillable land West is equal to one acre East, so that in agricultural possibilities we are nearly one and one-half times the East. In grazing lands we stand alone, there being none East of the river. In mineral lands we may be said to possess the entire area of the United States, as the minerals produced East are insignificant in comparison, also in timber, exclusive of Alaska, of which William Seward once said : "Alaska is destined to be the ship yard of America." That was because of the immense timber resources of that far off Territory of the United States. Every State and Territory west of the Mississippi except Kansas and Nebraska, are more or less producers of all the precious metals and coal. They each produce an inferior quality of coal, but are known as strictly agricultural States. The annual out-put of the mineral producing region West of the Mississippi river is estimated by competent authorities at about $1,000,000,000, about one-half of the value of the agricultural produce of the entire United States, and is estimated by competent authorities at about $1,000,000,000, about one half of the value of the agricultural produce of the entire United States, and much greater than the value of the West's present agricultural product. Dr. Strong in his publication entitled "Our Country," says: "Beyond a peradventure, the West is to dominate the East. With more than twice the room and resources of the East, the West will have probably twice the population and wealth of the East, together with the superior power and influence which, under popular government accompany them. The West will elect the executive and control legislation. When the center of population croses the Mississippi, the West will have a majority in the lower House, and sooner or later the partitions of her great territories, and probably some of the States, will give to the West the control of the Senate. When Texas is as densely peopled as New England it is hardly to be supposed her millions will be content to see the 62,000 square miles east of the Hudson send twelve senators to the seat of government, while her territory of 262,000 sends only two. The West will direct the policy of the Government, and by virtue of, her preponderating population and influence will determine our national character and therefore, destiny.

Since prehistoric times populations have moved steadily westward, as De Tocqueville said, "as if driven by the mighty hand of God." And following their migrations, the course of empire, which Bishop Berkeley sang has westward taken his way. The world's scepter passed from Persia to Greece, from Greece to Italy, from Italy to Great Britain the scepter is to-day departing. It is passing on to "Greater Britain." to our mighty West, there to remain, for there is no further West; beyond is the orient. Like the star in the East which guided the three kings with their treasures westward, until at length it stood still over the cradle of the young Christ, so the star of empire, rising in the East, has ever beckoned the wealth and power of the nations westward, until to-day it stands still over the cradle of the young empire of the West, to which the nations are bringing their offerings.

The West is to-day an infant, but shall one day be a giant, in each of whose limbs shall unite the strength of many nations."

The movement has been inaugurated that will lead to the formation of a Western Commercial Alliance or Congress that will concentrate the West and force Congress to do that for the West that the West asks for and is justly entitled to. The East will not much longer snub the West, and treat their modest requests with contempt.

The movement referred to above is the organized efforts to secure government aid to construct deep harbors on the Gulf Coast, briefly the following is a history of the movement :

For years Texas had been struggling to procure suitable national appropriations to secure deep water ports on the coast of that great commonwealth. One person was more active than many of the pronounced deep water men, viz., W. P. Caruthers, late of Corpus Christi, Texas, now of Denver, Colorado. The energetic young editor published the Corpus Christi Caller, and is still one of the editors. He advocated the measure in Texas untill he became disgusted with the dilatory methods of the so-called friends of deep water ports, and having made a visit to Denver about one year ago he became very favorably impressed with the "Chicago of the West," and settled here permanently. He made his plans and life-long ambitions regarding deep harbors known to the author of this work, and by the author's suggestion Mr. Caruthers presented the matter to the Colorado Real Estate Exchange, and after the second attempt succeeded in getting that body interested and after some delay it was determined to call an Inter-State Deep Harbor Convention at Denver. Fort Worth hearing of the contemplated action of Denver called a Convention at that place to meet July 10th, 1888, and requested the.

attendance of Colorado delegates, which invitation was accepted, and the following delegates from Colorado were in attendance . J T Cornforth. W. P. Caruthers, John C. Gallup, W. G. Sprague and F L. Dana, of Denver, General R. A. Cameron and W. E. Pabor, of Cannon City, Judson Bent, of Colorado Springs. General R. A. Cameron, of Cannon City was chosen chairman of that convention. The Colorado delegation succeeded in having a resolution passed by the Fort Worth convention requesting the Governor of Colorado (Alva Adams), to call an Inter-State Convention, which was done. The preliminary proceedings being as follows:

The Committee of Arrangements was composed of thirteen members of the Colorado Real Estate Exchange and thirteen members of the Chamber of Commerce of Denver, as follows W P. Caruthers. Theo. W Herr. F D. Morse. John Mattler, W. G Sprague, J C Montgomery F L. Dana, Jas. A. Jones. Henry Apple, A. C. Fisk, R. A. Gurley, O. J Frost and Frank W Gove, from Real Estate Exchange. I. B. Porter, M. J. McNamara, Joseph E. Bates, E. M. Ashley W N Byers, F. F Hallack, Geo A. Bushnell, Chas. A Raymond, J T Cornforth, Scott J. Anthony, Jas. A. Tedford, Thos. E. Poole and H. B Chamberlin from the Chamber of Commerce. The Committee elected I. B. Porter chairman, F L. Dana secretary, and E. M. Ashley treasurer.

By request of the Committee, Gov Alva Adams issued the following call

CALL FOR THE DEEP HARBOR CONVENTION, ISSUED BY THE GOVERNOR OF COLORADO,
STATE OF COLORADO, GOVERNOR S OFFICE,
DENVER, COLORADO, July 27th. 1888

I have the honor to invite your attention to the following resolutions, adopted by a Convention held at Fort Worth, July 10th, 1888

WHEREAS, All the States and Territories west of the Mississippi are interested in the pressing need of a deep water port on the coast of the State of Texas ; and-

WHEREAS, Denver, Colorado, being centrally located, and very accessible to all the vast sections of country interested, therefore, be it

Resolved, That the citizens of the City of Denver be requested by their delegates to this Convention, to call an Inter-State Deep Water Convention to be held in that city at such date as they may see fit, not later than August 28th, 1888.

In accordance with these resolutions, and in compliance with the request made by a committee of the Denver Chamber of Commerce and Board of Trade, and the Colorado Real Estate Exchange. I hereby call an Inter-State Deep Water Con vention of the States and Territories West of the Mississippi river, to be held at Denver, on the 28th day of August, 1888.

The basis of representation at that Convention will be as follows : Two delegates from each Senatorial district. to be appointed by the Governor of the State or Territory. One delegate from each county to be appointed by the Board of County Commissioners, or by the Chairman of said Board. Five delegates from each Chamber of Commerce, Board of Trade, or commercial body in the various cities. One delegate from each town having a population of 3,000 or less to be appointed by the Mayor or President of Trustees of said town. In each city or town having over 3,000 inhabitants, one additional delegate for each 5,000 or fraction thereof. Five delegates from each Editorial Association in the States and Territories interested. In all cases where deligates are appointed, an equal number of alternates shall be appointed by the same authority

The purpose of this Convention is to secure united and harmonious action of the middle and western states in a movement looking to the establishment of a Deep Water Harbor somewhere upon the Gulf of Mexico So important will be the influence of such a harbor upon the prosperity of every farmer, artisan, miner and citizen of the great West, that it should impel every official to whom this call is directed, to take prompt and effective action that will result in a great and influential Convention.

The Governors of the following States and Territories have been appointed Vice-Presidents o" the Denver Inter-state Deep Harbor Convention. Arkansas, Missouri, Iowa, Minnesota, Nebraska, Kansas, California, Texas, Oregon, Nevada, Colorado, Dakota, New Mexico, Wyoming, Montana, Washington, Idaho, Utah, Indian Territory and Arizona. ALVA ADAMS,
Governor of Colorado

The Committee made arrangements with Senator Tabor for the use of his Grand Opera House during the sitting of the Convention.

Opening of the Inter-State Deep Harbor proceedings.

Mr. I. B. Porter, Chairman of the Committee of Arrangements, called the meeting to order at 2 p. m. August 28th, 1888.

Mr. Porter said: Ladies and Gentlemen—It devolves upon me by the arrangements of th Executive Committee to call this Convention to order. I desire to t say that we have undertaken to allot the space on the ground floor of this hall as nearly in proportion to each state as we possibly could with the information that we had of the attendance. We may ascertain after a few moments that it is not properly apportioned, in which case we will re-apportion it and accommodate the delegates from each state and territory.

F L. Dana, Secretary of Committee of Arrangements, then read the call for the Convention issued by Governor Adams of Colorado, as appears above.

Chairman Porter then said: The Committee has invited Governor Alva Adams to welcome the delegates to Colorado:

GOVERNOR ADAMS' ADDRESS

Governor Alva Adams : Mr. Chairman and Gentlemen : To me has been given the pleasant duty of extending a welcome to the delegates to this Convention. Colorado welcomes you as partners in a great enterprise. She welcomes you as she extends her greeting to those who are bound and linked together in the same commercial destiny Before this Convention there is a great object to be obtained, and by its attainment there will come a rich and perennial harvest of prosperity. Transportation is the measure of the welfare of every American community, Every mile that is added, every cent that is added to the cost of transportation of our produce of our supplies is that much a tax upon the industry of our citizens. In recognition of this principle we have met here to-day so that we may counsel together and by our united wisdom we may find some way that will lead to the building of a Deep Water Harbor somewhere upon the Texas coast of the Gulf of Mexico. (Applause.) Where that harbor is to be is a matter of indifference to most of us, (applause), who are removed and distant from the influence of local competition and local rivalry. (Applause.) That point must be selected by competent hands. Let an honest, let a conscientious, let a scientific investigation determine which is the most feasible point, (applause), and then let every personal desire, every sectional interest, every local ambition be merged and forgotten in one patriotic effort for the general good. (Applause.) If more than one harbor can be obtained so much the better. (Applause.) But if one only can be secured, then let not its chances and its hopes be blighted and destroyed by the rivalry of other and dissapointed rivals. (Applause). But my friends, it matters not what course of action we may decide upon , it matters not what method we may elect to pursue here to-day, for between us and success their is a determined and bitter conflict, which will require our greatest exertions, our greatest ability and the greatest harmony to succeed. Every port upon the Atlantic coast will be arrayed against us. Every material interest of the great East and the North will be against us; and then there is another enemy, that has controlled legislation and has affected the weal or woe of the people to a serious extent in some cases, and that is the great lines of transportation leading from the West to the East over the lines of latitude. These are the Scipios who would like to see every port upon the Mexican Gulf filled up and ruined just as Carthage and Corinth were destroyed when their magnificence and their growing traffic began to cast a shadow over the supremacy of the imperial city. (Applause). As our mind takes hold upon the subject, as we begin to look into it and consider the extent of territory and the resources that will be encircled and benefitted by the building of a great harbor upon the north coast of the Gulf of Mexico, in which may float the commerce of the world, the greatness and the grandeur of this scheme are so imposing that its proportions seem to be described only by the words—sublime—magnificent. Wherever, my friends, shall be established a deep harbor upon the Gulf of Mexico, there we shall see spring up from the sands one of the most magnificent metropolises in this country. It will become the pride and the glory of the South, and it will at the same time be one of the richest jewels of that great circlet of cities which to-day adorn the bosom of our country. This is the city that will be erected there, and when we look into history, when we consider the seaports of antiquity, those who by their commercial supremacy have left an impress upon the annals of history, which time cannot efface, and for whose possession empires have been lost and won, when we look upon those ancient capitols and we come to examine the resources that fostered and nourished them, we find that they were insignificant compared with the wealth that now surrounds and is tributary to the western part of the Gulf of Mexico. (Applause). Nineteen states and territories will be direct beneficiaries of the deep water harbor, and these nineteen states and territories cover an area that is equal to one-third of our national domain, and decade after decade since this territory was won from the wilderness the inhabitants of that part of our country has almost doubled until to-day the population of this great region comprises nearly one-fifth of our many millions. And yet, great as has been the development, great as is the present population comparatively speaking, it is but the infancy of a mighty manhood. Our productions to-day are almost beyond our calculations, and for us to predict the possibilities of the future would be to strain the imagination and to build up a pyramid of figures that would seem almost fabulous. The statistician tells us of the production of this great country. He will tell you of the cotton, of the corn, of the grain and of the stock. He will tell you of the iron, of the coal, of the gold and the silver. Then let him take and compare the acreage from whence those marvels have been produced with the extent of virgin territory which to-day lies untouched by the ax or the plough, by the shovel or the hoe, and we then can begin to form some conception, and begin to grasp something of that greatness, something of that traffic, and of that tonnage which will roll its wealth down upon the wharves of this prospective port. (Applause). In the future this city will grow up and we will all be proud of it, and all be proud that we have been one of those who initiated the building, or the movement that has laid the foundation for the greatness that will come. Every interest that we possess is directly concerned in this movement. Our future pleads for its success. Nature has pointed the way which our traffic should go. The waters of this great region, the trend of the land is all towards the Mexican Gulf, and we thus have a great natural way for the future arteries of commerce, and any line of traffic, any method of transportation that will select these natural inclinations will find that it can perform its mission with less friction and at a minimum cost. If a deep water harbor is established upon the Texas coast, giving to us a direct and an air line to the sea, and to the markets that lie beyond, I believe that the saving in freight alone in one year after that harbor is opened will more than amount to the total cost of the building of the most extensive harbor upon the Gulf of Mexico. (Applause). But, my friends, in going through my calculations I have made no estimates that have not been based on the traffic that arises from American soil. But, back of that there are still great possibilities that lie on the west of the Gulf. Across the Rio Grande there lies another empire of wealth, and the greater part of the Republic of Mexico is naturally tributary to the Texas coast and port. (Applause). Mexico, my friends, I look upon as a natural and legitimate field for the enterprise and the hopes of our people (applause), and I do not think that I am doing violence to national faith when I predict an early abolition of every Mexican custom house by the peaceable conquest of the American flag over the dark hued millions of Mexico. (Applause).

Between the South and the West there should be an alliance. They are natural allies as against the balance of the Union upon great industrial questions, (applause), and if we join our hands together, and in accord and in harmony we work together, then will our voice be heard in the council chambers of the Nation. This, my friends, is what we should do here, work in accord and in harmony, the West and the South, joining in a great industrial alliance,—(applause)- that will bring to us an abundant harvest of prosperity in the time to come. We look to this Convention for wise and deliberate action. This Convention is not convened together for the consideration of little things. (Applause). It is not here to pursue and continue local conflicts. (Applause). We have met here to discuss problems and questions that affect a mighty empire, and it is not, my friends, a real estate scheme. (Applause). We are not bearing aloft the gaudy banners of any town site boomers. (Applause). But, as we come here we meet in faith, and we meet in the trust that great good will come from our deliberations. It is a question not for little men, or little things, but it is one that should call for the highest wisdom and the deepest thought of the statesman. It is worthy of the greatest effort. It is worthy of the most deliberate and conscientious action, and, my friends, I know that you will bring to your consideration and to this Convention all of those qualities which we look to from the great states that are here represented. I predict, my friends, although to-day success may not come, to-morrow it may be distant, but it will so surely come as we use wisdom, as we use discretion and firmness in the advocacy of our cause. (Applause). It will surely come, and while I want to see that success certain, I hope that this will be the initial movement that will bring us together upon every occasion when the interests of our great section of country are involved. (Applause). And I hope that not only success will come, my friends, but that the friendly alliances that you will form here, that this meeting together in social intercourse, in friendly communion, will result in creating a closer friendship and fraternal feeling between the citizens from all the states that stand represented before me to-day. (Applause).

The Convention then elected Ex-Gov. John Evans, of Denver, temporary chairman, and H. A. Lewis, of Dallas, Texas, temporary secretary. The permanent officers were Gov. John M. Thayer, of Nebraska, president, and F. L. Dana, of Denver, Colorado, secretary. There were present 752 delegates from 19 states and territories west of the Mississippi River. The result of the Convention after a four days' session was the adoption of the following resolutions:

WHEREAS, It is the sense of the States of Texas, Colorado, Kansas, Nebraska, Missouri, Iowa, Arkansas, California and Nevada, and of the Territories of New Mexico, Wyoming, Utah, Arizona, Dakota and Indian Territory, in Convention assembled at Denver, Colo., under the call of His Excellency Alva Adams, Governor of the State of Colorado, that the commercial, agricultural, mining, manufacturing and stock interests of all that part of the United States lying west of the Mississippi

River and the commercial and naval advantages of our country generally, demand, a permanent deep water port on the northwest coast of the Gulf of Mexico; therefore, be it

Resolved, First, That the senators and representatives in Congress, from the states hereinbefore referred to, and the delegates from the territories herein set forth, be and they are hereby most earnestly requested to procure at once a permanent available appropriation of the amount necessary to secure a deep water port on the northwest coast of the Gulf of Mexico, west of the $93\frac{1}{2}$ degrees west longitude capable of admitting the largest vessels, and at which the best and most accessible harbor can be secured and maintained in the shortest possible time, and and at the least cost.

Second—That for the purpose of carrying into effect the foregoing resolutions, committees, to consist of five from each state and three from each territory, representative in this Convention, be appointed by their respective delegations; that it shall be the duty of said committees to see that the object of said resolution be properly presented and vigorously urged before Congress, and to that end and with the view of co-operation and concert of action, the chairmen of the respective committees shall be and they are hereby constituted and created a central committee.

Third—That the states and territories, and commercial bodies represented in this Convention approve the idea of securing deep water on the Gulf Coast of Texas by private capital, and they do hereby respectfully request and respectfully urge their senators, representatives and delegates in Congress to lend their united support to such bills as may be introduced for such purpose with proper safeguards for the protection of the government; provided that the port or point suggested be one desirable for the location of a deep water harbor.

WHEREAS, The need of a deep water harbor on the coast of the Gulf of Mexico, directly and vitally affects nearly one-fourth of the people of the United States, we deem the request contained in the foregoing resolutions, of such great and paramount importance as to justify their early reference to the official notice of the President of the United States, in order that he may be duly and fully informed and be able, as contemplated in the Constitution of the United States, to "give to Congress information of the state of the Union, and recommend to their consideration such measures as he shall judge necessary and expedient;" therefore be it

Resolved, That a copy of the foregoing resolutions be transmitted to the President of the United States, and that he be requested to make in his next annual message to the Congress of the United States, such recommendations with reference to the location of a deep water harbor on the northwest coast of the Gulf of Mexico as to him shall seem proper and expedient; and

WHEREAS, It is of vital importance to all that vast region of country between the Mississippi River and the Pacific Ocean, including Minnesota, Oregon and Washington Territory on the north, and Arkansas, Texas and California on the south, that a harbor deep enough to float any vessel that sails the ocean, and ample enough to protect the fleet that may be required to handle the commerce of this whole region of country, nearer to it than any other Atlantic seaport, be constructed on the northwest coast of the Gulf of Mexico as soon as practicable; and,

WHEREAS, Such a harbor is of such great national importance that it is worthy of an ample appropriation from Congress for its construction; and,

WHEREAS, We have already adopted a request to the present members of Congress to favor such appropriations, but would make that request more emphatic; therefore,

Resolved, That the legislatures and people of all the states and territories included in the region described be earnestly requested hereafter to elect no senators, representatives or delegates to Congress except such as are known to be heartily in favor of such an appropriation, and will earnestly and faithfully work for it until such harbor is completed.

The following committeemen were appointed, as provided in the first resolution, as a permanent committee:

ARKANSAS—T. F. Sorrells, Pine Bluff, Chairman; Wm. Fishbach, Fort Smith; Gov. Simon P. Hughes, Little Rock; J. W. T. Tiller, Pine Bluff; Wm. M. Duffy, Princeton.

TEXAS—J. A. Carrol, Denton, Chairman; Walter Gresham, Galveston; G. W. O'Brien, Beaumont; John Hancock, Austin; Uriah Lott, San Antonio.

COLORADO—John Evans, Denver, Chairman; C. C. Davis, Leadville Secretary; Alva Adams, Denver; A. Wilson, Durango; W. S. Jackson, Colorado Springs

KANSAS—Howel Jones, Topeka; Alexander Caldwell, Leavenworth; W. E. Hutchinson, Wichita; J. S. Emery, Lawrence; Marsh M. Murdock, Wichita.

WYOMING—Francis E. Warren, Cheyenne; J. M. Carey, Cheyenne; Fred J. Stanton, Cheyenne.

MISSOURI—D. H. Armstrong, St. Louis; A. L. Tomblin, Stanberry; Col. H. F. Fellows, Springfield; J. S. Logan, St. Joseph; W. W. Anderson, Louisiana.

UTAH—E. Willden, Beaver; Chas. T. Stoney, Beaver.

NEW MEXICO—W. W. Griffin, Santa Fe; Frank C. Plume, Taos; Numa Raymond, Las Cruces.

NEBRASKA—Champion S. Chase, Omaha, Chairman ; O. E. Goodell, Lincoln, Secretary; Joel Hull, Minden; Herman Kountze, Omaha; W. N. Nason, Omaha.

IOWA—James M. Pieree, Des Moines, Chairman; A. P. Chamberlin, Des Moines, Secretary; Dr. W. O. Kulp, Davenport ; D. W. Smith, Des Moines ; B. Zevely, Council Bluffs.

ARIZONA—W. E. Stevens, Mayor of Tueson; A. Leonard Meyer, Phoenix; Royal A. Johnson, Tucson.

Later, on meeting of General Committee the following officers were elected: President: John Evans, Denver, Colorado. Secretary: F. L. Dana, Denver, Colo. Treasurer: Alva Adams, Pueblo.

Later, on meeting of Central Committee, the same persons were chosen as officers of the Central Committee.

At this time arrangements were made for a subsequent meeting of the committee at Dallas, Texas, October 17th, 1888. The meeting was held, resolutions passed providing for a systematic effort to get the Federal Congress to take preliminary steps to rapidly complete the harbor work in progress on the Gulf coast at the earliest possible moment. A committee was provided for to proceed to Washington to urge immediate action by Congress. The Hon. Walter Gresham, of Galveston, Texas, was the only member of that committee present at Washington, and to his untiring efforts the Great West is indebted for a Board of Engineers being ordered to select the most eligible site for a deep harbor on the Texas Gulf coast, and a small appropriation to defray their expenses. While the recognition by Congress was small, it shows that the Inter-state Deep Harbor Committee has succeeded in starting the wedge that will ultimately accomplish the object sought.

The Inter-state Committee is a basis for the building up of a Western Commercial Congress that will represent all the states and territories west of the Mississippi River, before the National Congress, and demand increased appropriations for general internal improvements; besides encouraging or aiding inter-state commerce, and thereby increase the business of their several states.

A PLAN FOR A WESTERN COMMERCIAL CONGRESS.

It has been the author's opinion that the Western States and Territories should select delegates to a Commercial Congress, with representation in proportion to the commercial importance of each, in a lower house, and an upper house, composed of committeemen from the various legislatures, as follows: The lower house to be composed of business men, members of some commercial organization, appointed by the Governor of the State or Territory. A just proportion of delegates from each state at this time would probably be Missouri 75, California 60, Iowa 50, Minnesota 40, Texas 36, Kansas 30, Louisiana 20, Arkansas 10, Nebraska 7, South Dakota 3, Colorado 4, Oregon 3, Washington 3, Montana 3, North Dakota 3, Idaho 3, Utah 3, New Mexico 3, Arizona 3 and Indian Territory 3; giving a total representation of 361 members.

The upper house (or senate) to consist of six delegates from each state and territorial legislature; three from the lower house and three from the senate, amounting to 114 members, who would be sent as committeemen at the expense of their respective states and territories. A precedent has been established for such committees in St. Louis from various Western States and Territories to discuss the subject of beef inspection and quarantine.

In joint session a President of the Congress should be chosen, and duties prescribed. Each house then assemble separately, and select their presiding officers, clerks, etc. Resolutions and recommendations should be thoroughly discussed by both houses, and passed by a majority before receiving the signature of the President. The proceedings would form a basis for a report to the several legislatures by their committeemen. Questions discussed would be confined to that which affects the Great West, or any portion thereof. The expenses of the members of the lower house should be borne by their respective states in the way of appropriations, similar to that made by the late Colorado Legislature for the expenses of the members of the Inter-state Deep Harbor Committee. That committee is composed of representative men from nearly all of the states and territories comprising the Great West, and having an organization, should meet and take steps to provide for a Commercial Congress, turning over to the new organization the responsibility of securing deep harbors on the Gulf of Mexico.

IRRIGATION RESERVOIRS AND DUTY OF WATER.

From Report of State Engineer, of Colorado, relative to reservoirs and duty of water, which is applicable to all the arid region, we quote the following:

The construction of reservoirs for the storage of water for irrigation has received a greater impetus during 1888 than during any other period in the history of the state. On the 16th and 17th of March of this year, there convened in the City of Denver, pursuant to a call made by the Governor, upon the request of a few wise and patriotic citizens, a large number of men representing various water districts, communities and organizations, and interested in the storage of water for irrigation. This assembly took the name of the "Storage Reservoir Convention." Papers pertinent to the matter under consideration were read, and discussions of the questions in this way presented followed. The work of the convention culminated in a memorialization of Congress. The result of this and kindred efforts on the part of those interested in the progress of agriculture in the region of the west dependent upon irrigation, is embodied in "An act making appropriations for sundry civil expenses of the government, for the civil year ending June 13th, 1889, and for other purposes," whereby it was provided (*inter alia*) that there be appropriated, "for the purpose of investigating the extent to which the arid region of the United States can be redeemed by irrigation, and for the selection of sites for reservoirs and other hydraulic works necessary for the storage and utilization of water for irrigation, and the prevention of floods and overflows, and to make the necessary maps, including the pay of employes in field and in office, the cost of all instruments, apparatus, materials, and all other necessary expenses connected therewith, the work to be performed by the Geological Survey, under the direction of the Secretary of the Interior, the sum of $100,000 or so much thereof as may be necessary," and that "the Directors of the Geological Survey, under the supervision of the Secretary of the Interior, shall make a report to Congress on the first Monday in December of each year, showing in detail how the said money has been expended, the amount used for actual survey and engineer work in the field in locating sites for reservoirs, and an itemized account of the expenditures under this appropriation. And all the lands which may hereafter be designated or selected by such United States surveys for reservoirs, ditches or canals for irrigation purposes, and all the lands made susceptible of irrigation by such reservoirs, ditches, or canals, are from time to time henceforth hereby reserved from sale, as the property of the United States, and shall not be subject, after the passage of this act, to entry, settlement, or occupation, until further provided by law; *Provided*, That the President may, at any time in his discretion, by proclamation, open any portion or all of the lands reserved by this provision to settlement under the homestead laws."

It is not necessary to support at this late date the advisability of the construction of reservoirs in Colorado. It is shown by the discharge sheets accompanying this report that the streams are at flood tide in the spring, and carry but small quantities of water during the fall and winter months. It is fortunate that, since the greatest flow of the streams is not confined to the irrigating season, it should occur during or just before that season. The time that the greatest quantity of water will have to be stored is thus short, so that the percentage of water that will be lost from the reservoirs by percolation and evaporation will thus be quite small compared with the percentage of loss that would accompany the storage of water in the fall and winter months. It is in the securing and presentation of a knowledge of the water supply in certain portions of the state that this department has endeavored to advance the cause of reservoir construction. Such information as this office contains has been placed at the disposal of the Director of the Geological Survey. What has already been accomplished in the direction of reservoir construction is only partially shown in the plates accompanying this report and in the tabulated statements before given. There is no doubt but that many reservoirs are being constructed outside of the district platted, and of which no notice has been filed in this office.

The portion of the precipitation in the mountains which is available for irrigation on the plains is the excess of the total precipitation over these quantities of water utilized by plants and animals, absorbed by or percolating into the earth, and evaporated, and any measure that would result in the decrease of this loss would increase the available water for irrigation, and *vice versa*. The quantity of water which passes into the soil by absorption or percolation is, of course, not known, but it may be assumed to be small and beyond the power of man to materially affect. But the quantity of water evaporated and utilized by plants is by no means beyond man's ability to modify. Evaporation is the re-vaporization of water; it takes place from wet surfaces exposed to the air; is more rapid, as a rule, on a clear day after a heavy shower, and is most rapid if, besides these conditions, there is a strong, dry wind. Other things being the same, evaporation is greater the higher the temperature. It is, in general, greater from the surface of water than from land, and it is said to be one-third as rapid from the surface of trees as from the surface of water.

Attention has hereinbefore been called to the fact that east of the Continental Divide, the precipitation of snow and rain in the mountains is much greater, in fact double, that upon the plains and valley lands, and that it is from this precipitation that the streams are directly or indirectly supplied. Just what proportion of this mountainous precipitation is lost, is not known, but the loss is probably not far from 60 per cent. of snow and rain-fall for average years. It would seem to be in excess of that for the years of minimum, and less for the years of maximum precipitation.

It can be determined by calculating from the area of the water-shed and the natural discharge of those streams, about what depth of water over the entire water-shed of the stream is equivalent to the discharge of the streams in any one year. If this be done for the years of mean precipitation, and the water be taken from the corresponding depth over the water-sheds, as indicated by the precipitation records, it may be found what depths of water over the water-shed is lost to the purposes of irrigation.

This information may be used as a basis from which to estimate the discharge of streams which have not been measured. Of course, such an estimate is only roughly approximate. The area of the water-shed, not only of the streams measured, but of all of the streams running from the mountains of Colorado, can be quite accurately determined from the topographical maps and atlas of Colorado, prepared by F. V. Hayden, United States Geologist.

It is to be regretted that records of precipitation have not been taken at numerous places in the mountains. The record at Pike's Peak can only furnish a basis for a very rough estimate of the precipitation in the mountains east of the Continental Divide.

The evaporation from the surface of water on the plains of Colorado is, as a rule, between one-eighth and one-quarter of an inch per diem. These matters have been been set forth as a preface to a theory recently advanced by Major J. W. Powell, Director of the Geological Survey, concerning the effect of the removal of our mountain forests upon irrigation, which it seems desirable to present, in connection with the consideration of storage reservoirs, since, as is readily seen, it is intimately connected therewith. As Major Powell's view of this subject has been recently made known, so that time has not been afforded for the mature consideration of it; as it involves questions concerning which but little is known, and the importance of which is too great to permit of hasty conclusions, and as the consideration of the subject naturally falls to the State Forest Commissioner, it is only briefly set forth, and the position is indorsed here to that extent only which is indicated by a strict interpretation of the remarks made in connection therewith. This new theory is in direct opposition to the prevailing belief that the preservation of our mountain forests is necessary to the welfare of irrigation, and may be stated in two parts as follows:

PART I.—By reason of the mountain forests in Colorado, the total quantity of water flowing through the canons of the streams is less than would be the case were the forests removed.

PART II.—The quantity of water available for late irrigation on the plains would be materially increased by the removal of the mountain forests.

These are, no doubt, startling statements to many. Our forests have for so long been credited with the benevolent purpose of holding around their roots the precipitation upon the mountains until the proper time arrives to permit the water to gravitate towards the channels, and thus to the plains for the benefit of late irrigation, that it is hard in one breath to divest the mind of a belief in their generous qualities, and feel assured, as this theory requires, that they selfishly thrive, at the expense of the weaker, but more valuable vegetation which irrigation fosters.

The old theory that the removal of the mountain forests is prejudicial to irrigation interests, seems to rest primarily upon the assumptions that the forests tend to increase the rainfall, and that they equalize the flow of water in the streams throughout the year, and that in consequence thereof more water is caused to fall than would otherwise fall, and that not only a greater supply of water is thus furnished the streams, but that it is furnished later in the irrigation season when most needed, for the reason that the snows lay long in the shade of the forests and are slowly melted. It is held, however, by recent able writers and students of the subject, that forests exert no appreciable influence on the rainfall. This is, for certain reasons, connected with the relation borne by currents of air to high peaks, more likely to be true on the mountains of Colorado than in most other localities, and as a general principal, it would seem to be sustained by the fact, that the most careful observations, extending in some cases over hundreds of years, have failed to indicate with reference to any country where irrigation has been practiced, that by reason of the vegetation so fostered, however luxuriant it may have been, any increase of rainfall has been occasioned. That forests (especially those which are deciduous, *i. e.*, drop their leaves) situated on low mountains, such as those at the head-waters of the upper tributaries of the Ohio river, tend to equalize the flow of water in the streams, and especially to prevent floods, it is believed no one denies. The forests, situated near the summits of the ranges in Colorado, are especially effective in keeping up a late flow of the streams, is admitted by all, for reasons that will shortly appear.

The new theory would seem to rest upon the assertions that the late water now furnished for irrigation by the streams come chiefly from the great drifts of snow above timber line; that the mountain forests of Colorado prevent, to a great extent, the snows falling below timber line on our mountains from drifting into deep chasms and ravines, and consequently prevent the formation of additional great snow drifts; that there is less loss by evaporation from the snow gathered in drifts than where the snow is not so collected, on the same principle that a greater evaporation occurs from a given quantity of water exposed in a broad and shallow basin than occurs when the water is confined in a deep and narrow depression; that there is a much greater loss by evaporation from the snow sheltered by the trees, and spread out for long periods to the action of the air ever circulating in currents over the mountains, than from snow exposed to the sun, and permitted to melt rapidly, and that the moisture absorbed by the forests of the mountains is very considerable, and if carried to the plains would nourish a very great acreage of crops.

In this connection it may be observed, that the late water for irrigation furnished many of the streams, does come chiefly from the great snow drifts above timber line, though other streams—Bear Creek, for example—are supplied during the late season almost entirely from springs; that the forests do prevent, to a very great extent, the mountain snows from drifting into deep ravines; that the mountain forests do absorb a large amount of moisture; that spring floods do bring down great quantities of water; that in some of the streams more water is carried during a few days of the spring than during the entire succeeding period embraced between the 15th of August and the 15th of October; that the evaporation of snow gathered in drifts is much less, as a rule, than from snow not so collected; that forests protect the snow beneath them by choking the high winds, which sometimes evaporate in a few hours great fields of snow from areas not protected by trees.

A great diversity of conditions is observable in Colorado, even above the 9,000-foot contour line, where are presented southern exposures and northern exposures, localities visited by easterly winds, others by westerly winds, some by dry winds and some by comparatively moist winds, and localities where the snow, if slowly melted, would seep into the soil, re-appearing at lower levels as springs, and others where the snow, if so melted, would percolate into the porous strata and never appear again upon the surface; localities where, if the mountain forests were removed, the snow would, perhaps, be lapped up by dry winds, to be precipitated beyond the confines of the state, while in other places, if the forests were removed, the snow might be blown into great drifts on the ragged breasts of great mountains where the sun could scarcely melt it during the entire season.

These diversified conditions presented in Colorado, considered in connection with the theories and remarks pertaining thereto, above given, would seem to indicate that neither theory is in harmony with the peculiar conditions observed in all portions of the state.

It may not be amiss to call attention here to the fact that the laws governing water, in whatever form we find it, are most difficult to fathom, and that no theory based upon experiments and observations of it under certain conditions, can be applied without modification to water under different conditions. To illustrate this, water in an ordinary ditch of economical cross-section flows most rapidly in the center of the channel and just below the surface. It might be assumed that such would be the case in a rectangular flume also, yet in some rectangular flumes (where the depth is about equal to the width), the maximum velocity of water is found near the bottom. It is evident, at any rate, that the removal of the mountain forests will materially affect the quantity of water supplied to the streams, and that the effect of this removal of the forests will be different in different portions of the state.

Looked at in the light of the new theory, the application to beneficial use of the forests of certain portions of the state may be welcomed, for it will be felt that the moisture they absorb and encourage to evaporate will be rendered, by their removal, available for irrigation, and thereby there will, in effect, be transported from the inaccessible mountain tops to the accessible plains, many thousands of acres of fertile lands. On the other hand, it would seem that the removal of the forests from certain portions of the mountains would be but an invitation to dry winds to carry with them to unknown regions, large quantities of the moisture which is so much needed by the irrigator, or cause the waters of these portions of the mountains to flow to the plains in floods at seasons when they were not the most needed.

Whatever the beliefs which are entertained on this subject may be—and an effort has been made to state them and the reasons therefor impartially, though this has of course been done imperfectly, since the proper presentation of them would require great time and research—the rapid removal of our forests is actually taking place, and results beneficial or injurious will certainly accompany this change. The ordinary floods observable in our streams may, beyond doubt, be attributed chiefly to this cause. These flood waters, during a portion of the season, are not used directly for irrigation. They will, unless stored, be lost to the use of the irrigator. To store the excess of flood water will require a great expenditure of money. Before this money can be wisely expended, a great deal of information will have to be collected and furnished the people of the state. It is the policy of other irrigating counties to collect such information, and no doubt will be of Colorado. But this state may delay the securing of this desirable information until after the failures of extensive projects by its citizens, occasioned by lack of this information, shall force the attention of the legislature to the subject, or, it may profit by the experience of other irrigating countries, rapidly push the collection of statistics pertinent to reservoirs, and be ready to meet in this respect the demands shortly to be made for this information. Of primary importance, in this connection, is a collection of information concerning the water supply; the demands already made upon this supply; the evaporation from water surfaces not only on the plains, but in the mountains; the evaporation from the soil; the precipitation throughout the various portions of the state; the character of the sediment in our streams and the laws governing the motion and deposit thereof, and the duty of water in various districts throughout the state.

APPENDIX.

DUTY OF WATER.

By the duty of water is meant the efficiency of a known quantity of water in the irrigation of crops. It is usually expressed in the number of acres that a cubic foot of water per second, running as long as needed during the irrigation season, will irrigate. The cubic foot of water per second of time, sometimes called the second foot, has been previously described herein, and stated to be the unit of measurement adopted in the distribution of water from the natural streams of the state into the irrigating canals and ditches. There has recently come into use, though not yet recognized by our laws, a new unit of measurement, applicable more especially to the consideration of water stored in reservoirs, which is designated the acre foot of water or acre foot. By the acre foot is meant 43,560 cubic feet, or the quantity of water which will exactly cover one acre of surface to a depth of one foot. Any statement in which the duty of water in Colorado is expressed as a definite quantity is arbitrary. As previously remarked, the laws governing water under certain conditions are not applicable to water under different conditions. For example : The observed duty of water in northern Italy, where the mean annual precipitation is about thirty-eight inches, and where the atmosphere, which bathes and in part sustains plant life, is quite humid, can be only very remotely indicative of what the duty of water is or should be on the plains of Colorado, where the mean annual precipitation is only about fifteen inches, and the atmosphere very dry. Since the annual fall of rain on the plains of Eastern Colorado varies from about ten to about twenty inches, the same quantity of water will not be required each year for the irrigation of any given acreage of crops, or a given quantity of water distributed, under otherwise similar conditions, will irrigate a greater area during the years of maximum precipitation than during the years of minimum precipitation.

Some kinds of crops require more water than others, and the same crops on some soils require more water than on other soils. Two cubic feet of water per second carried on to a field in one body will, under conditions otherwise the same, irrigate more than twice the area that one cubic foot per second carried alone would irrigate. Many additional statements might be made showing that the duty of water, when expressed in the number of acres that can be irrigated by a second foot of water running during the irrigating season, differs with each year, each character of crops, soil, sub-soil, etc.—in fact, with the slightest change in any of the governing conditions.

As there is a demand for general results in this matter, it may be stated, relative to the duty of water on the plains of Colorado, measured where distributed to the land, that one second foot, running throughout the irrigating season, in addition to about five inches of rain-fall during April and May, and 4.5 inches during June, July and August, if distributed with fair care to diversified crops, on what might be called average land, would irrigate from sixty to seventy acres. It is noticed that, to accomplish this duty, it must be measured where placed upon the land. This is not always considered in speaking of the duty of water. A second foot of water diverted from a stream at a point some miles from the land to which it is designed to distribute it, might, by reason of evaporation and seepage, never reach the land. It is sometimes convenient, however, to refer to the duty of water of certain streams or canals, when reference is had to the quantity of water flowing in the stream, usually at its canon, or permitted to enter the canal.

As in ditches of considerable length, twenty-five to thirty miles, it is not uncommon to lose by evaporation and seepage 25 to 30 per cent. of water turned into the ditch, the estimated duty of the water turned into the ditch might be placed at say fifty acres. But as the ditches are used, they lose less water, as a rule, from year to year by percolation; and the lands to which they supply water need, after several applications of the water, in some cases at any rate, less water than at first; and since as water increases in value, it is more economically used, the duty of water, whatever be the locus of the measurement, is continually increasing in Colorado, and it is thought that when distributed with the greatest care, and in sufficient quantity to be handled without great waste, during the seasons of average rain-fall, and to crops and soils fairly conditioned for its economical use, that the duty of water should approach ninety acres to the second foot. If the duty of water in connection with some of our streams is considered, it will be found that, notwithstanding all losses by seepage and evaporation, the efficiency of the water can be placed at over one hundred acres per second foot. This is accounted for by the return of much of the water diverted by the upper ditches to the channel of the stream, and its re-diversion by lower ditches, so that portions of it are again and again distributed to the land. With more storage reservoirs this duty will be still further increased.

There are methods of distribution by which water can be caused to effect a duty far surpassing that possible with the best surface irrigation, which is the form of irrigation considered above. One of these methods which is peculiarly adapted to fruit culture, and the cultivation of garden vegetables, is that wherein perforated pipes are laid below the surface of the ground and distribute water to the roots of plants and trees. The attention of this department has been called by Mr. F. E. Farish, of Arizona, to the remarkable success obtained by the use of this method of cultivation, applied to his orchards in Yuba County, California, by the late Hon. G. G. Briggs, who has been known to declare that one acre of land irrigated in this way would yield returns the net value of which was equivalent to that obtainable from fifty acres of land irrigated on the surface. Sediment in the water distributed to the perforated pipes, it may be observed, is fatal to the success of this plan, so that the water must be settled before being used.

MAJOR J. W. POWELL'S REPORT ON STORAGE RESERVOIRS UNDER THE GEOLOGICAL SURVEY.

The following is the report in full of the Geological Survey on the division of the waters of the Platte and Arkansas rivers and their tributaries for purposes of irrigation:

I have the honor to acknowledge the receipt of the following Senate resolution, with instructions endorsed thereon:

IN THE SENATE OF THE UNITED STATES,
August 29, 1888.

Resolved, That the Secretary of the Interior be directed to inquire and report to the Senate at its next session the extent to which the diversion of the waters of the Platte and Arkansas Rivers and their tributaries in Colorado for irrigation and other purposes, affects the flow of the waters of those streams in the lower valleys, and especially during the growing season; and whether, in his opinion, the title conveyed by the government to lands fronting on said stream covers the privilege of diverting water therefrom beyond that necessary for use thereon for irrigation and mining purposes, and to report what action is needed to protect the rights of riparian owners along the waters of said streams in the states of Kansas and Arkansas, and what measures can be devised to increase the flow of water in those streams during such seasons.

(Attest). ANSON G. MCCOOK, Secretary.

[Indorsement].
DEPARTMENT OF THE INTERIOR,
September 1, 1888.

Copy. Respectfully referred to the Director of the United States Geological Survey, with request that he will make the inquiry as requested by the resolution, as to the extent and effect of the diversion of the waters of the streams specified, and what measures can be devised to increase the water in such streams, and report the result to this department. WILLIAM .F. VILAS, Secretary.

In compliance with the above instructions the following brief preliminary report is submitted:

It is not possible to report fully and satisfactorily on the subject at the present stage of its investigation, as accurate observations have not yet been made to a sufficient extent to give good quantitative results. The work of the survey of the arid lands now in progress will ultimately give good data for the solution of the problem, and at such time it is probable that a satisfactory report can be made.

REPORT.

The Platte and the Arkansas have their sources in the mountains of Colorado and Wyoming, but after passing the Colorado and Wyoming lines, they receive great additions to their volumes from the storms and streams of the lower country; so that but a small portion of the water which these rivers discharge into the Missouri and Mississippi comes from the mountain regions. In Colorado and Wyoming all agriculture is dependent upon artificial irrigation, as the water which comes direct from the heavens to the agricultural lands is insufficient to produce crops. The same is true of the western portion of Kansas and Nebraska. In this portion of the arid region under consideration, embracing a part of Colorado, a part of Wyoming, a part of Nebraska, and a part of Kansas, agriculture is possible only by diverting the water of the streams out upon the adjacent lands; and the real question is this: What effect will the development of irrigation in Colorado and Wyoming have upon irrigation in Nebraska and Kansas? The North Platte, the South Platte and the Arkansas present distinct problems; they must therefore be considered separately in this statement.

The Platte has two branches—the North Platte, draining a large area in Wyoming; the South Platte, a large area in Colorado. Much of the region drained by the North Platte in Wyoming is at so great an elevation above the sea, that agriculture cannot be made profitable—that is, the climate is too cold and the season too short to cultivate as profitable series of crops; but some portions of the Wyoming region lie at lower altitudes, where profitable agriculture can be carried on. The area of such lands, however, is not sufficient to utilize all the waters of the North Platte. Ultimately a large volume of this water can be used across the line in Nebraska to better advantage than in Wyoming, and the storage of the waters of the North Platte, which will be chiefly in Wyoming, will greatly benefit Nebraska—in fact, Nebraska is far more interested in the storage of the waters of the North Platte than Wyoming, for in general the storage of the waters of the North Platte will benefit Wyoming to a very slight degree. It must be understood that irrigation can be practiced without storage by using the waters of the running streams during the season of irrigation, which is very short, usually averaging for various crops about two months in this region. Storage increases the area of irrigable lands by holding back in reservoirs the water that would otherwise run to waste during ten months of the year. It is this water, to be stored about the headquarters of the North Platte, by which the people of Nebraska are to be chiefly benefited.

The South Platte has its source in the mountains of Colorado. In that state irrigation is already greatly developed, so that practically all the water of the South Platte which flows from the mountains during the season of irrigation is already used in critical seasons. Whether this water should be surrendered by the people of Colorado to the people of Nebraska; whether the agricultural industries along the Platte and its tributaries in Colorado should be destroyed in order that new industries in Nebraska may be created, is a question that every one can easily answer for himself. But there is a further condition worthy of consideration. If the waters of the South Platte now used in Colorado were used in Nebraska, the area brought under cultivation in the latter state would be very much smaller than the area now under cultivation in Colorado by the use of the same waters.

This fact results from well known physical conditions. In that arid region the rain is condensed on the mountains; comparatively little falls on the arid plains, not enough to produce perennial streams. When the waters debouch from the mountains into the plains their channels are radically changed; they are narrow, deep and clear; where they run across the plains they are wide and shallow, and their waters are loaded with mud. The muddy waters are spread out below in wide channels of sand. A stream may be several hundred yards wide and only a few inches deep. The water permeates these sands and a large portion is evaporated; so that a stream steadily diminishes in volume from the mountains across the arid plains until a more humid region is reached, where it again increases in size. It is for this reason that the waters of the South Platte will irrigate a much larger area in Colorado near the mountains than in Colorado near the Nebraska line; and the area which they will irrigate in Nebraska is still smaller.

MEASURING THE FLOW OF WATER.

It is probable that three acres can be irrigated near the mountains of Colorado where only one acre can be irrigated in Nebraska. This must be understood, however, as an estimate, and not as actually determined by stream gauges.

The waters of the South Platte flowing through the irrigation season, are already substantially used near to the mountains, and the important question to be determined is what effect will storage have upon the supply of water from this stream? It has already been stated that the waters of the North Platte can be advantageously and economically stored in the mountain region, but this is not true of the South Platte. With some important exceptions the waters of the South Platte must be stored below, as the declivity of the mountains drained by that river is in general too great to afford favorable places for their storage; they will therefore have to be stored in the foot hills and on the plains.

All of this stored water will decrease the volume of the South Platte where it crosses the Colorado-Nebraska line during the non-irrigating season, but when the mountain waters of the non-irrigating season are stored in this manner, and poured upon the lands of Colorado, and used for agricultural purposes, a part of this stored water will be evaporated to the heavens, but another part

—and a large part—will be returned to the Platte, where it can be recovered and again carried to the irrigable lands further down the stream in Eastern Colorado and Western Nebraska.

This general statement may therefore be made: The use of the water which falls as rain during the irrigating season near to the mountains in Colorado, as it is now chiefly used, greatly diminishes the volume in Western Nebraska; but, on the other hand, the storage of water during the non-irrigating season, to be used during the irrigating season will greatly increase the water available for Nebraska during the irrigating season. Taking the facts as they are, namely, that the waters of the South Platte falling during the irrigating season are already used in Colorado, the prospect for irrigation from the South Platte in Western Nebraska depends upon the storage of the waters falling during the non-irrigating season. The greater the amount of water stored in Colorado, the greater will be the area irrigated in Nebraska.

The waters of the Arkansas that flow during the irrigating season are partly used in Kansas, but chiefly in Colorado; so that already in critical seasons the river runs dry near the Colorado-Kansas line. The future development of irrigation in the valley of the Arkansas therefore depends chiefly upon the storage of water. This storage can be accomplished with advantage, in fact with great economy, in the mountain regions of Colorado. Along the headwaters of this stream in the mountains there are many mountain meadows and morainal valleys, where lakes can be created to store large bodies of water at small expense. When the waters of these mountain streams are stored in the upper regions, where they are comparatively clear, the reservoirs have a permanent value, from the fact that they will not be speedily filled with sediment; but if reservoirs be constructed below on the plains, and the rivers taken out where they are muddy, and excessively muddy, as is the case with the Arkansas, the storage basins will be speedily filled with sediment and destroyed. If stored on the plains, as in the case of the South Platte, the water must be diverted from the natural channels where they debouch from the mountains and carried in canals to the storage basins. This adds greatly to the expense of storage.

But there is another consideration affecting this question of great importance. In the lowland reservoirs the evaporation from the surface would be 50 to 75 inches, and the lowland reservoirs would therefore lose a large body of water in this manner, while in the highland reservoirs the evaporation would probably be not greater than 25 inches, and might often be less. Whenever highland reservoirs are possible, the water must be stored in the upper regions, and these conditions control in the case of the Arkansas River. The waters of the Arkansas cannot be taken out within the boundaries of the State of Kansas and stored in reservoirs, from the fact that they contain so much silt that the reservoirs would be speedily obliterated. The flow in waters in the irrigating season is already provided for. All additional irrigation from these waters would be so small that all state interests may be neglected.

The irrigating season on this river is, on an average, something more than two months, while the waters run to waste for more than nine months. It is this waste water that is to be stored in the mountains. Whatever is thus stored will decrease the volume passing the Kansas-Colorado line during the non-irrigating season; but will greatly increase the volume passing the line during the irrigating season; and as in the case of the South Platte, the prospect for irrigation in Western Kansas depends upon the storing of water in Colorado. The greater the storage the greater will be the area irrigated in Kansas.

It must be understood that in the above statement the primary facts and principles have been set forth, and general results given. Exact quantitative results cannot be given at this stage of the investigation; but if the work of the irrigation survey is continued until the survey is completed, practical quantitative results will be afforded.

When the investigation was begun under the instructions of the Secretary, I had not carefully considered the subject, and had made no collection of the available facts relating thereto; and I supposed that the waters of the South Platte and of the Arkansas falling in Colorado would be wholly or chiefly utilized in Colorado; and I reasoned in this manner from the consideration that the people of Colorado are already engaged in these industries, and are more likely to specially develop irrigation industries than are the people in Kansas and Nebraska. But there was another consideration which engrossed my attention for the time. On the arid

Opening the Water.

plains no perennial streams are born. The water which falls from the heavens is in the main evaporated back to the heavens, though when great storms, fall storm waters, collecting for a few hours, or a few days at most, flow into the perennial streams that head in the mountains and cross the plains; and I suppose that like results would follow from the spread of irrigating waters on the lands. But experience in California, in Utah, in Colorado, and on the Gila in Arizona, abundance exhibits the fact that the waters used in irrigation are but partially evaporated, and that a very large quantity finds its way again to the streams. It is thus that the facts of experience have modified preconceived hypotheses.

Ultimately a very large area in Kansas and Nebraska will be irrigated by impounding the local storm waters of that region, and the topographical conditions are very favorable for such enterprises. But besides the irrigation which it is possible to accomplish through the impounding of storm waters, considerable areas will be irrigated through the utilization of the waters of the North Platte, the South Platte and the Arkansas—all contingent, however, upon the condition that the waters of these streams are stored above.

It must be remembered that the upper Arkansas, the North Platte and the South Platte are not navigable streams. They are all exceedingly broad, muddy rivers, having great declivity, and so shallow as to be practically impassible for even canoes during the greater part of the year. They are thin sheets of mud tumbling down a highly inclined plain; so that the interests of navigation are in no way affected by the use of these streams for agriculture.

The use of these streams for agricultural purposes will have no practical effect upon their uses as powers in Kansas and Nebraska. Because of the great amount of sediment which they carry, they have little value as powers; for if hydraulic works were constructed along their upper courses, it would be at an enormous expense, on account of their great width, and because they run through vast accumulations of sand; and if the streams were dammed, and ponds created, they would speedily be filled by the enormous inflow of sand. There is yet a further consideration. The rain which falls in Kansas and Nebraska furnishes a sufficient volume of water for the Platte and Arkansas alike for all possible prospective use as mechanical powers.

From the above statement it will appear that the question of the use of the Platte River and of the Arkansas, is one affecting agriculture only, and that the amount of irrigable lands redeemed in Nebraska and Kansas by the waters of the Platte and Arkansas depends upon the amount of water stored in Colorado and Wyoming.

Commissioner of the General Land Office, Stockslager, makes the following report on the same subject:

I have the honor to return herewith the resolution of the Senate of the United States of August 29th, 1888, which you referred to me on the first of September, 1888, with a request for the expression of my views "upon the inquiry as to whether the title conveyed by the Government to land bordering on the streams specified, conveys the privilege of diverting water therefrom beyond what is necessary for use thereon for irrigation and mining purposes, and what action is necessary to protect the rights of riparian owners along the waters of said streams in Kansas and Nebraska."

This resolution refers to the diversion of the waters of the Platte and Arkansas Rivers and their tributaries for irrigation and other purposes in Colorado, and inquiries, first, to what extent such diversion affects the flow of the waters of those streams in the lower valleys, and especially during the growing season; second, whether the title conveyed by the Government to lands fronting on said streams covers the privilege of diverting water therefrom, beyond that necessary for use thereon for irrigating and mining purposes; third, what action is needed to protect the rights of riparian owners along the waters of said streams in Kansas and Nebraska; fourth, what measures can be devised to increase the flow of water in these streams during such seasons.

Of these matters only those embraced under the second and third heads come within your request for an expression of my views.

In reference to the former, I have to state that the title conveyed by the Government carries with it the right to the enjoyment of the water privileges attaching under the common and statute law to the proprietorship of the land. This right is affected by certain provisions of the acts of Congress of July 26, 1866, (14 Stat., 253) July 9, 1870, (16 Stat., 217), and May 10, 1872, (17 Stat., 91) now embodied in sections 2339 and 2340, United States Revised Statutes. These sections read as follows:

Sec. 2339. Whenever by priority of possession, rights to the use of water for mining, agricultural, manufacturing or other purposes have vested and accrued, and the same are recognized and acknowledged by the local customs, laws and the decisions of courts, and the possessors and owners of such vested rights shall be maintained and protected in the same; and the right of way for the construction of ditches and canals for the purposes herein specified is acknowledged and confirmed;

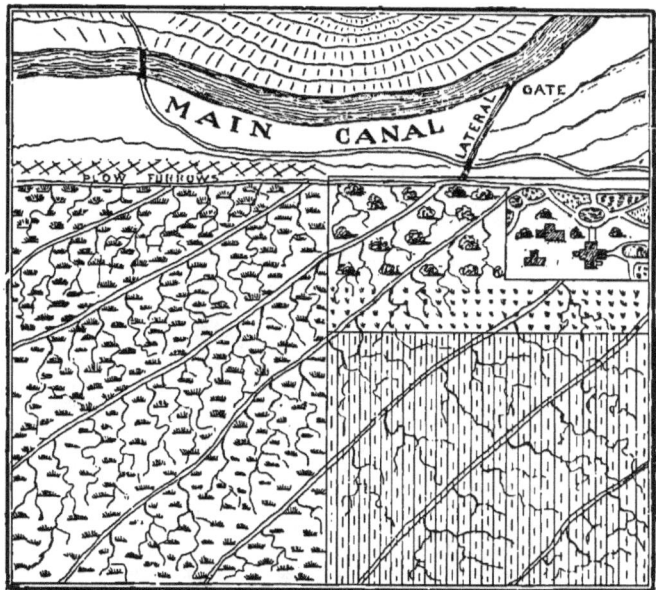

Diagram showing Main Canal and Lateral.

but whenever any person, in the construction of any ditch or canal, injures or damages the possession of any settler on the public domain, the party committing such injury or damage shall be liable to the party injured for such injury or damage.

Sec. 2340. All patents granted, or pre-emptions or homesteads allowed, shall be subject to any vested and accrued water rights, or rights to ditches and reservoirs used in connection with such water rights as may have been acquired under or recognized by the preceding section.

The foregoing statutes recognise the rights subsisting under the "local customs, laws, and the decisions of courts," to the use of water for mining, agricultural, manufacturing or other purposes, and enact that the possessors and owners thereof shall be maintained and protected in the same, and the right of way for the construction of "ditches and canals" for the purposes specified, is acknowledged and confirmed. All patents granted, or pre-emptions, or homesteads allowed, are made subject to the rights so recognized, acknowledged and confirmed.

The statutes of Colorado, which provide elaborately for the regulation and protection of such water rights, may be found in the General Statutes, State of Colorado, of 1883, page 560 *et seq.*, and for information on the general subject, Gould on Waters, sections 226 to 240, inclusive, may be consulted.

The "local laws, customs and decisions of courts," so far as I am able to ascertain, appear to admit of the diversion of water from streams to an extent beyond what is implied in the expression "necessary for use on the lands fronting on the streams for irrigation and mining purposes." They seem to contemplate the conveying of the water for use beyond the land fronting immediately on the streams, and even for use in reservoirs, for mining, agricultural, manufacturing and other purposes.

In reference to the inquiry touching the right of riparian owners, I can only suggest, with the limited data in my possession, that the question, having reference to the vested rights of owners under existing laws, does not appear to be one for legislative or departmental action, and that in case of controversy the courts are open for the adjudication of the rights of such parties, whatever they may be, under the law and the facts of the particular case.

BURLINGTON & MISSOURI RAILWAY.

The first spike of the above road was driven in 1869, at Plattsmouth, Nebraska. This road has 1,265.90 miles of main line, 1,516.33 miles of branches, and 372.04 miles of sidings and double tracks, making a total of 2,782.23 miles of road, including 35.71 miles operated jointly with the Kansas City, St. Joe and Council Bluffs Railway. The important cities connected with this line are Denver, Colorado; Cheyenne, Wyoming; Omaha, Lincoln, Hastings, Beatrice, Nebraska City and Grand Island, Nebraska; Concordia and Atchison, Kansas; Des Moines, Burlington, Keokuk and Dubuque, Iowa; St. Joseph, Kansas City and St. Louis, Missouri; St. Paul, and Minneapolis, Minnesota; Galesburg, Peoria, Rockford, Aurora and Chicago, Illinois. The above list of important cities on this line is an evidence of the important part this road has taken in the development of the Great West. The traffic department reports the following: number of tons of freight hauled in 1888, 2,556,-715; number of passengers carried, 1,547,461; number of freight cars hauled 1 mile, 60,712,555; number of passengers hauled 1 mile, 12,752,676. The company owns the following excellent equipment: 95 passenger coaches; 75 baggage, mail and express cars; 220 locomotives; 6,141 freight cars of all kinds. They have recently added dining car service through to Denver from Chicago, and free chair cars.

This company has connecting points with other lines as follows: Cheyenne, Wyoming; Denver and Sterling, Colorado; Hastings, Kearney, Grand Island, Edgar, Wilcox, Alma, Minden, St. Paul, Ord, Loup City, Fairmont, York, David City, Columbus, Seward, Crete, Lincoln, Beatrice, Pawnee City, Schuyler, Wahoo, Dunbar, Louisville, Omaha, Nebraska City, Auburn and Falls City, Nebraska; Atchison, Washington and Concordia, Kansas; St. Joseph, Missouri.

This company has about recovered from the greatest single railroad strike the world ever saw, and is fast regaining its former prestige in the passenger line. The B. & M. have always been in the front rank when convenience and comfort of passengers have been considered, and their present equipment is unsurpassed in the land.

A Flume in the Main Canal.

TABLE OF RAILROAD MILEAGE AND TRAFFIC OF THE "GREAT WEST."

1887. STATES.	Miles of Road.	Passengers carried.	Passengers carried one mile.	Freight, tons, handled.	Freight tons, One Mile.
Louisiana	1,754.37	1,783,288	57,655,992	2,877,414	253,549,754
Missouri	7,818.58	8,800,717	332,107,165	17,238,514	2,316,443,616
Arkansas	2,208	814,310	34,058,459	1,202,177	194,334,168
Texas	7,214	2,549,832	141,748,502	4,501,387	743,744,946
Kansas	8,104.33	5,236,381	284,406,727	7,833,166	1,337,399,001
Colorado	3,013.52	914,988	74,959,240	2,764,207	318,687,230
New Mexico	1,210	114,998	56,007,753	208,000	151,521,042
Iowa	7,907	1,705,298	61,895,000	4,501,098	367,319,282
Minnesota	8,446.79	8,510,387	326,377,496	13,400,905	2,221,070,520
Nebraska	3,703	2,770,664	222,060,375	5,234,250	1,191,231,910
Dakota	3,555	672	6,720	5,000,000	1,000,000,000
Wyoming	833.30	325,000	580,000	510,000	145,619,000
Montana	1,062	100,000	3,500,000	750,000	22,208,700
Washington	923	32,240	650,000	340,705	6,814,100
Oregon	1,519.04	499,952	36,618,895	732,005	143,450,490
California	4,265.00	15,348,760	559,744,127	9,281,279	2,254,213,458
Nevada	954	80,000	2,300,000	396,237	10,250,000
Arizona	988	12,953	205,000	51,624	1,896,800
Utah	1,307.98	495,000	27,565,000	1,065,200	119,250,000
Idaho	811	....	....	....	....
Indian Territory	422	....	....	....	....
Totals	68,348.19	50,175,480	2,223,136,571	78,038,168	12,794,098,087

We will not vouch for the accuracy of the above table owing to the many errors we have detected therein. It is just as we take it from "Poor's Manual of Railroads, except Dakota, and that we estimated. The table is approximately correct, though not absolutely. Idaho and Indian Territory are each omitted in estimates of freight and passenger business; Oregon, Washington, Nevada and Arizona are manifestly much under-rated. We took the liberty of correcting Mr. Poor on the railroad mileage of New Mexico, Texas, Arkansas, Iowa, Nebraska, Dakota, Montana, Washington, Nevada, Idaho and Arizona.

The table is up to July 1st, 1887, only; since that time nearly 20,000 miles of railway have been constructed in the United States, nearly all of which is credited to the territory west of the Mississippi River, and brings the grand total of railway mileage of the Great West to approximately 85,000 miles, or within a very small amount of being one-half of the railway mileage of the United States. More than that of Germany, Great Britain and Ireland, France, and Russia combined, and nearly as much as all of Europe combined. Is it any wonder, then, that we call the Great West "A Vast Empire?"

ST. LOUIS & SAN FRANCISCO RAILWAY COMPANY.

The St. Louis & San Francisco Railway includes main line and fifteen branches, covering 1,321.16 miles of road, extending from St. Louis, through Missouri into Kansas, Arkansas, Texas and the Indian Territory.

This company purchased the property of the Atlantic & Pacific Railway Company, sold under foreclosure, September 8th, 1876. In connection with the Atchison, Topeka & Santa Fe this company controls the Atlantic & Pacific, and the Wichita & Western Railways. This company is the largest owner of the bridge across the Arkansas River at Van Buren, bonded for $474,000. January 30th, 1888, this company took possession, under lease, of the Kansas Midland, 107.20 miles, between Wichita and Ellsworth, Kansas.

The company owns 189 locomotives, 135 passenger and express cars, and 6,285 freight cars. Business for 1887 was as follows: carried 859,703 passengers, or 49,516,497 passengers one mile. Freight moved, 1,407,841 tons, or 309,496,860 tons one mile. This line has, ever since its organization, gradually increased its mileage and equipment, until to-day it ranks well up with its older competitors, and is a very popular line with passengers and shippers.

NORTHERN PACIFIC RAILWAY.

This magnificent system of railway has grown up since 1870, at which time the first spike was driven by Governor R. D. Rice, at a place in Carleton County, Minnesota, now known as Northern Pacific Junction. This system includes 3,411.27 miles exclusive of sidings, making direct connection with each of the following splendid commercial cities: Ashland and Superior, in Wisconsin; Duluth, St. Paul and Minneapolis, Minnesota; Winnipeg, Manitoba, Grand Forks, Fargo and Bismark, in Dakota; Helena and Butte City, in Montana; Spokane Falls, Seattle and Tacoma, in Washington, and Portland, Oregon.

This company handled, in 1888, 2,597,897 tons of freight, or 704,772,506 tons one mile, using freight cars equalling 108,788,322 moved one mile. Passenger coaches 20,100,150, moved one mile; passengers carried, 1,343,737, or 159,483,895 one mile. The equipment of this line is first-class in every particular, and consists of 390 locomotives, 186 passenger coaches, 9,617 freight cars.

This road intersects only two important systems throughout its entire course—the St. Paul, Minneapolis & Manitoba system, and the Union Pacific system; and practically controls a larger agricultural region than any other two or three railway systems in America combined. It passes through the lumber section of Minnesota, the farming section of Dakota, the grazing and mineral sections of Montana, the mineral section of Idaho, and the mineral and farming sections of Washington and Oregon. It has 27 branch lines shooting off from the main line of the road, at convenient points, like branches are sent out from the main trunk of a tree, to feed and support the parent stem, this being as essential for the success of a road as for the life of a tree.

The Northern Pacific has been ably and conservatively managed during the past few years, as is evinced by the splendid financial condition of the road. The track is in good, safe condition, and rarely do we hear of an accident to a passenger train.

In 1887 this line was first opened for through travel without transfer, and the large number of passengers carried is evidence of its growing to be the popular summer route to and from the Pacific Coast. One feature alone will cause thousands to choose this route, viz: the branch line to the Yellowstone Park, which leaves the main line at Livingston and terminates at the Park limits.

THE CHICAGO AND NORTHWESTERN

RAILWAY SYSTEM.

Co-ordinate with the growth of the Great West, and generally in advance of permanent population, has been the progress of the great highways, among which stands the Chicago & Northwestern, justly pre-eminent as the

PIONEER ROUTE.

The Chicago & Northwestern was first to establish through service between Chicago and the Pacific Coast; first to place in Western service the vestibule cars now so universally popular among long distance travelers; first to establish a solid vestibule service between Chicago and Denver; first to inaugurate through dining car service between the Rocky Mountains and the Great Lakes; in short, the first to recognize and adopt every modern improvement and device that will add to the traveler's comfort and enhance the pleasure of a journey.

The people of the Great West, remote from Eastern friends and, perhaps, childhood's home, may comfortably, and even luxuriously, revisit old scenes and renew old associations through the medium of the generous facilities offered by this enterprising modern railway.

A few years since the journey was a thing to be dreaded, a task to be performed only when absolutely necessary; time was long, hanging heavily on the traveler's hands, and at the end of the pilgrimage the sufferer worn, tired and exhausted. All this has been changed like magic, by the genius of man and the keen enterprise of the railway company. No longer are there more thorns than roses in a railway experience, but, like the flight of an eagle, swift, sure and steady, the modern palace on wheels glides across prairie, meadow and stream, annihilating time and carrying in its bosom all the comforts of home and luxuries of wealth. The destination reached, finds the contented traveler better, both physically and mentally, than when starting; old friends are greeted with warmer affection; familiar localities meet the eye with keener interest; the trip has been a draught of elixir, arousing new energies and giving new life.

The Chicago & Northwestern has been foremost of all in bringing about this happy change; its management has been ever in the van in the effort to give the public immediate advantage of every advance made in the direction of railway improvement; its aim is to *lead* all others, and its constant and growing popularity attests its success.

To this great railway no small part of the credit of developing the Great West is due; its lines have been pushed steadily forward into unoccupied territory, thus opening new fields constantly and enabling the tide of emigration to flow into sections that would otherwise have lain dormant for years. The sagacity of this policy to-day stands revealed, and enables the Chicago & Northwestern Railway to safely rely upon the intention of the people to patronize this early and constant friend of the Great West.

WHY SHOULD I GO TO MONTANA?

Great Reservation.—Because 18,000,000 acres of free Government land, with a delightful climate, and equally suited for general farming and stock raising, have just been opened to the home seeker, in the Milk River Valley, and near Benton and Great Falls.

Stock Raising.—Because the favorable climate and superior grasses of Montana make it the natural home of horses, cattle, sheep and other domestic animals; and because winter feeding is not required, as stock grazes at large the year round.

General Farming.—Because a rich soil and abundant summer rains produce wheat, oats, rye, barley and the grasses and vegetables of a quality, size and yield unsurpassed.

Mining.—Because Montana produces more of the precious metals than any other state or territory, and abundant opportunities remain to secure valuable properties at nominal cost.

Immigration.—Because the Great Reservation is the meeting point of settlers from the Pacific Coast and from the Eastern States, and is the only extensive tract of good land left suitable for settlement.

Business. Because the rapidly growing towns along the St. Paul, Minneapolis & Manitoba Railway offer splendid opportunities to engage in business.

Manufacturer.—Because the 1,000,000 horse-power at Great Falls, the extensive coal veins, the wool, mineral and grain raising resources of Montana offer exceptional opportunities to the manufacturer.

Tourists.—Because the canon of the Gates of the Mountains, the Great Falls of the Missouri, the Giant Fountain and Continental Divide offer the most sublime and diversified scenery to be found on the Continent. Take a summer tour.

Why Travel by the St. P., M. & M.?—Because only by it can you travel through the largest body of free land left for settlement. Because it reaches the Great Falls, with the largest water-power on the Continent. Because it reaches Helena, the richest city of its size in the world; and because it is the shortest and best route to Butte, the largest mining camp on earth. Special tourists' and land-seekers' rates. Daily trains through solid to Montana. Choice of three routes to the Pacific Coast. Find out all about it by writing for "The Great Reservation, and "Tourists' Summer Guide.

For further information, rates, maps, etc., apply to F. I. WHITNEY, G. P. & T. A., St. Paul, Minneapolis & Manitoba Railway, St. Paul, Minn.

Denver & Rio Grande
EXPRESS.

SIMPLEST, QUICKEST, SAFEST, CHEAPEST

MONEY ORDERS

Payable at over 13,000 places in United States and Canada, and the principal cities of Europe.

RATES FOR DOMESTIC ORDERS:

Not over $5.	5 cents.
Over $5 to $10,	8 cents.
Over $10 to $20,	10 cents.
Over $20 to $30,	15 cents.

RATES FOR FOREIGN ORDERS:

Not over $10,	10 cents.
Not over $20,	18 cents.
Not over $30,	25 cents.

G. W. KRAMER, Manager.

THIRD EDITION.   JULY 1889.

PRICE 50 CENTS

COLORADO SCENE ON THE LINE OF THE B. & M. R. R.

THE GREAT WEST
A VAST EMPIRE
BY F. L. DANA.
SECRETARY INTER-STATE DEEP HARBOR COMMITTEE

DENVER, COLO.

NEB. — SCENE ON THE LINE OF THE B. & M. R. R.

ENTERED AT DENVER POST OFFICE AS SECOND CLASS MATTER

"ROCK ISLAND ROUTE."

Chicago, Kansas & Nebraska R'y,

(Chicago, Rock Island & Pacific R'y Co., Lessees.)

SOLID VESTIBULE TRAINS

—AND—

FREE RECLINING CHAIR CARS

BETWEEN

Chicago and Denver, Colorado Springs and Pueblo,

VIA KANSAS CITY AND ST. JOSEPH,

WITHOUT CHANGE OF CARS.

Union Depots at all terminal points, and close connections East Bound, for St. Louis and all points East and South, and West Bound for Salt Lake City, San Francisco, and all Pacific Coast Points.

For Tickets, Maps, Folders, or any desired information, apply to your nearest ticket agent, or address

JOHN SEBASTIAN,
General Ticket and Passenger Agent,
Topeka, Kansas.

G. F. LEE,
Genl. Agent Pass. Dept.
Denver, Colorado.

www.ingramcontent.com/pod-product-compliance
Lightning Source LLC
Chambersburg PA
CBHW020911230426
43666CB00008B/1407